THE DRUIDS

The Druids

Ronald Hutton

hambledon
continuum

Hambledon Continuum is an imprint of Continuum Books
Continuum UK, The Tower Building, 11 York Road, London SE1 7NX
Continuum US, 80 Maiden Lane, Suite 704, New York, NY 10038

www.continuumbooks.com

First published 2007

British Library Cataloguing-in-Publication Data
A catalogue record for this book is available from the British Library.

ISBN 978 1 85285 533 8

Typeset by Egan Reid Ltd, Auckland, New Zealand
Printed and bound by MPG Books Ltd, Cornwall, Great Britain

Contents

Illustrations

Introduction

This book seeks to reverse the priorities of those that have hitherto been written on its subject. The typical author of a book on Druids published in English since 1950 has taken as its main preoccupation the 'original' people who bore that name, the figures from the ancient world, and devoted most of the text to an attempt to recover what can be known of their character, beliefs and activities. This is equally true of archaeologists such as Stuart Piggott, Anne Ross and Miranda Aldhouse-Green; an expert in medieval Irish and Welsh literature such as Nora Chadwick; or freelance writers interested primarily in recovering ancient wisdom (Ward Rutherford), promoting Celtic nationalism (Peter Berresford Ellis) or providing images and ideas to modern spirituality (John Matthews). A few of them have devoted a section of their text to people who have taken the name of Druid since 1700, whether scathingly, in the case of Stuart Piggott, or respectfully and objectively, in that of Miranda Aldhouse-Green. In such cases, however, this treatment has always been subordinate to the primary task, of investigating what can be known of ancient Druidry.

In rejecting this model, I have no intention of denying value to it, because it has achieved interesting results in every case, and insights of enduring importance in some. I have attempted something different because of a conviction that a new perspective is likely to show up important issues that have been obscured by the traditional approach; and also because it is the one in which I personally most believe. In this book I argue that we can know virtually nothing of certainty about the ancient Druids, so that – although they certainly existed – they function more or less as legendary figures. By contrast, we can know a great deal about the ways in which Druids have been regarded, and acted out, in modern times, counting the latter as beginning in the years around 1500. There are excellent records for these, which, collectively, provide important insights into aspects of social, cultural, intellectual and religious history. The forerunner whose book has come closest to my own in its approach was A. L. Owen, whose doctoral thesis, presented at Oxford University, was published as *The Famous Druids* in 1962. This looked at the way in which Druids were represented in British literature – including scholarly works, poetry and drama – from the early sixteenth to the early nineteenth century. It was based upon a large amount of pioneering research, to which my own work has been indebted at many points. It was, however, confined to literary sources, and ends just as the popularity of Druids as figures in the British imagination was reaching its greatest extent. I have built upon it by uncovering more texts for Owen's own period and area of interest, by looking at the manner in which Druidry has been acted out as well as described, and by covering a considerably longer span of time.

I am well aware that Druids have played an important part, often in many different ways, in Irish, French, German, American, Canadian and Australian culture, and probably that of other nations as well. To deal with them in British sources alone has, however, been a very large project, and the one to which my own position and resources have been best suited. It can also be suggested that the British have, cumulatively, shown more interest in Druids than anybody else, and that their interest has had a knock-on effect upon most of the other nations mentioned above.

This book is intended to be the first of a pair, based on the same research. Until now, I have tried to satisfy two different kinds of reader at once: an academic one, and anybody in the general public who is interested in my subject and reads academic work. To an extent, I seem to have succeeded, but in the past few years I have started to receive letters from people wanting to know about the kinds of thing on which I write, who complain that my books are too hard for them. It may be, simply, that those books have started to attract the attention of people for whom they were never designed, and could never be designed, because our interests and approaches are so different. On the other hand, I felt that there might be some merit in splitting my work, on this occasion, and seeing if I could try to please two different audiences separately, by concentrating on the needs of each. This book is the more obviously accessible of the two: it uses language that anybody can understand; it is relatively short (by my standards); it has plenty of visual material; it consists of edited highlights from the mass of my material and arguments; it has a discussion of sources at the end instead of numbered notes; and it takes a thematic approach to the subject. Having said that, it should still have plenty to interest the most expert fellow scholar. The division of the chapters by theme allows me to discuss issues that cannot as plainly be considered in any other way, and there are things in it that will not appear anywhere else. The source materials used are named, section by section, and every quotation in the text is given a precise reference.

The larger book that is to follow will also be accessibly written, and is intended, in part, for those who have enjoyed this one and wish to follow up the subject in more detail. Most of the information in this book will be found in that one, but approached in a different way: in a chronological format rather than a thematic one, so that particular periods can be studied as a whole. In addition, much more material will be provided, and discussed more deeply, with a full endnoting of sources and a proper analysis of their nature and assessment of their value, and a guide to their location if they are scarce. People already interested in the modern history of Druids will find there answers to questions that may have occurred to them from the present text: why William Blake is never mentioned; why I state that the first modern Druid order was founded in 1772 instead of in 1717 as is commonly claimed at present; and what happens in all those periods in which I state that large numbers of texts were published on Druids, of a particular nature, without spending more time on them. What the present book does best is look at developments and transitions; when many writers tackle the same theme at roughly the same time, and it typifies a period, I note the fact and move on to when things change. In the other book I shall be able to look at the 'golden ages' of particular ideas in more depth, as well as at times in which attitudes are altering.

It will be noted that I speak of 'Druidry', to mean 'things that Druids believe and do or are thought to have believed and done'. I have chosen this over the more traditional 'Druidism', partly because I think it a nicer word, but also because the older term carries a lot of baggage, in the shape of associations with formal religious systems (often of a particular kind), with which I wanted to dispense. The term 'Druidry' is much more recent – I think that it was coined by Ross Nichols in the 1960s – but is now well established, and has much looser and more general connotations which are more convenient to me. I also employ the usage 'BCE' and 'CE' instead of 'BC' and 'AD' for periods of time, for reasons explained in a previous book, and, in the traditional manner of British writers of my time and many past, use Latinised versions of ancient Greek names. Some definitions of general concepts used in the book may also be helpful. 'Religion', in my usage, is a belief in the existence of spiritual beings, who are in some measure responsible for the cosmos, and in the need of humans to form relationships with them in which they are accorded some respect. 'A religion' is a framework of doctrine and observations intended to put this belief into effect. 'Spirituality' is a belief on the part of humans that they need to accord importance to a non-material world, or to non-material aspects of the apparent world. 'A spirituality' is a system designed to facilitate that belief.

At times in the writing of this book I was covering such large spans of time so fast, and taking material from so many sources, that I was reminded embarrassingly of those Victorian antiquaries who ransacked prehistoric burial mounds at high speed, one after another, in the name of science. Like me they would take a few plum finds from each and then move on, without showing any interest in the patient and thorough reconstruction of context that has subsequently come to characterise archaeology. In the same way, the sources on which I have drawn would furnish the means of writing scores of carefully constructed microhistories. Clearly I believe that broad-brush history also has its value, which is why I have chosen to work on such a book, but the consideration that really salves my conscience is that history does not operate like archaeology. Historians are not obliged, in the course of practising their discipline, to destroy the source material on which they depend. Nobody can ever hope again to excavate a mound despoiled by Victorian diggers and obtain from it the information that it would have yielded had they left it alone. By moving swiftly across so many periods, and by proposing a framework within which to set the study of attitudes to Druids since 1500, I hope, by contrast, to be drawing the attention of colleagues and successors to issues and sources which they may then tackle to better effect.

Acknowledgements

'Acknowledgements', in this context, is a somewhat bloodless way of saying 'heartfelt thanks'. My first batch are due to the Arts and Humanities Research Council, for supplying most of the funding on which the work for this book was based. It also provided me with a research assistant, Joanne Parker, who turned up hundreds of potential sources for me – some of which proved invaluable – while engaging in her own demanding research project, teaching three course units, completing an existing book for the press, and organising two conferences related to our respective interests. She also turned out to be a perfect copyeditor. Behind my application to the AHRC lay my own department at Bristol, who encouraged it and then supported the subsquent programme of work to the best of its ability during an unprecedentedly difficult and demanding period for all its members.

A different debt of gratitude is owed to the Order of Bards, Ovates and Druids, and in particular to its Chosen Chief, Philip Carr-Gomm and, at one remove, its patron, Dwina Murphy-Gibb. Dwina funded a system of Mount Haemus awards for research into the history of Druidry, and Philip bestowed the first of those upon me, to support my preparatory work before the AHRC grant was made. He also lent me a cache of books from his own library, and photocopied and sent to me a long series of documents from his order's archive, built up slowly during his tenure of the post of Chief by acquisitions from outside. As one of the inevitable consequences of my work was to question aspects of the legendary history of his own organisation, this was action of the noblest and most altruistic kind, and I hope that my tribute here, as well as some of the material in the book, may do something by way of compensation.

I have also relied heavily on the personnel of the large number of libraries and archives in which I have carried out the research, and who have been helpful in every case. Those of four institutions, however, stand out among all the rest:

the staff of the Wiltshire Archaeological and Natural History Society Library at Devizes, Wiltshire, and of the Salisbury and South Wiltshire Museum; Peter Keelan, keeper of the Salisbury Collection of Cardiff University Library; and Hywel Matthews, the reference librarian at Pontypridd. For courtesy, kindness and intelligent interest I have never encountered any better than these. I shall tell one story about Hywel Matthews to prove my point. I once got to Pontypridd for a spell of work, to find that it was the one weekday on which the library closed for the afternoon. As the fateful hour drew near, he told me that, if I wished, he would lock the door and allow me to work through till the end of the day, under his supervision, in order to make best use of my visit; in other words, he was willing to give up his own free time to assist my research. Mercifully, I completed everything that I needed before the formal opening period ended; but I shall never forget that gesture of generosity, and it was one of many.

I have other people to thank for particular kindnesses, but have scattered these tributes through my comments on source material, so they can be specific, rather than put them into a generalised list here. I would, however, like to conclude by giving due honour to Ana Adnan, whose contributions of information and inspiration were recognised in various endnotes to my last book for Hambledon and London. In the case of this one, she left her own home for weeks on end to nurse me through my recovery from major surgery, in the course of which confined period most of the text was written, and the whole thing completed. To state that, I think, says more about her, and what I owe her, than any formal dedication.

The Patriotic Druids

Patriotic Druids were there to inspire their people to resist invaders and to preserve their identity as free inhabitants of a land that they had made their own from time immemorial. Spiritually, they were part of an organic relationship with the natural world within which they lived and which would itself be – by implication – polluted and damaged by its conquest at the hands of brutal foreigners. As part of their training as religious and moral leaders, they were able to employ powerful skills in rhetoric and in the understanding of human nature, and of the worlds beyond the human, to incite their fellows to resist attack with strength, courage and commitment. As the historians and priests of the communities whom they served, they preserved and communicated a sense of all that the past, the deities and the land itself had provided to make up an inheritance worth defending to the death. Should the initial fighting go the way of the invader, then they could become the leaders of continued resistance, melting into the woods and mountains, or slipping over the new frontier into lands yet free, to keep the flame of hope and pride burning. It helps this image considerably that the foreign aggressors whom ancient Druids actually faced were always the Romans, rulers of the greatest empire of the entire ancient world and equipped with a far more advanced technology and state system than the tribes whom the Druids served. Druids could thus feature as the champions not merely of liberty but of a simple and natural way of life, threatened with unprovoked attack by an enemy who sought to extinguish all independence, variety and choice in the known world. With that enemy came tyranny, military occupation, heavy taxation and comprehensive economic exploitation. Its soldiers marched in step and built in reinforced concrete. The leaders who came with them created towns where there were green fields, straight, hard highways where there were wandering lanes, and streets laid out on uniform grid patterns between red-tiled houses where there were friendly huddles of thatched huts. In opposing all this, therefore, the Druids became Che Guevara, Joan of Arc, the Jedi and almost any hero played by Mel Gibson, rolled into one.

This image is absolutely indispensable to the popularity that Druids have had in the modern world, which is why it is considered first in this book. It was, however, very rare in ancient times. This is not for what might, at first, seem to be the obvious reason: that all the records of Druids left from the times in which they actually existed were made by their enemies, the Romans, or collaborators with their enemies, the Greeks. Had rich descriptions survived of them in the act of opposing Roman aggression, even if cast as villains, then it would be necessary simply to reverse the sympathies of the modern reader; as, for example, has now often been done with accounts of the destruction or subjugation of other traditional peoples, such as native Americans or Tasmanians. The problem is, rather, that Druids are almost never portrayed in this fashion. The Roman and Greek writers made it plain, as will be discussed far more in later chapters, that they were the leading priests, judges, diviners, intellectuals and teachers of the peoples of Gaul (modern France and Belgium, and Germany west of the Rhine), and were also found in Britain, presumably with the same importance. As such, they *should* have featured prominently in the Roman descriptions of the conquest of these areas; and yet they are almost wholly invisible. No historian, to date, has been able to provide a wholly convincing explanation for this.

The single exception to the rule has, therefore, been given a huge weight of importance in modern times, and he was one of the most intelligent and admired of Roman historians, and one of the few to be interested in the native peoples of northern Europe: Cornelius Tacitus. He dealt with Druids as resistance leaders (or, at least resistance supporters) twice in his work. He did so when discussing a great rebellion against Roman rule by the tribes of northern Gaul in 69 CE, commenting that Druids had used their reputation for reading omens to encourage it. He provides no details, however, and some modern commentators have pointed out that he may just have been repeating a rumour that had reached Rome, and was inspired by prejudice against Druids. Much more famous, and significant, is his second reference, which is one of the best known in ancient literature, if only because it is the only point in that literature in which Druids are actually portrayed in Britain (or at least right next to it).

It occurs at a point in his *Annals* at which he describes an expedition mounted, at the opening of the 60s CE, by the then Roman governor of Britain, Suetonius Paulinus. He had been provoked to jealousy by a rival commander, who had won some striking victories at the other end of the empire, in Armenia, and wanted to pull off a success to match him. He therefore decided to attack the large and fertile island that lies off the coast of the north-west corner of what became Wales, known in Roman times as Mona, and still called Môn by the Welsh but Anglesey by the English. It had become a refuge for people fleeing from areas already conquered by Rome, and a base for those who encouraged further resistance to Roman rule; so Suetonius (as historians abbreviate his name) resolved to take it out. Anglesey is separated from the Welsh mainland by a narrow strait of the sea, and this is the sight described by Tacitus that greeted the soldiers crossing this water towards the island. It is so important to later perceptions that it deserves to be translated in full:

> On the shore stood the enemy host, with its dense array of armed men, among whom dashed women clad in black attire like Furies, with hair dishevelled, waving flaming torches. All around were Druids, raising their hands towards the sky and shouting dreadful curses, which terrified our soldiers who had never seen such a thing before; so that, as if paralysed, they stood still and exposed their bodies to wounds. Then, swayed by an appeal from their general and their own mutual encouragements not to be scared by a bunch of frenzied women, they carried the standards forward, cut down all resistance and burned their enemies with their own torches. An occupying force was imposed on the conquered people, and their groves, dedicated to inhuman superstitions, were destroyed. The natives had believed it, indeed, a duty to drench their altars in the blood of prisoners and to seek signs from their deities in the patterns of human entrails.

Tacitus begs a number of questions in this description that modern readers would like to have answered, and never can. Was Anglesey already a special centre of Druidry, or were Druids simply gathered there as part of the temporary concentration of refugees on the island or brought in as spiritual reinforcement for the army gathered to fight Suetonius? What was the status of those terrifying women? Were they spiritual dignitaries of equal rank to the Druids, or inferior or superior to them? What was it that the Romans initially found so unfamiliar and appalling in the sight? In one sentence Tacitus says that it was the Druids who surprised and shocked them; which has serious implications for any argument that Druids were normally prominent in resistance to Rome. In another, however, he seems to indicate that it was the women who scared the soldiers; in which case they were the novel element in the situation. Or was it both together? If Tacitus himself ever knew the answers to these puzzles, he was not interested in them. As it stands, the panorama that he does provide is still a superb one for later authors wishing to pick up and run with the image of the patriotic Druid. Here we have holy people doing what patriots are supposed to do: deploying their spiritual authority courageously against a brutal and militarily superior invader. Furthermore, the resistance is given a feminist dimension in the presence of those amazing women, garbed and equipped like Furies (the Greek and Roman spirits who stirred up war and demand vengeance) or, indeed, their local equivalents, the war goddesses who feature in medieval Irish literature. The futility of all this display just serves to make it the more poignant. There is, of course, that unpleasant couple of sentences about the bloody religious rites that were abolished as one of the achievements of Suetonius's victory, but these can be brushed away as Roman propaganda or misunderstanding.

Behind these issues, however, is a larger one: that it may never have happened at all. We can be reasonably sure that Suetonius did lead an expedition to north Wales, as both other historical sources and archaeology provide a good context for one; and had he done so then Anglesey would have been an obvious enemy base for him to capture. The problem is whether the advancing Romans ever actually saw what Tacitus says that they did when they approached the island. On the surface of things, there should be no problem. This is an account left by a highly intelligent and very well-connected author, himself the son-in-law of a former governor of Britain, working only fifty to sixty years after the events described. He had potential access to both written accounts and those taken directly from surviving witnesses; so that his description of the attack on Anglesey may well have been provided by a veteran who had fought among the legionaries of Suetonius on that fateful day, or taken from a despatch sent home by the general himself. In this sense it may seem that Tacitus was in much the same position as a historian writing about the Second World War in the 1990s. Such a parallel would, however, be dangerously misleading, for ancient historians simply did not work according to the same priorities and conventions as their successors in the twentieth century. They were less concerned to establish the exact truth of the past than to propose lessons from it, of utility to present and future readers.

In this context, it is very clear what this particular passage is there to do. For one thing, it livens up the narrative of events at that point and entertains a civilised readership with a vivid account of wild tribespeople in action. For another, it makes specific points about the nature of what it was, or should be, to be Roman. Several of the traditional charges made against barbarians were that they were influenced by women, deeply superstitious, given to noisy, overblown and superficial displays of military valour, and engaged in horrible religious customs. Tacitus's cameo of the fall of Anglesey manages to cover the lot, very economically. It also shows how Roman soldiers, encountering such opponents, might initially be daunted; but that they need not be. Suetonius himself never loses his nerve (and he was a commander whose reputation Tacitus was concerned to defend), and his men themselves manage to recover their courage in part by their own efforts. So true Roman grit, comradeship and reason win the day over the flamboyant but superficial menaces of savages, and the deliverance of the island from the grip of a bloodthirsty religion provides the ultimate moral reason why it should do so. The end of the account also implies, very clearly, the ghastly fate that would have awaited the Romans had they not pulled themselves together, and had they let themselves be taken prisoner in defeat.

None of this in itself proves that the account is not objectively true; what it does do is supply good reasons why it need not be. In this context, it is interesting to bring in the views of two experts in Roman literature who have recently made independent analyses of Tacitus's treatment of events in Britain: E. W. Black and David Braund. The former shows that there is no evidence that Tacitus ever used eye-witness reports, and much that he relied on earlier written material, of very variable quality; and concludes that he is a dangerous source to use for British affairs. The latter carefully examines the way in which Tacitus employed historical issues to make moral and emotional points, while emphasising that we can never know the truth of the actual episodes that he portrays. The combined insights of these classicists fit into a recent pattern of scholarship concerned with the manner in which Tacitus's work in general – in which Britain plays a very small part – creates or recreates perceptions, and represents beliefs, rather than recording reality. The actual evidence for Druids as heroic champions of native independence, or indeed for their existence in Britain at all at the time of the Roman conquest, therefore consists of a molehill of completely unreliable material. On this a mountain of literature was to be built.

It took a very long time to build. During the middle ages there was one part of Europe in which Druids occupied a prominent place in literature: Ireland, where they were built into the heroic tales and saints' lives that made up the collective memory of the native past. Works in the Irish language, however, made little impact on the rest of the medieval world, being ever less likely to make any as first Viking and then Anglo-Norman invasions forced native culture back into the hinterland of the island. The subjection of the Irish to the medieval English crown also prevented Ireland from being united into a single political unit, and so operating as an independent force in European affairs which would have made Europeans more aware of its cultural traditions. Elsewhere, there was just nothing much for patriotic Druids to do. They did not promote the glory of Christendom, or the claims of royal or noble families, or of towns or monasteries. They did not inspire knights to achievements of chivalry and military prowess. They were not prominent enough in the ancient texts to force later readers to take notice of them; and indeed some of the most significant of those texts had actually been forgotten. One of these was the *Annales* of Tacitus, which was rediscovered only in the fourteenth century. In short, the people of the middle ages did not, in general, know about them, and those few who did had no use for them.

This was still very much the situation in the year 1480. Within three centuries, however, it had altered completely. All over north-western Europe, Druids became regarded as important ancestors. They were absolutely central to concepts of European prehistory and were major characters in works of history and creative literature alike. Nowhere was this more true than in Britain, and especially in its least Celtic area, England. The subject of this whole book is, by and large, how this change came about, and what were its consequences and implications.

The easy part of the job is to say that the European interest in Druids awoke as part of the transition from the middle ages to the early modern era, as part of that phenomenon that many people still call, although now with some controversy, the European Renaissance. The change was so dramatic, in fact, that it could be argued that to have an awareness of Druids was and is part of what it is to be modern, and that the appearance of such an awareness was an aspect of that shift from being medieval to being modern embodied in the old-fashioned concept of what the Renaissance was supposed to be. Part of that concept was the appearance of a new sense of national identity, defined by common languages and cultures and powered by a new intensity of research into the ancient past. First off the mark in using Druids for this purpose were, ridiculously, the Germans. I call this ridiculous because, if there was one thing on which the ancient writers agreed about Druids, it was that the Germans did not have them. By the 1490s, however, some of the most influential writers in Germany were Rhinelanders. Whereas the Romans had defined Germany as being the area of central Europe lying east of the Rhine, by the end of the middle ages the German-speaking region had long been extended to include the entire Rhine valley, with large areas that had once been part of the Roman province of Gaul. In the ancient texts, Gaul was the land of Druids *par excellence.*

Furthermore, the Germans of the late fifteenth century were acutely aware both that they had achieved huge economic wealth and cultural sophistication and that the rest of western Europe, and expecially the Italians, still regarded them as barbarians, in the style of the classical writers. This fuelled precisely the mixed sense of pride, ambition and resentment which was to make Germany the launch-pad of the European Reformation. One lesser result of the same emotions was to forge a link between ancient Druids and modern national identity. As the Druids happened to be the only northern Europeans who had impressed the Greeks and Romans with their learning, it was essential for the Germans to have them. In the years on either side of 1500, a set of Rhinelanders – led by the poet Conrad Celtis and the scholarly abbot Trithemius – began to extol them as the ancestors of German civilisation: a group of wise and pious holy men who had prepared the land for Christianity. These writers actually referred to themselves as Druids, though in jest. They got round the historical problem by declaring cheerfully that, when the Romans suppressed the Druids in Gaul, the latter fled across the Rhine to the free German tribes, who welcomed them with open arms and kept them for good. There was not, of course, a shred of actual evidence for this, but (as many an author has found before or since) if you claim something for which there is no evidence at all, it cannot easily be disproved.

The idea of the Druids as national ancestors soon became popular in Germany, and within ten years the French had woken up to the fact that the Germans had just engaged in a piece of large-scale cultural larceny. The kingdom of France covered most of ancient Gaul, and its rulers had ambitions to take all of the rest, which they subsequently almost achieved. As soon as the Germans made Druids worth having, the French wanted them too, with a vengeance. By 1508 Symphorien Charpentier had started the work of bringing them into national history, something which gathered strength all through the remainder of the century. In 1556 Jean Picard produced the first extended discussion of them in French, and in 1585 Noël Taillepied devoted the first book in it to them; by then, French authors had come to accept the Gallic Druids as the wisest and most enlightened people in the entire ancient world, and the most ready for the coming of Christ. They were aided in this opinion by an Italian friar generally called Annius of Viterbo, who had stunned the scholarly world in 1498 by launching into it an edition of hitherto unsuspected texts by genuine, but obscure, ancient writers. They were unsuspected because they had just been forged, probably by Annius himself. What they did was to fill in the history of northern Europe between the Book of Genesis and the coming of the Romans, which had hitherto been a complete blank. They did so, moreoever, with wise and kindly kings, who sponsored a sophisticated civilisation in what became Germany, France and Britain, led by Druids, who taught people like the Greeks all that they knew. This was, of course, exactly what the contemporary Germans and French wanted to hear, and they subsequently made extensive use of his work. Annius's revelations made his reputation in his own country as well, and he duly received the wages of sin, by being made secretary to the Pope. Unfortunately for him, the Pope concerned was Roderigo Borgia, whose court was one of the more dangerous places on the planet. Within a short time Annius was dead, allegedly by poison.

His work lived on, in a fantastic flowering of pseudohistory that reached its apogee in the second half of the sixteenth century.

For the French, there was just one problem with all this, and it was that the most important of all ancient authors who wrote about Druids, Julius Caesar, stated categorically that Druidry had originally come from Britain. Taillepied tried to head off this problem by saying that he meant Brittany; but everybody knew, or should have known, that this was linguistically impossible. French scholars were therefore looking nervously over their shoulders at times, wondering when their traditional rivals, the English, were going to wake up to what they were missing, and cash in; but the English did not. Part of the reason for this lay in the complicated ethnic nature of the British Isles. The kingdom in them which traditionally had the strongest links with France was Scotland. Through most of the late middle ages the Scots had regularly found an alliance with the French to be a promising way of making life harder for the English and safer for themselves. As a result there were, as usual, a number of Scots studying at Paris during the period in which the French were getting drunk on Druids, and one of them – Hector Boece, known to the international scholarly community as Boethius – brought them home with him. This was a period in which Scottish historians were going in for some uninhibited mythologising of their own, glorifying their nation's past with the invention of scores of non-existent kings. Boece wrote a national history which incorporated all of them and added a lot more material, bringing in the Druids to act as a learned pagan clergy serving Scotland in the manner of his own, pre-Reformation, Catholic Church. He also engaged in a piece of intellectual larceny of his own, by stealing Mona from the Welsh. He identified it as the Isle of Man, traditionally part of Scotland, and thus turned the people who had defended it against Suetonius into good Scots.

Boece's history was published in Latin (for the European market) in 1526, and translated into Scots (in both prose and verse) during the next decade. Its influence established the Druids as respected features of the Scottish national past for the next two hundred years. The Reformation made no difference to this; when the primate of the reformed Kirk of Scotland, Archbishop Spottiswoode of St Andrews, wrote a religious history of his country in the following century, he merely transformed them into prototypes for Protestant ministers. The

Scots were, however, alone in their enthusiasm. The Welsh had a better claim
to be the true heirs of the ancient British than anybody else, because they were
directly descended from them in language and blood, and had the real island
of Mona. By the reign of Elizabeth, moreover, they were involved in a boom
of history-writing of their own, led by scholars such as Humphrey Llwyd, Sir
John Price and Maurice Kiffin who were making their nation's story fit a new,
Protestant, identity. That story was, however, centred on their medieval bards,
the professional poets who had defined an enduring sense of Welshness in the
course of their people's long struggle against English conquest. They did not
need the Druids, who seemed much more remote, ambivalent and mysterious.
Llwyd was anxious to recapture Mona from the Scots, but his sympathies were
not with the Druids whom Tacitus had portrayed upon it, whom he summed up
as having practised an 'absurd religion'. As late as the 1690s, a prominent Welsh
poet, Henry Vaughan, could answer an enquiry by stating that, as the Druids had
left no writings, nothing genuine could be known about them and there was no
reason to suppose that they had anything to do with the medieval bards who
truly represented the Welsh heritage.

The Irish should also, in theory, have been exceptionally well placed to share
in the new continental enthusiasm for Druids, given their increasingly strong
links with Roman Catholic nations abroad, made as part of a great renewal of
Irish Catholicism that began in the late sixteenth century. This was provoked by
a fresh wave of English conquest, itself partly produced (and largely justified)
by the desire to turn the island Protestant and so safeguard the English (and
Welsh) Reformation from a stab in the back. With Druids so firmly and clearly
embedded in Irish medieval literature, unlike that of the Welsh, there should have
been ample material available to turn them into national heroes. The new Irish
nationalist writers, however, went in precisely the opposite direction; as part of
reaffirming the identity of their people as loyal and pious Catholics, they turned
Druids into the enemy who came before Protestantism; heathen priests who had
been defeated in the first triumph of the true faith.

All this left the Tudor English in a muddle of ignorance and doubt. That the
French and Scots were keen on something was in itself a good reason for the
English to have doubts about it; in this context the Druids could look as suspect

as haggis or garlic. It also did not help matters that, by chance, the first author to deal with them in England, Polydore Vergil, was a pedantic Italian, the second, John Leland, went mad before he could publish, and the third, John Bale, hated what little he had heard of Druids. For whatever complex of reasons, nearly a hundred years passed before English historians took Druids on properly, but then they were pressed into service by the great rewriting of national history which occurred in the later part of the reign of Elizabeth. Druids appeared in both of the key works of this process, which were produced with different aims and for different audiences. One was Holinshed's *Chronicles*, a multi-volume patriotic history designed by a committee for a not very discerning home audience. It was more concerned with inspiring the newly Protestant English with a sense of historical mission than with matters such as source analysis, and so, when dealing with Druids, it simply cobbled together the fantasies of Annius and Boece with the writings of Greek and Roman authors. The other great work of Elizabethan history-writing was the *Britannia* of William Camden. This, designed for a learned international audience, applied the highest standards of scholarship. It had no truck with writers like Annius and Boece, and used only the genuine ancient texts. Both histories had it in common that they made Druids major figures in the earliest known past of the land that became England. In this manner, they arrived at last in the consciousness of the English by the opening of the seventeenth century. During the following two decades, two of the leading political theorists of the reign of James I, Sir Edward Coke and John Selden, took them up as national heroes: Coke made them the people who had established, or at least nurtured, the common law, while Selden hailed them as founders of that tradition of free assembly which was to give rise to the institution of Parliament.

None of this really worked. For every English writer of the seventeenth century anxious to extol Druids in the French and Scottish manner, as honourable forbears, there were one or two who denied that they were either honourable or – properly speaking – forbears. Much of this debate belongs to later chapters of the present book. For now it is sufficient to note that it went on, and also that, while intellectuals wrangled over them, the Druids failed to establish a secure place in the popular imagination. Shakespeare, that instinctive crowd pleaser, totally ignored them, even though he took much of his idea of history from Holinshed and wrote a play, *Cymbeline*, set in ancient Britain. The first playwright actually to put them onto the London stage was Henry Fletcher, sometime in the 1610s, and he made a complete hash of it. His subject was the rebellion of the native British queen, Boudica, which – after some remarkable successes – had eventually been crushed by that same Suetonius Paulinus who had taken Anglesey. In Fletcher's blood-and-thunder melodrama, Druids get totally mixed up with bards and reduced to singers of heroic tales. There was not much better understanding of them in the highest expressions of contemporary theatre, the royal court masques. When Thomas Carew wrote one of these for Charles I in 1633, he vaguely personified the spirit of ancient Britain as 'a chorus of Druids and rivers'. At the mid-point of the century, Elias Ashmole, founder of the Oxford university museum, saluted and dismissed them with the telling phrase 'the famous and mysterious Druids'. By the end of the century things were, on the surface, no different. In 1713 even an educated Englishman like the poet William Diaper was still hazy enough about them to confuse them with the dryads, ancient Greek tree-spirits.

By then, however, things were very much altering beneath the surface of appearances. The catalytic event was the revolution of 1688 in Britain, when a neat combination of the right personalities and the right weather toppled the main royal house of Stuart from the thrones of England and Scotland. The exiled royal family drew most of its remaining support from Ireland and the north and west of Scotland, which is the main reason why, during the next twenty years, the British Isles were drawn together into a superstate dominated by England. In 1691 Ireland was placed firmly under the control of Protestants of English origin who looked to the mother country for support and kept in subjection the Roman Catholic majority of the population. In 1707 England and Scotland were formally united as a single kingdom with one government and Parliament. One of the problems of this new superstate was that there was no obvious history to support it. The group identities of its modern peoples had been formed largely in conflict with each other, and the heroes of them, from Fionn Mac Cumhail, Alfred the Great and Kenneth Mac Alpin, to Edward I, Henry V, Robert the Bruce and Owain Glyndwr, had won their glory in what now looked like civil wars. Suddenly the Druids seemed to provide a set of people common to every part of the islands, for whom impressive claims could be made as mutual ancestors and upon whom a genuinely shared identity could be based. It also helped that, although they kept some vigour in German and French historical tradition, the Renaissance love affair of those nations with them was subsiding, and they were no longer so obviously identifiable as major figures from other people's stories.

The vital conditions were now in place for Druids to take their place as major figures in the historical consciousness of the newly United Kingdom. For those conditions to be effective, however, they needed an advocate, persuasive enough for people in general to pay attention and to accept the message. A number of candidates swiftly lined up for the role in the years just after 1700, but they all had disadvantages. For one thing, none of them was English, and England was both the dominant nation in the new superstate and the centre of cultural fashion. All were from the Celtic lands of the British Isles, attempting to bring the importance of their own cultures to the attention of the English and Lowland Scots. Two, Edward Lhwyd and Henry Rowlands, were Welsh, one, Martin Martin, was a Highland Scot, and the fourth, John Toland, was a Gaelic Irishman by birth and upbringing. Rowlands, Martin and Toland all dealt directly with the Druids, but their personal associations, with what to most of the British were alien cultures, may have had the effect of keeping the ancient holy men looking marginal and foreign. In addition, Toland was not only the liveliest and most provocative writer among them but one of the most controversial and unpopular of his time, because of his attacks on established religion. He tried desperately hard to secure aristocratic sponsorship for a comprehensive book on Druids, promising in succession three very different approaches to the subject, but failed completely to secure it. The final misfortune shared by all four men was that they all died before they could make a sustained impact; and so the Druids reached the 1730s with not much more relevance to the British in general than they had possessed a hundred years before.

For a moment in the 1730s it looked as if things might change, because of the work of another Scot. This one was much better qualified: he came from the Lowlands, with a culture much closer to the English. He had moved south to become part of the London literary world, and he was making his mark as one of the most influential British poets of the century. This was James Thomson, and in 1736 he published a poem entitled 'Liberty', which hailed the new Britain as a realm that had managed to combine national greatness with individual freedoms. He attributed this remarkable achievement to a tradition that began with the Druids, who had inspired the free British tribes to patriotic courage. They admittedly got no more than a single verse, in a very long work, but Thomson was clearly pointing a way forward, which many were subsequently to follow.

Perhaps that was all that was needed, together with enough time for the British to read and digest the relevant writings of earlier authors such as Toland; but such a hypothesis is impossible to substantiate, because a different figure now intervened, and decisively. He was a physically chunky, incurably romantic, Anglican parson called William Stukeley, who will feature repeatedly in the remainder of this book. Stukeley was the person who was to put Druids firmly, and indelibly, into the physical and mental landscapes of the British as a whole, and did so because of a number of unique qualifications. First, he had a tremendous personal enthusiasm for the Druids themselves. Secondly, he enjoyed generally robust good health and long life, giving him the time and energy to survive early checks to his literary career and to get his books published and his ideas known. Thirdly, he was an English gentleman, son of a Lincolnshire lawyer from a long-established landed family; he was therefore one of the ruling class of the dominant nation in the new superstate. Fourthly, he was socially and intellectually well connected, having aristocratic friends and patrons and membership – at various times – of most of the learned societies of the capital in which knowledge of the ancient world was discussed and increased. Fifthly, he had wide interests, covering what are now called the natural sciences, history and prehistory, and is generally regarded as the most significant of all the forefathers of the discipline of archaeology in England. Sixthly, he became a member of the clergy of the established Church, which still ran the universities and was the most powerful and influential cultural force in the nation. Seventhly, he was (eventually) of independent means, marrying enough money to provide a sum which, combined with the profits of a wealthy parish, enabled him to publish beautifully-illustrated books at his own expense.

In his two great volumes on the prehistoric monuments of Stonehenge and Avebury, which appeared in 1740 and 1743, he convinced most of the British, once and for all, that structures of this sort were the work of their native and prehistoric ancestors, and not of the Romans, the Vikings or the wizard Merlin. He identified complex ritual landscapes from the remote past that few had hitherto suspected to exist, and coined enduring technical terms for kinds of ancient monument and aspects of them. In the shorter term, he associated these impressive remains with the Druids, whom he portrayed as admirable in every way and as being ancestors of whom the modern British could be proud and with whom orthodox Christians could feel comfortable. In doing so, he persuaded several generations of country vicars and gentry that they and their culture were respectable objects of research.

It is important to observe the apparent effect on the perceived connection between Druidry and British identity. At some time before his death in 1744 (and probably soon before it), the English poet often later considered the most talented of his generation, Alexander Pope, began working on an epic set in early Britain. It was based on the medieval legend that held Britain to have been settled by refugees from the city of Troy, led by a hero called Brutus after whom the island was named. In Pope's version, Brutus's brave, sturdy and rational warriors arrive to find it dominated by Druids, gentle priests who love the natural world and are able to see the future. This last talent enables them to predict that the newcomers will be good for their country, and so to welcome them; and indeed the mixture of the different qualities represented by the Druids and the Trojans provides a perfect balance. In 1747 a lesser but still famous poet, William Collins, imitated Thomson with an 'Ode to Liberty'. This portrayed the Druids as patriots on two metaphysical levels, showing them first exhorting the chiefs of ancient Britain to defend their country, before a shrine to freedom, and then continuing to praise them for their efforts in a celestial paradise to which all have now gone. During the same year appeared *The Modern Druids*, an appeal to all true Britons to nurture the Royal Navy which was the basis of their present greatness and security. They were urged to do so by by taking care of the land in the manner of their ancient counterparts, and especially the woods that supplied the dockyards with timber. By the end of the decade, therefore, and almost a quarter of a millennium after they had fulfilled the same function for the Germans, French and Scots, the English had finally taken the Druids on in the role of heroic and definitively national ancestors, as part of the process of becoming British.

This process actually consisted of three different, though interlocking, developments. The most important, which has been the focus of a celebrated book by Linda Colley, consisted of defining the inhabitants of Britain against external enemies: specifically, against the forces of Roman Catholicism and political tyranny which were believed to combine (conveniently) in the great contemporary foreign rivals of the British: the French. The English, Scots, Welsh and Cornish could therefore be given a common cause as Protestants, with the same constitutional monarchy and framework of civil liberties, menaced by an identical, mighty and dangerous neighbour. The second development took the form of an effort by the non-English peoples in the new consortium to convince the English (and, to a much lesser extent, each other) of their distinctive cultural achievements, so that their partners could come to understand, respect and value them better. The most sensational figure in this movement was a Highland Scot, James Macpherson, who was treated as a child to an unusually intense experience of the growing pains of the new Britishness. His clan territory had been occupied, and devastated, by soldiers from the British army as part of the repression that followed the rebellion on behalf of the exiled Stuart king that had been led by Bonnie Prince Charlie. Macpherson emerged from youth, and the Highlands, with an ambition to persuade the English and Lowland Scots to admire his own parental culture instead of despising it as barbaric and threatening. Between 1760 and 1763 he published three books of poetry, allegedly translated from the Gaelic and supposed to be epics composed in Scotland in the third century. They became a Europe-wide sensation, hugely admired and influential. They also immediately attracted charges that Macpherson himself had forged the material, starting a controversy which has only recently started to subside, around an agreement that he worked up genuine Gaelic stories into more imposing pieces and claimed them to be much older than they were. During his lifetime Macpherson was defended by many friends and followers, and wholly succeeded in his original aim, in that even people who doubted all of his claims for the poetry found it moving and inspiring in itself.

Auctori d.d. Observantiæ ergo J.V.gucht. Sculptor.

1. William Stukeley's self-portrait as a Druid, with the name Chyndonax, the frontispiece to his book on
   Stonehenge. It perfectly captures his extrovert, romantic, intelligent, obsessive and emotional nature.

2. Suetonius's Romans massacre the Druids (and their female companions) on Anglesey, although none are armed and one touchingly still clutches his harp. Painted by R. Rogers and engraved for Smollett's *A Complete History of England* in 1758.

Engraved for The Complete English Traveller.

Murdering the DRUIDS and Burning their GROVES

3. Another Georgian treatment of the massacre on Anglesey, engraved for "The Complete English Traveller". This time the Druids are not only unarmed, but half-dressed, and their sacred groves as well as they themselves are being burned in the background.

4. Iolo Morganwg on the road, in old age, as drawn for the recollections of him published by his friend Elijah Waring. As usual, he is reading even as he walks.

IOLO MORGANWG, A PERSONAL RECOLLECTION.

Below: 5. This is how Owen Morgan ('Morien'), a successor of Iolo, imagined the latter's Gorsedd of Bards as having appeared in prehistoric times. All involved are suitably gentle and reverent, and bareheaded as Iolo prescribed; though why the harper is costumed as the Roman god Mercury is never explained.

The Druid Fathers at their Public Prayers, led by the Archdruid. The Pristine Gorsedd in its original purity.

6. Another Druid dies at the hands of a Roman invader, this time as the frontispiece to Thomas Love Peacock's *The Genius of the Thames*; his killer's expression is a suitable mixture of fear and guilt, as the expiring man predicts the fall of Rome and greatness of Britain.

7. Perched on the natural podia formed by oak tree roots, a pair of Druids incite their tribespeople to resist Rome, in an engraving from the 1892 version of the *Illustrated History of England*.

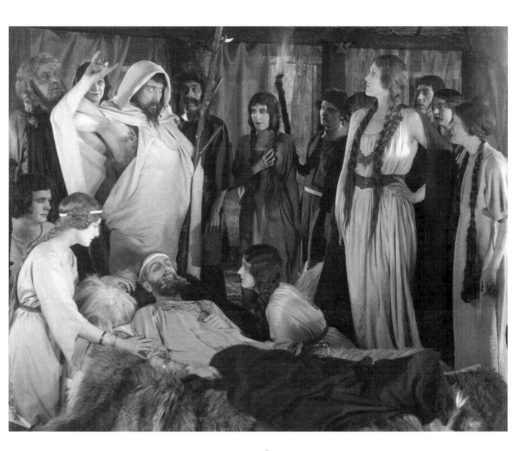

Above: 8. Boudica listens to a Druid warn her against Rome, eyes blazing, in the manner of the one immortalized in William Cowper's poem.

9. Royalty is incorporated into the Welsh Gorsedd, in way that would have warmed Iolo Morganwg's heart: Princess Elizabeth, subsequently the present queen, being led to the stone circle for initiation as an honorary member.

10. The Gorsedd, in turn, incorporates the religious leader of the English Church: Rowan Williams, archbishop of Canterbury, after his initiation as a Druid.

Below: 11. A view of the Neolithic circle at Loanhead of Daviot, one of the 'recumbent stone' circles in the hinterland of Aberdeen, which may have inspired the Scots to be the first nation to connect megalithic monuments to Druids. The characteristic huge horizontal stone, between its tall pillars, is visible on the far side, to the right of centre.

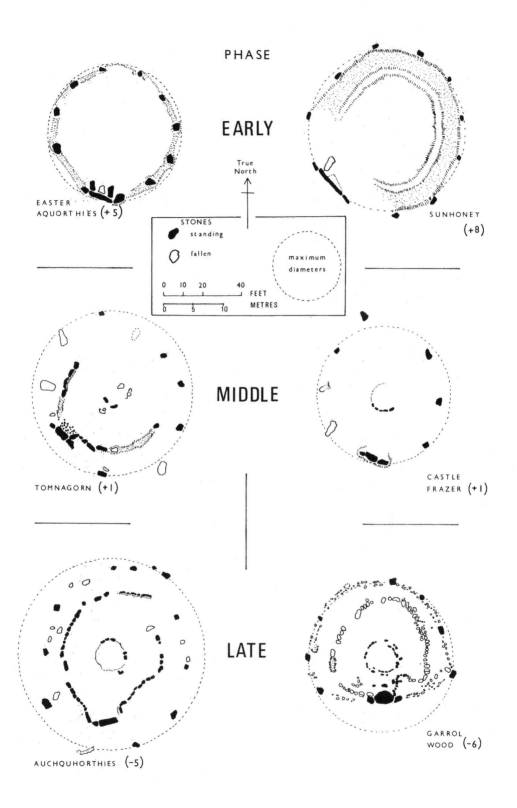

PHASE

EARLY

EASTER AQUORTHIES (+5)

SUNHONEY (+8)

True North

STONES

standing

fallen

maximum diameters

0 10 20 40 FEET

0 5 10 METRES

MIDDLE

TOMNAGORN (+1)

CASTLE FRAZER (+1)

LATE

AUCHQUHORTHIES (−5)

GARROL WOOD (−6)

12. Plans of six recumbent stone circles, collated by the prehistorian Aubrey Burl, showing the remarkable uniformity of the design.

13. John Aubrey, the Wiltshire gentleman antiquary who began the process of associating megaliths and Druids in the minds of the English and Welsh. Painted at about the age at which he 'discovered' Avebury, his lifelong qualities of sweetness and irresolution seems to show in his face.

14. This is the illustration, from Aylett Sammes's illustrated history of Britain, in 1676, which established the enduring British image of a Druid (and wizard). It was taken from an English reference to a German description of statues, almost certainly of Greek philosophers, at a Bavarian monastery.

The third process represented the same aim as the second, but approached from the opposite direction: it was a new interest in traditional Welsh and Scottish culture on the part of English intellectuals. Apart from showing a sporting readiness to promote the British partnership, it promised an immediate cultural benefit, by opening up hitherto unexplored old literatures to English authors and artists who were getting jaded with the traditionally admired Greek and Roman classics. The outstanding figure in this enterprise was probably the poet Thomas Gray, whose credentials as a leader of English taste – being a Londoner who had settled at Cambridge – were impeccable, and whose enthusiasm for Welsh culture, in particular, was passionate and sustained. In 1757 he seized the imagination of the British with a poem called 'The Bard', based (unwittingly) on a seventeenth-century Welsh nationalist myth that the medieval English king Edward I had ordered the extermination of the native Welsh bards. The idea was that by destroying them he would crush the soul of Wales. Gray portrayed the last surviving bard, as cornered on a crag above the River Conway and choosing to leap to his death in it rather than yield to foreign tyranny. It was a useful reminder of the centrality of poets (like Gray) to national life, but also a remarkable cultural achievement: to portray to a largely English audience an episode in which their own ancestors and nation featured as villains, and enlist their sympathy for the victims. The poem succeeded completely, achieving a wide readership and proportionate acclaim, and inspiring at least ten works of art.

Druids could play a prominent role in all three processes, and did, from the 1740s onward. For the rest of the century, their link with patriotism was recognised in a succession of odes, plays, masques and prose works, and inspired two masterpieces. The first was put before the public in 1759, at the height of the Seven Years' War against the French. This was William Mason's epic poem 'Caractacus', commonly regarded as the most celebrated piece of heroic literature produced in Georgian England. Its impact, and influence, was certainly tremendous, and may be said to have completed the work that Stukeley had commenced, of making the Druids household names among the English. Mason was a former Cambridge don turned country clergyman, ambitious for fame as a writer and a great admirer of Gray, who repaid him with the snide if accurate comment that Mason 'reads little or nothing, writes abundance, and that with a design to make a fortune in it'. The poem was based on Tacitus's account of the attack on Anglesey, but mangled even the presumed historical facts beyond recognition. It transported the patriotic British hero Caractacus there from a different generation, credited the Romans with a gallantry and mercy completely missing from Tacitus's story, and dismissed the charge of human sacrifice with the claim that it had resulted from a piece of Roman confusion: only French Druids did such awful things. What Mason did was give readers, as Pope had aimed to do, the best of two different worlds: in this case, the eventual joyous union of Briton and Roman adds the blessings of civilisation and reason to the native British qualities of heroism and nobility, and the resulting combination is (eventually) unbeatable. No wonder his epic went into a second edition before the end of the year, and four more before 1777, when it was turned into a stage play as well.

The second really significant work was also a poem, much shorter and by a very different kind of person. This was William Cowper, a writer who lived in retirement enforced by bouts of depressive illness, leavened by an enthusiasm for evangelical Christianity, reforming causes and his nation. In 1780 he wrote an ode, 'Boadicea', which was published two years later. It concerned the rebellion of Boudica, the queen who had led what was briefly the most successful resistance ever offered by the southern British to Rome. No ancient source mentioned Druids in connection with it, but if they *had* been associated with patriotic opposition to the Romans then they *should* have been involved. Cowper made one of them the precipitating force behind the uprising, a 'hoary chief' among them, 'sage beneath a spreading oak'. When the queen pours out to him the outrages that Roman officials had committed upon her and her tribe, he flies into a tempest of rage and grief. Like previous writers, Cowper enhanced the figure of the Druid by crossing it with that of the bard, so he now speaks a prophecy, while playing 'his sweet but awful lyre'. It is of the eventual decline and destruction of Rome, and the glorious future of Britain, which would come to build an empire of its own greater than any of which the Romans dreamed. Mason had turned the interaction of Roman and Briton into one of balance and complement, the fruitful combination of very different, and opposing, qualities. Cowper chose a vehemently contrasting course, making Rome the epitome of all that was foreign, intrusive and tyrannical, and pronouncing the innate qualities and particular destiny of the British sufficient to ensure them an unprecedented glory. His poem was to be reproduced, and taught in schoolrooms, down to the twentieth century.

The image of Druids as ancestors for the British reached its peak in the second half of the eighteenth century, in the poetry and prose of Scottish, English and Welsh authors alike. They were almost always assumed to be wholly male: the black-clad women in Tacitus were at once too enigmatic, too disorderly and too difficult to relate to any parallel figures known to Georgian culture. The Druids were commonly shown as functioning as clergy did in any military system: by blessing and encouraging the troops. They were also, however, assimilated to another variety of holy men familiar to the age from its favourite literature: the Hebrew prophets of the Old Testament. Cowper's one was clearly in this mould. By the end of the century a poet called William Sotheby could add a further twist to patriotic legend by adding them to the traditions of King Arthur. It had long been said that the king and his knights slumbered in a cave, waiting for the moment when their country most needed them again, and that they would awake and go to its aid. Sotheby now put Druids into that cavern as well, awaiting the same mission.

By that date, however, forces were already working against the newly found sense of the Druids as common property, and as straightforwardly admired national forbears, for the different peoples of the unified British state. The process of state unification was generally accepted as necessary and desirable, and as a success, by the late Georgian period. It also, however, inevitably imposed strains on the self-images and identities of the component peoples, especially on those traditionally fewer and militarily weaker, than the English who dominated the combined kingdom. The price of acceptance and partnership seemed to many of them to be absorption: at best to lose their historic identities completely and become part of a homogeneous Anglicised culture, and at worst to be regarded as slightly comic and debased varieties of Englishness. Accordingly, from the end of the eighteenth century a centrifugal force set into the British state to balance those working for union and assmilation. The Scots and Welsh adopted symbols and traditions that set them off from the English literally at a glance: national costumes, songs, instruments. institutions and literatures. In this process, Druids had sharply differing fortunes. They played almost no part in the revival of Scottish nationalism, because they had already been given up by it as part of the cost of Britishness, together with an independent government and Parliament. It had been the Scots, after all, among all the peoples of Britain, who had first incorporated Druids into a sense of nationhood and who had seen them taken on by the English as part of the new Britishness. Scottish cultural separatism now abandoned them to that overarching British identity, and instead developed new symbols, such as the kilt, clan tartans and bagpipes, all drawn from the part of their nation geographically furthest from England and most alien to it: the Highlands. It was the Welsh who took on the Druids as part of a cultural counterattack.

The early modern Welsh had not needed Druids, because they had much more satisfyingly solid and directly relevant figures on whom to focus national pride in the shape of their bards, the professional poets who served the native ruling classes. This was the easier in that the bardic tradition enjoyed a last great flowering in the early sixteenth century, just before the boom in the writing of new Welsh nationalist histories encouraged by the Reformation. Between 1560 and 1660, however, it went into steep and terminal decline, and by the end of the seventeenth century it was gone. The reason was that the gentry, upon whose patronage it had traditionally depended, no longer wanted it. What they wished to buy into, instead, was a general culture of gentility that united most of the wealthier landowners of western Europe, and to break out of the cultural backwater in which their medieval way of life had left them. Welsh scholars and poets who wished to preserve traces of that way of life by 1660 found comfort in two considerations; but both of these largely evaporated over the next hundred years. One was that an ancient and distinctive national culture still survived among the lesser landowners and common people; but much of this disappeared in turn as the rest of society 'modernised'. The other was that the traditional bardic verse could be collected and written down before it was forgotten and so preserved for posterity. The trouble here was that, by the early eighteenth century, much of what was contained in that verse could no longer be understood; it depended largely on complicated and oblique symbols and references, which the old bards had learned as part of their training but to which they had not left any guide. As a result, when Welsh patriots turned to the task of reviving a distinctive national culture with ancient roots, in the second half of the eighteenth century, they found themselves lacking most of the necessary materials for it.

None the less, they rose to the challenge with energy and ingenuity, collating, editing and studying the manuscripts of bardic verse and encouraging the production of new Welsh literature and music. By the last two decades of the century the greatest centre for this work was London, where Welsh people both tended to be most homesick and most conscious of their status as a minority in the new Britain. They were also best equipped there to earn the money needed to sponsor cultural events. In particular, the societies founded by Welsh Londoners, the Cymmorodorion and the Gwyneddigion, acted as powerhouses for this work. From 1789 the Gwyneddigion set about systematically reviving the medieval institution of the eisteddfod, a gathering of poets and musicians to compete for prizes, and organised a number of these in north and central Wales. Druids were co-opted into this general programme of national renewal as part of the British boom in enthusiasm for them. They could, after all, be deemed to have had a specially close potential relationship with the Welsh, the most obvious direct descendants of the ancient British in race and language, and their new popularity could rub off on Wales with some adroit management. Furthermore, by the beginning of the eighteenth century, the tug of war between Welsh and Scottish scholars over which nation possessed Tacitus's island of Mona had been resolved firmly in favour of the Welsh. A Druid appeared as a supporter of the coat of arms adopted by the Cymmorodorion at their foundation in 1751. The most learned Welsh scholar of the mid eighteenth century, Evan Evans, identified Druids with bards, and wrote a long poem in 1772, 'The Love of Our Country', which called them the first defenders of the Welsh nation and the founders of its poetry. The very obscurity of much of the medieval bardic verse could actually be turned to advantage in this situation, by suggesting that it had preserved some of the mystical teachings of the Druids themselves. Henry Rowlands had first made this point in 1722 Evan Evans repeated it.

The problem was that it was, by its very nature, impossible to prove. So, although by the 1780s some English and Welsh writers were prepared to grant

Wales a special relationship with Druidry, the evidence to clinch this was lacking. The missing material was now provided by an artisan called Edward Williams, best known to history by the bardic name on which he eventually settled: Iolo Morganwg ('Eddie from Glamorgan'). Iolo was the second really important person in the relationship of the modern British with Druidry, after William Stukeley, and like Stukeley will reappear in subsequent chapters. One recent scholar, Ceri Lewis, has hailed him as an authority on architecture, agriculture botany, geology, music and theology, as well as an accomplished poet and the greatest expert of his day on the history of Welsh literature, with an unrivalled knowledge of the surviving manuscript sources: in short, 'unquestionably the most remarkable figure in Welsh literature'. Another, Prys Morgan, has termed him 'the true spiritual father of modern Welsh nationalism' and the most learned Welshman of his generation. A third, Geraint Jenkins, has called him 'a stunningly learned and many-sided genius'. His occupation was, by turns, that of stonemason, shopkeeper, builder and farmer, but his dream was always to establish himself as an author of poetry and works of scholarship. Given his abilities, credentials and ambitions, he was the obvious person to rediscover any records of Druidic custom and belief preserved in medieval Welsh tradition. He duly announced complete success in the task.

Between 1791 and 1794, when he was living in London as a prominent member of its Welsh immigrant society, he revealed to the world a ceremony, a liturgy and a body of moral and religious teachings that had been handed down to the medieval Welsh poets and scholars by the ancient Druids, and a history to explain and support these. A central feature of this system was that it perfectly reconciled the figures of the bard and the Druid. It made bards, the traditional representatives of Welsh culture and the people with whom the patriots of the Georgian revival most identified, the central characters in ancient British society. They had the joint tasks of preserving and transmitting the existing native cultural tradition, and of encouraging further achievements, and Druids were represented as always having been just one category of bard, with a special concern for religious and ethical matters. Iolo declared that Welsh literature alone preserved their lore and that the ancient accounts of them were both inadequate and faulty. He accordingly made it plain that the modern Welsh were both their natural heirs and the only people equipped to study them and represent them to the world. In the records described by Iolo, they were also revealed as splendid ancestors, with beliefs and customs that most modern people could admire. Iolo had, in fact, through the power of his scholarship and devotion of his patriotism, solved most of the problems of the contemporary Welsh cultural revival and grabbed back for Wales a particular association with Druids just as they had become most respected as figures built into the new fabric of British nationalism. There was just one problem with all this, and it is summed up in another, resounding, superlative bestowed on him by Ceri Lewis: that 'he was, beyond doubt, the most accomplished and successful forger in literary history'. Having failed to uncover the material that he needed for his task, he had composed it himself.

Forgery (and extensive 'enhancement' of genuine sources) has already featured in this story, in the cases of Annius of Viterbo and James Macpherson; it was also to play a prominent role in the creation of modern Scottish national identity, as a pair of English brothers invented most of the 'historic' clan tartans. The late eighteenth century was a particularly fertile period for it, because of the combination of an energetic historical scholarship, making frequent genuine discoveries, with an as yet immature ability to distinguish true from false documents. Iolo's achievement, however, went well beyond the norm, and left an enduring mark on Welsh cultural life. This requires some explanation. Part of the reason lay in his own psychopathology: like all really great imposters, including famous actors and actresses and effective spies, he seems to have had the ability to blur the boundary between fiction and reality in his own mind. Mary-Ann Constantine, examining his personal papers for clues to his mental processes, has found 'few or no' indications of any self-awareness of his identity as an inventor of evidence; it is possible, though not proven, that he really was trapped in his own fantasy world. Geraint Evans has pointed to a particular aspect of his lifestyle that greatly enhances this possibility: his addiction to opium. He took it as medicine, for the later three-quarters of his life, to control chronic asthma; the precise form that he used was that of laudanum, in which the drug is drunk dissolved in alcohol. This was freely available as a sedative in his time, but extremely potent, and he consumed it in enormous doses. Certainly this would have aided the blurring effect described above, though it could only have acted to enhance an already remarkable degree of personal psychosis.

Another aspect of the latter was his driving ambition, which could be described as expanding outwards through three concentric circles of aspiration. First, and most urgently, he wanted glory for himself. Prys Morgan has supplied a very neat case-study of this impulse in action and how it related to his talents as a forger. It focuses on the sixteenth-century legend of a medieval Welsh prince called Madoc, who was said to have sailed to America and settled there. The foundation of the United States gave the London Welsh a new interest in this, and in 1790 a respected minister among them, John Williams, published a book on it. As soon as this attracted attention, Iolo faked some documents to corroborate Williams's version of the story and thrust himself forward with them, posing as a greater expert than Williams himself. The unfortunate cleric was forced to produce a second volume of his book, incorporating Iolo's bogus material. From this and other examples, Morgan concluded that 'Iolo mimicked and invented pieces of literature all his life – poems, chronicles, texts, stories – often without any motive whatsoever save to prove to himself that whatever any other person produced, he could do better'.

His second circle of ambition was to inflate the reputation of his native Glamorgan, which had in fact long been one of the more Anglicised parts of Wales and one of the least prominent in the medieval resistance to English conquest. It had also been marginal to the main medieval bardic tradition, its poets only having become prominent near the end of the middle ages, and only ever including one (Lewis Morganwg, in the Tudor period) who could be regarded as a figure of national status. The true heartland of national pride, and of resistance to conquest and Anglicisation, had lain in the north since the end of the twelfth century, and there it remained at the time of the modern cultural revival. The London society most active in promoting that revival, the Gwyneddigion, meant 'those from north-west Wales', and the eisteddfodau that it sponsored were all in the north. Iolo, a prominent member of that society during his time in London, was often teased in it for his southern Welsh accent. It was therefore a particularly sweet revenge to claim, as he did, to have proved both that the bards of Glamorgan were the only people in Wales to have preserved the authentic medieval bardic and ancient Druidic teachings, and that he himself was the only person left alive to have been initiated into it. This claim was acceptable to many because of the third circle of his ambitions, which was to advance the reputation of Wales in general to be a land of uniquely long, rich and unbroken cultural tradition, one which preserved what had once been common to all north-western Europe. In Prys Morgan's view, Iolo's Welsh nationalism chimed with another aspect of his psychopathology, his 'persecution mania, which made him invent a dramatic version of Welsh history full of ogre-like conquerors and vengeful attackers'. It may be suggested here that the failure of his literary ambitions in London, forcing his return to Glamorgan for life in 1795, would only have sharpened this characteristic.

A second reason for his success as a forger lay in his unrivalled knowledge of medieval and early modern Welsh literature, which allowed him to ground his fabrications in genuine, and already familiar, texts. A favourite technique of his was to take a known but obscure bard or scholar, or a figure from genuine literature, and attribute forged work to one of the first two, or compose a new body of legend surrounding the latter. For example, he claimed to have found much of his information on Druidic teachings in a manuscript made by a genuine sixteenth-century Glamorgan copyist, Llywelyn Sion, of whom little had hitherto been known. Iolo added that he had found (and left) the manuscript in the possession of a genuine scholar in modern Glamorgan, Richard Bradford of Bettws; but Bradford had died by the time that anybody thought to look for it. More of the ancient lore that he revealed was said to have been discovered in another Tudor text, compiled by Llewelyn Sion and two other actual scholars from the period. Rachel Bromwich has studied Iolo's use of the classic Welsh literary form of the triad: a saying which groups three things together that have a common characteristic. Much genuine medieval bardic lore was contained in triads, which had become the focus of much attention in the course of the modern revival. Iolo built on this by rewriting genuine medieval triads to incorporate moral and religious teachings, and composing many that were completely original. In the process, he carried on the work of fleshing out figures who were known only from passing references in the real literature. For example, Dyfnwal Moelmut was a leader found in early medieval genealogies, whom Geoffrey of

Monmouth, the twelfth-century composer of romanticised history, had turned into a king and a codifier of law. Iolo composed a series of triads that set forth his laws, and which in turn embodied the view of ancient British history that Iolo was inventing. Hugon le Fort (Hugo the Strong) had been a character in the romances associated with the early medieval continental emperor Charlemagne. Iolo found a reference to him in a poem by the late medieval Welsh bard Iolo Goch, under the slightly transmuted name of Hu Gardarn, and developed him into the founding figure of Welsh culture. He claimed to have found many of the triads that he published in a manuscript compiled in 1601 by the famous scholar Thomas Jones of Tregaron, given to Iolo by one friend (now dead) and lent by him to another, who had died before he could return it, so that it had become lost.

Another reason for Iolo's success was that he often wrapped up his own work in that of others, which disguised the trail that led back to him as author. His first victim in this regard was an honest and patriotic Welsh schoolmaster working in London, William Owen, who was another prominent member of the cultural revival. One of Owen's earlier projects was to produce a complete edition of the work of Dafydd ap Gwilym, the poet often considered to be the best medieval Wales had produced. Iolo wrote a set of poems in the same style, imitating it brilliantly, and sent them to Owen as newly-discovered work by ap Gwilym. Owen gratefully included them in his edition, and spread the news of Iolo's discovery around the capital, launching his reputation there. Three years later Owen produced an edition of the poems of another celebrated medieval bard, Llywarch Hen. This time Iolo contributed as a preface to it his first forgery of the teachings of the ancient bardic and Druidic order After this stealthy approach, Iolo felt ready in 1794 to publish his own first book of poems and add a further catalogue of alleged Druidic teachings. The reception of this was disappointing enough to send him back to Wales and into further concealed methods of planting his ideas. The most effective was provided by another leader of the London Welsh community, a prosperous fur and leather merchant called Owen Jones, who had helped to sponsor Owen's editions of medieval poetry. He subsequently provided money for a much more ambitious project: a bumper edition, in three volumes, of all the chief Welsh medieval texts, which would introduce ordinary

Welsh people to the best of their cultural heritage. Iolo was one of the most active members of the editorial team. The first volume appeared in 1801, fulfilling all of the original design. The second came in 1803, but now Iolo had begun to sift his own forgeries into the genuine, and valuable material. The third, following four years later, consisted almost entirely of his bogus texts. By behaving in this manner, he had betrayed not only his friends and sponsors but his country, by preferring that its people should read his own fraudulent work to the real literary heritage of their forebears. To give some sense of the damage done, it needs to be appreciated that the material intended for the fourth volume of the series was that which was later to become known as *The Mabinogion*. By now, however, the money had run out, squandered on Iolo's deceptions, and almost half a century was to elapse before the most famous collection of all Welsh medieval literature saw print. These deceptions account for the bitter metaphor used repeatedly of Iolo Morganwg by scholars in the late twentieth century: that he polluted the wells of source material on which Welsh scholarship depended.

The final reason for Iolo's ability to deceive lay, paradoxically, in his own failure as an author. From the early 1790s he often talked of publishing his comprehensive history of the British bards, and of the Druid system that they had incorporated, but never completed it. Instead he spent his old age in a cottage at the little village in which he had grown up – Flemingston, among the softly rolling pastures and woods of the Vale of Glamorgan – making more and more notes and drafts for it. He wrote to William Owen in 1803 with the admission that 'There is in some sort of chaotic existence such a mixon [sic] of papers scribbled from time to time by me as materials for the History of the Bards, but of which, beyond this, I know nothing at all, remember not a single idea or syllable'. Geraint Jenkins has suggested, very plausibly, that this incomplete and jumbled work was another characteristic of chronic opium addiction. As a result, at his death in 1826 he left a vast mass of manuscripts, most purporting to be transcripts from medieval and early modern sources, in which his system of Druidic tradition was developed still further. His skill as a forger, and perhaps the drug-induced disorder of his mind, caused him to make several different versions of some key texts and at times to add notes claiming that he himself did not understand the contents. To the unwary, or even to the fair-minded, such touches seemed powerful arguments that – whatever the authenticity of his sources themselves – he was innocent of any conscious deception. As a result, his collection of papers was treated by many as a treasury of information taken from old (and now apparently lost) sources. In the forty years after his death, selections were published in five successive volumes, which incorporated between them most of his material on the Druids and gave it a new lease of life in the nineteenth- and twentieth-century imagination.

From the beginning, doubts were expressed about Iolo's claims for bardic history. These multiplied with the publication of his papers after his death. Critics sometimes went as far as accusing him of having made them up, while others settled for suspecting the late medieval and Tudor bards, on whom he had (apparently) relied, of making the inventions. Before he could be properly unmasked, however, a much better knowledge was required of Welsh medieval texts, a stage only reached at the end of the Victorian period, with the work of Sir John Morris-Jones. The job was only truly accomplished with the appearance of a scholar prepared to devote a lifetime to it, equipped with the most thorough possible expertise in both the medieval and early modern bardic texts (especially those of Glamorgan) and Iolo's own papers and biography. This was Griffith John Williams, who set to work in the 1910s and completed his task in the 1950s, by which time no doubt whatever remained of the true extent of Iolo's inventiveness and duplicity; and so, as Williams was anxious also to emphasise, of his genius. The result was that, to most Welsh scholars for most of the twentieth century, the trickster from Glamorgan was regarded as a traitor and a villain. Only recently have some, whose names are cited above, felt able to acknowledge fully the second part of Williams's conclusion and recognise him as a major cultural figure in his own right. Ironically, his reputation has remained higher in England, and outside the university system, for the simple reason that Morris-Jones and Williams both published their findings in Welsh whereas Iolo's key texts have long been printed in English. During the late twentieth century, a rumour circulated among English Druids, in particular, that nobody had ever worked through the full mass of his papers, long housed in the National Library of Wales, and that they contained original texts that proved the truth of some, at least, of what he had asserted. Another story, in the same circles, held that scholars had now found plenty of ancient material in his writings but had not yet completed the work of separating it from his additions. Neither is true: there are genuine early modern bardic manuscripts in his archive, but they contain none of his 'Druidic' teachings, and the references to real texts and characters in own writings have no relevance to Druidry in themselves. He always added the relevance himself, by creating the evidence.

Iolo's most effective contribution to Welsh nationalist culture was not a doctrine, or a body of literature, but a ceremony which he named 'The Gorsedd of the Bards of the Isle of Britain', *gorsedd* being a Welsh word generally meaning a high seat or mountain top, but which he chose to translate as 'sublime moot'. To him, it was an event for the awarding of formal honours to Welsh people who had excelled in the arts, sciences and religion, and for a display of the abilities of some. He staged the first on Primrose Hill, London, in 1792. Full details survive of the one held at the autumn equinox of that year, which show the basic elements of the ritual fully developed: a circle of small stones was laid out with a larger one at the centre. A drawn sword was placed on this and all the participants assisted to sheathe it as a sign of the identity of true bards as heralds and ministers of peace. Bardic traditions and several poems were then recited. On his return to Glamorgan, Iolo took the custom of the Gorsedd home with him and founded a number of such meetings around Wales. What gave them much greater force, and importance, was a new movement among the Welsh clergy of the established church. By the end of the eighteenth century the process had begun that was to transform the people of Wales, hitherto some of the most religiously conservative in Britain, into the most enthusiastic followers of the dissenting Protestant sects who worshipped outside the official church: the chapel was replacing the parish church as the centre of Welsh devotion. Faced with this challenge, some of the official clergy decided to put themselves at the head of the new cultural revival, in the hope of having their flocks identify them, and their institution, as the finest embodiment of Welsh nationalism. Their chosen vehicles were local associations known as Cambrian Societies, founded in each region of the country and centred on the institution of the *eisteddfod*, revived so recently by the London Welsh associations. Their leader was Thomas Burgess, Bishop of St David's. He was himself a Hampshire-born Englishman, but that only added fervour to the enthusiasm with which he championed the customs and arts of his newly-adopted nation.

The critical moment for the process came in early July 1819, when the first of these bodies, the newly-formed Cambrian Society of Dyfed, gathered at the Ivy Bush Inn, Carmarthen, to hold an *eisteddfod*. Burgess presided over the opening session, and the organising committee consisted entirely of churchmen. The bishop made it a principle, adopted by all his clerical lieutenants, to welcome a partnership with Protestants of all kinds; they intended to build a set of national institutions which they would lead by example and moral authority, rather than a sectarian one identified wholly with their own denomination. As part of this canny and liberal approach, Burgess welcomed the now aged Iolo into the team of organisers of the eisteddfod. This was an unholy alliance if ever there was one, because Iolo himself – as he had repeatedly made clear – did not believe in established churches; but each was willing to take advantage of the other. Iolo duly held a Gorsedd ceremony in the garden of the inn, assisted (among others) by three of the bishop's young parsons. Iolo then admitted a succession of people to membership of the Bards of the Isle of Britain, tying ribbons of different colours around their right arms to indicate the cultural service for which they were being honoured. In his system, Druids were simply bards who happened also to be ministers of religion, and so the rectors and vicars of Burgess's Church could be absorbed into it – along with any other kind of Welsh clergyman – without difficulty.

Regional cultural societies now spread across Wales, with the *eisteddfod* as their focus and the Gorsedd commonly added as its ritual element; a ceremony which, in itself, embodied Iolo's version of history. For a time the established churchmen retained prominence in the leadership of such events, and none did so with more vigour than a young rector called John Williams, who took the bardic name 'Ab Ithel' after a celebrated bard from whom he claimed to be descended. For much of his working life, he served the parish of Llanymawddwy, in one of the bleakest parts of the Cambrian Mountains. He did so with a reckless devotion, riding or walking out on winter nights to visit the sick and the troubled, sometimes being swept off his feet by streams in flood. When his parish was afflicted by an epidemic of fever, and all the surrounding settlements cut off contact with it, he remained at his post, ministering to the sick and dying. Such a lifestyle took its toll: he sometimes fainted when returning home from his tours of duty, once passed out in the pulpit, and for the last ten years of his life was never really well. In view of all this, the energy with which he pursued his literary career is the more remarkable: he published books of history, piety and poetry, edited and translated some of the key medieval Welsh texts, and co-founded first the Cambrian Archaeological Society, with its journal *Archaeologia Cambrensis*, and then (when he fell out with it) the Cambrian Institute, with another periodical, the *Cambrian Journal*. He also became one of the most committed and tireless disciples of Iolo Morganwg, to whom he gave the same devotion he showed to his parishioners, reading through Iolo's archive, publishing several articles based on it, and eventually editing the most important of the remaining texts in it dealing with the nature of ancient Druidry. He brought them out in two volumes, in English translation to reach the widest possible audience, under the ringing name of *Barddas* ('bard-knowledge'). They became the most widely-read and influential of all the publications of Iolo's work.

Ab Ithel was therefore at the very centre of Welsh cultural life in the mid nineteenth century, and his greatest dream was to help create an institution at that centre which would draw together all the components of the revival now flourishing at a regional level: a National Eisteddfod. This was achieved in the year before his death, though ironically organised and controlled by more sober individuals who were reacting against his wilder ideas and anxious to tone down some of the 'Druidical' touches that he envisaged for the event. Iolo's Gorsedd ceremony was, however, retained as an indispensable element. The National Eisteddfod collapsed between 1868 and 1880, but then returned permanently and with added glamour. The Gorsedd now had an Archdruid in charge, and in 1894 members of the ceremony adopted robes in the colours of their particular grades in it. This act opened the flood gates of pomp, so that the next year the Slade Professor of Fine Art at Oxford University, Herbert Herkomer, was brought in to design standard robes for the grades, a ceremonial sword (with a copper-gilt hilt set with crystal) for the sheathing ritual, and regalia for the Archdruid: a crown of metal oak leaves and acorns, a copy of a Bronze Age breastplate and a crystal-headed sceptre. Next year there appeared a blue and gold banner, wrought with crystals, and a drinking horn (actually from an African buffalo) covered in silver. In 1902 the Gorsedd was effectively made the House of Lords of the National Eisteddfod, without whose consent the event could not be held and subjects could not be chosen for competitions. By this period, too, the small stones that were carried in to represent those needed for the Gorsedd circles were replaced by megaliths, erected for the purpose and often left standing as a permanent memorial of the event, and perhaps available for reuse should the Eisteddfod (which rotated around Wales) return to the town or city concerned at a future date.

It is an obvious irony that, even as the Gorsedd was growing ever more power-ful, ornate and impressive-looking, its historical claims were being undermined by the exposure of its creator as an imposter. This latter process was given a still sharper relevance by the fact that both of the scholars involved in discrediting Iolo, Morris-Jones and Williams, were also critics of the Gorsedd itself as a conservative force in Welsh life and letters. Its members reacted and adapted with commendable speed, so that by 1923 its Recorder felt able to declare that neither the ceremony itself nor even its name dated back as far as the middle ages, let alone to Druidical times. None the less, he could still argue, with justice, that since history began bards had engaged in contests, and that the Gorsedd could therefore claim to represent a native tradition of bardic arts stretching back to pre-Christian times. During the rest of the twentieth century the Gorsedd settled down comfortably into the character of a colourful and popular piece of modern pageantry: in Prys Morgan's words, the public face of the Welsh-language 'establishment'. As such it is a textbook example of an 'invented tradition': one that relied upon an original foundation myth that has subsequently been disproved but has made itself worthy of respect in its own right.

Even as modern pageantry, there is nothing particularly pre-Christian about the Gorsedd. It opens with a prayer to 'God', written by Iolo. From the late nineteenth century onward it began to add celebrations of natural produce and beauty – the presentation of blooms, fruits and crops, and a dance by children wearing flowers. Though these may have echoed the (then) prevailing fashion among scholars to imagine ancient paganism as primarily made up of fertility cults, they have far more obviously in common with the love of the vanishing countryside, something which became a feature of mainstream southern British culture from the late Victorian period, as the British, with terrifying speed, became predominantly an urban and industrial nation. The widespread adoption of harvest festivals in churches and chapels, and of May Queens and maypole dances in schools, were other manifestations of this. Although the leadership of patriotic Welsh culture by established clergy did not survive the middle decades of Victoria's reign, the Archdruids of the National Eisteddfod have mostly been ministers of the main Welsh Protestant denominations. The consecration of Rowan Williams, Archbishop of Canterbury, as a Druid at the National Eisteddfod in 2002 was entirely in keeping with the tradition, kept up since Iolo's time, which regarded that grade as being a kind of honorary degree awarded to a churchman. In 1928 a parallel body, the Gorseth, was established in Cornwall as a focus for the growing Cornish cultural revival, with the sponsorship and support of the Welsh Gorsedd. It dispensed with Druids altogether, being wholly a gathering and council of bards, with no formal representation of religion among its members.

Iolo's concept of an unbroken bardic and Druidic tradition in Wales, represented by the Gorsedd, achieved rapid attention and some acceptance in the English and Scottish parts of Britain as well as in his own land. As a result of the contacts he had made in the metropolitan literary world, English writers such as Robert Southey and Thomas Love Peacock put it into their work, and it spread far through that of scholars from the rest of the island. It became a familiar – though never an entirely uncontroversial – part of Welsh national identity, together with the female costume of steeple hat and red cloak, the harp as chosen instrument, the *Mabinogion* as the greatest piece of traditional literature, and the national anthem 'Hen Wlad Fy Nhadau' ('Land of my Fathers'), all of which were brought together into a system in the mid nineteenth century, marking off the Welsh as strongly as the kilt, tartan and bagpipes signified the Scots. In 1887 a campaigner for home rule for Wales could use it as an argument for the superior and older civilisation of his people. When George Borrow's classic account of the Welsh countryside, *Wild Wales*, was put into an edition in the popular 'Everyman' series, in 1906, the English critic Theodore Watts-Dunton was asked to contribute an introduction. It commenced, automatically, by hailing Wales as the 'land of Druidism'.

All this made it the easier and more natural for the rest of the British to shake the Druids off. Having been built into the identity of the new Britain in the mid eighteenth century, Druids found fewer and fewer people inclined to regard them as a part of its heritage in the nineteenth. Other factors than Iolo's genius were working towards this end. An important one is that the images of Druids that had come down from the ancient world were often too negative to provide comfortable material for patriotism. Another is that the Victorians began to doubt whether, admirable or not, they had actually been that important in British prehistory. Two others derived directly from the complex process of building and sustaining a sense of Britishness, the earlier parts of which have been discussed above. One concerned the image of Rome itself, against which that of the patriot Druid was most often pitted. Medieval Europeans had defined themselves largely as the heirs of Rome, and, as the greatest empire of the ancient world and the fount of much later European civilisation, admiration for it remained strong during succeeding centuries. It took on a new lease of life in the Victorian period, as the British acquired a huge empire of their own, most of it consisting of native peoples whom they considered to be backward or barbaric by their own standards; much as the Romans had once regarded the British themselves.

It was thus very easy for many to identify more with the conquerors of Roman Britain and Gaul than the conquered. This was aided further by the new, linked, concepts of the evolution of species and of the inherent tendency of human beings (or at least of their more advanced races) to economic, technological and moral progress. According to these new views ancient Britain (Druids and all) represented a rather grubby and disgraceful childhood, out of which the natives had grown with the aid of the Greeks and Romans, who had passed on to them the sacred duty of advancing humanity further. The other relevant development was the home-grown English reaction to the desire on the part of the Scots and Welsh to find symbols that could mark themselves off at a glance from a generalised, anglocentric, new Britishness and so preserve their separate national identities. A quest for a distinctive Englishness, commenced in response, led easily and directly to the Anglo-Saxons, who could be portrayed as honest, simple and robust people, uncontaminated by the corruption and decay that had beset the overcivilised Romans and their subjects. According to this view, the early English had nurtured (in their German forests and farmlands) a natural attachment to liberty that was to flower on British soil into the common law, the jury system and representative government. This concept of history rebranded the native British (once again, Druids and all) as 'Celts', a breed inclined to moral and political weakness, instability and unreliablity. It grew with particular force between 1850 and 1875. A particularly vicious edge was put upon this abuse when it was deployed against the Irish, who had been brought into the United Kingdom in 1801 and thereafter manifested an increasingly strong and sustained desire to reject the Union and get out, reinforced by their own national cultural revival. Druids were built into the Irish literary heritage and accordingly featured prominently in the works of the nationalist revival: all the more reason for English and Scots to cease to identify with them.

None the less, the shift was a slow one. Nineteenth-century plays, sculptures and paintings still praised Caractacus and Boudica as national champions, and thousands of schoolchildren were still taught older works such as Cowper's poem, which embodied Druids in the same role. In the first half of the century new poetry was still produced along the same lines. Iolo had shown no interest in the great iconic event of patriotic Druidry, the defence of Anglesey, partly because the island was not in (or off) Glamorgan and partly because it came from a Roman source. Most of his design was to convince everybody that the classical references to Druids were worthless, and that the only solid information was in Welsh texts of which he was the discoverer and publicist. That left Tacitus's portrait as the mainstay of a more generalised British role for ancient Druids. The most widely-read female English poet of the century, Felicia Dorothea Hemans, wrote a 'Druid Chorus on the Landing of the Romans' (on Anglesey) during the 1820s. Two of the century's most famous male writers, Thomas Love Peacock and Alfred Tennyson, also composed works in the same decade, spoken by doomed or dying Druids on the island and predicting the fall of Rome and British greatness. In 1827 Cambridge University offered a prize for the best poem offered by undergraduates on the Druids. Both the winning entry and the runner-up were published, and the latter was by a student at Corpus Christi College, Thomas Edwards Hankinson. It depicted the sole survivor of the massacre on Anglesey, mourning his dead comrades in the following terms:

We fought for thee, my country: 'twas the strife
Of desperate rage – the struggle of despair –
The last wild stroke for liberty and life:
We braved the invader in his fierce career,
Thy Druid daughters with their flowing hair,
Poured in mad onset on the foe, and high
Raised the shrill shriek, – and tossed the torch in air:
Thy grey rocks, echoing back their thrilling cry,
Sent the dread war-note forth – 'To death or victory':
'The time will come: – the veil is half withdrawn –
The future's veil of gloom – I see – I see
The horizon purpling with thy glory's dawn,
My native land! – thy sons shall yet be free –
And brave, – but not in vain – thy name shall be
The rallying-shout of nations – heard afar
In distant lands, and thundered o'er the sea:
Thy blood-red standard, victory's beacon star
Shall stream with meteor flash along the clouds of war'

This shows vividly the sort of image of Druids that still fermented in the minds of some upper-class Englishmen by this date. It was given a further impetus, and the prominence of female Druids further emphasised, six years later when Vincenzo Bellini's opera *Norma* arrived in London. The libretto, by Felice Romani, portrayed Druidry as the mainstay of resistance to the Roman occupation of Gaul. As such, it was perhaps intended to encourage Italians to rebel against the foreign powers and despots who between them divided up their nation at that period. It certainly had that effect. The story-line centred on the idea that Druidic priestesses, like Roman Catholic nuns or pagan Roman Vestal Virgins (but not, according to any ancient author, like Druids), were vowed to virginity. The heroine, or anti-heroine, thus transgresses a double set of conventions by becoming the mistress of a Roman governor. The story ends in one of the great melodramatic climaxes of opera, when she chooses to confess her guilt to her people and she and her lover are burned to death together. It was, and remains, one of the classic works of sung music. The British loved it: it returned to London in 1837, an English version was produced in 1841, and it was performed at Covent Garden annually between 1847 and 1861.

Perhaps buoyed up by it, a lady at the gracious midland town of Leamington Spa, trying to raise funds for a local hospital, published a poem in 1838 which portrayed the Roman conquest of Anglesey as a disaster for humanity. This time it is a lone bard who survives to mourn that

> One common slaughter lights the pile,
> The Bards are gone, the Druids dead,
> No more upon this sacred isle
> Shall bright religion raise her head.
> The moral code, the mysteries deep,
> That taught us how the seasons roll,
> The virtues that in herbs may sleep,
> The powers of the immortal soul!
> The knowledge of each mystic truth,
> And poetry, and laws, are o'er;
> Nor age is seen, nor bright-haired youth,
> O desolate, abandoned shore!

In 1851 another Victorian female poet, Esther Le Hardy, had a dying Druid utter another prophecy of British greatness: with his last breath he contemplated his country and

> Bless'd her with beauty, wealth and power;
> Bless'd her with virtue's richest dower;
> Bless'd her with one, who turns to bless
> In deep affection's faithfulness;
> Bless'd those fair beings to earth has bound her,
> Springing in ecstasy around her;
> Bless's those she loved, and bless'd the day
> When Britain own'd Victoria's sway.

This came close to suggesting that the success of Victorian Britain may actually have been due in part to the benedictions of the ancient Druids; but it was a swansong in a double sense. After this date the forces working against a place for Druids in a generalised British patriotism became so strong that such voices became very rare. *Norma* continued to shake the Druidic flag for a time, but during the 1860s the opera disappeared as well. Its extravagant romanticism was less to the taste of the new generation, a fact was underlined when it was sent up thoroughly by William Schwenk Gilbert, who was subsequently to become half of the partnership that was to represent the essence of late Victorian Britishness to much of posterity: Gilbert and Sullivan. In his comic opera *The Pretty Druidess*, staged in 1869, the contribution of Norma and her fellow priestesses to the overthrow of Rome consisted of sewing garments to be sold at a Druid fête to raise funds for the resistance movement, and of making attempts to convert the Romans to their own faith: a satire on do-gooding Victorian ladies. The final tragedy of the original was averted by the cheerful revelation that every one of them had taken a Roman boyfriend, providing too many prospective executions to be practicable. The male Druids were made into parodies of Anglican clergy, preoccupied with the intricacies of their vestments, the necessity of getting their curates to do most of the actual work, and an uninhibited love of food and drink. Their chief announces a ceremony with the invocation:

> Now lo the mystic sucking-pig draw near,
> Uncork the sacerdotal ginger beer!
> Incomprehensible rice pudding try!
> Attack the sacrificial rump-steak pie!

There are few glimmers of their former role as national heroes during the remainder of the century. In 1883, for example, the poet Mackenzie Bell used a hillside in Kent as the focus for a pageant of historic characters who might have stood upon it in the past, thus making a point about the enduring quality of Englishness. He included a Druid, praying before going to fight the Romans 'in his dear country's cause'. His poem may, however, have been composed long before its date of publication. When Rudyard Kipling came to treat the same sort of theme two decades later for his children's books *Puck of Pook Hill* and *Rewards and Fairies*, on a much bigger scale and in a Sussex setting, it is the Romans who are admired and the British priests are missing. This was in keeping with the disquiet voiced by another English nationalist, Thomas Hughes, the author of *Tom Brown's Schooldays*, writing over twenty years before Bell. Contemplating the White Horse carved in the chalk of the Berkshire Downs (which has since been proved to be Iron Age in date and so quite conceivably 'Druidic'), he comforted himself with the tradition that it had been made on the orders of Alfred the Great: 'One wouldn't care so much about it if it weren't made by the Saxons and their great king. The Druids don't seem akin to us somehow.'

When patriot Druids reappeared full-bloodedly in a British context, it was in a work isolated enough to seem eccentric. This was Marie Trevelyan's *Britain's Greatness Foretold*, published in 1900 to rally nationalist feeling in the wake of the string of defeats just inflicted on British armies in the Boer War. It was a novel about Boudica's revolt, dressed up as history and making an overt comparison between Boudica and Victoria. Its inspiration was, equally openly, from Cowper's Georgian ode, and it treated the Druid's prophecy in the ode as an actual historical event rather than a modern poetic fiction. As befitted the work of a modern woman author, Druidesses were as prominent in it as Druids, leading choruses of graceful maidens at royal courts. Trevelyan was, however, not only a lone voice but a writer heavily influenced by Welsh tradition. In any case, within two decades of her novel's appearance, the horrors of the First World War had swept away wholesale the sort of strident nationalism, drawing upon figures and images from the past, in which Druids could find a place.

What was left was a sense of Druidry as an intrinsic part of Welsh identity. When the playwright Emlyn Williams wrote a comedy about contemporary Welsh life in 1944, set in and around a rural pub, the latter (like the play itself) was called 'The Druid's Rest'. The production is best known now for having launched the actor Richard Burton on his way to stardom. Nine years later a much more famous Welsh author, Dylan Thomas, completed his 'play for voices', *Under Milk Wood*, set in the fictional, and archetypal, small seaport town of Llarregub. Images drawn from the Gorsedd are intrinsic to it: within three consecutive pages the town chapel's minister (inevitably also a poet), 'intricately rhymes ... in his druid's seedy nightie', while on the hill above the port stands a 'small circle of stones, made not by druids but by Mrs Benyon's Billy'. In the 1970s three quintessentially English television comics, Tim Brooke-Taylor, Graeme Garden and Bill Oddie (known collectively as 'The Goodies') screened a show satirising the Welsh, in which the heroes found themselves tied up within a Gorsedd circle, with a guest comedian (Jon Pertwee) attired in Druidic robes and surrounded by acolytes in similar garb, conducting a religious ceremony in which the English guests are destined to be the sacrifices. In the 1990s the most talented and successful British author of comic fantasy, Terry Pratchett, introduced a nation known as Llamedos, modelled on Wales, into his imagined world. The very name is a tribute to Dylan Thomas (those innocent of these matters should try reversing 'Llareggub' and 'Llamedos'), and, sure enough, the entire religious and cultural life of the country revolves around Druids and bards, working in stone circles. This miscellany of references, drawn from different decades, places and genres, shows how deep the association runs. Iolo had thus succeeded brilliantly in his immediate aim, but had failed in the greater one that had lain behind it: he had made Wales the land of Druidry, but in the process the Druids had lost most of the wider symbolic value which had made them worth having.

There is, however, a further twist to the story. All these characterisations of patriotic Druids identify them with a parent country against foreign enemies. They ignore the fact that the term 'patriot' has also at times been appropriated by subjects of a ruling government who claim to understand and represent the interests of their country better than its rulers. As such, it is employed against a regime by opponents within the same nation. The figure of the Druid has long been associated with this other form of patriotism as well, and during the twentieth century, as the old-fashioned forms of nationalism declined, it has come to feature in it more strongly.

The Wise Druids

Wise Druids were the priests, philosophers, scientists, judges and teachers of their people, and reached a standard in each of these fields that at least equalled, and probably exceeded, that of any other practitioners in the ancient world. They were as sophisticated in their organisation as in their knowledge, having different divisions of expertise served by specialists with different names, and annual meetings in which Druids from all the different tribes of a particular region assembled to discuss matters of common interest. Their religious teaching inspired people to courage and virtue; their knowledge of the natural world was based on close, intelligent and accurate observation; and their arbitration of civil disputes and judgement of criminal cases were regarded as final, so absolute was the respect in which they were held by the communities whom they served. They were exemplars of personal sanctity and sagacity, working within a tradition of received wisdom, training and mutual support that brought out the best of which humans were capable.

These Druids are actually those found longest and most consistently in the ancient sources, spanning a period of six hundred years, and have an afterlife in the medieval Irish literature that gives them eight hundred more. They are the earliest kind of Druid actually encountered, in two works, by Sotion of Alexandria and an unknown writer later mistaken for Aristotle, produced in the Greek world around 200 BCE. Both are lost but were quoted by a later scholar, and included Druids among a list of wise or holy men belonging to non-Greek peoples. This sort of list continued to be made by Greek scholars, and in particular those living in the greatest city of their world, Soton's Alexandria, until the end of ancient times. Sometimes they glossed it. Dion Chrysostom, writing around the year 100 CE, said Druids were concerned with all branches of wisdom, and were the true rulers of their societies because kings depended so heavily on their advice. About a century later, the Christian saint Clement claimed that Greeks had originally learned much from the scholars of peoples whom they had subsequently despised as barbarians, including the Druids. Soon after Hippolytus reversed the flow of knowledge, claiming that Druids had become especially devoted to one branch of Greek philosophy, that of Pythagoras, which they had been taught by a missionary. This philosophy suggested that the universe was constructed on a system of sacred numbers, geometrical patterns and musical notes which humans could learn to understand, and that when they died, their souls were reborn on this earth in new bodies. In the fourth century a Roman writer, Ammianus Marcellinus, quoted another lost source by a Greek, to the effect that Druids were 'men of a higher genius, members of the secret fellowship of the Pythagorean teaching; they were uplifted by investigations into secret and profound things; and with contempt for mortal lot they pronounced the immortality of the soul'. To this Greek chorus of praise can be added an original comment from a Roman author, Valerius Maximus, who said that the Gallic tribes in the country behind Marseilles believed firmly that human souls were immortal; and again drew the parallel between this and the teachings of Pythagoras. He added that (allegedly) their faith in an afterlife was so absolute that they lent each other money that could be repaid in the next world.

All this adds up to an impressive set of references. The problem is that all were produced by writers living far away from actual Druids, and mostly at a time when the latter had disappeared from the societies with which they had any contact at all. They were reliant on the testimony of others, and there is no indication of how accurate that was. It is easy to dismiss them as intellectuals constructing a myth of noble savages with which to criticise or compliment their own civilisation, or projecting their own concepts onto badly-understood foreign traditions. On the other hand, it is equally easy to defend them as sophisticated, learned and objective writers, less contaminated by prejudice and propaganda than those living closer to Druids in time and place. The latter were heavily implicated in the Roman project of devaluation and conquest of native peoples; those who emphasised Druidic wisdom were not. There is no test by which either judgement can be established as the fairer.

Other ancient sources provide more detail of Druidical learning and organisa-tion. The fullest was left by the only author who was himself an eyewitness of the societies that had Druids at a time when the latter ought still to have flourished in them. He was the most famous of all Roman politicians and soldiers, Julius Caesar, whose conquest of Gaul in the mid first century BCE added to the empire the very land with which Druids were most commonly associated by ancient writers. He also left the longest description of them. In this he commented that they were concerned with all matters relating to religion, acted as teachers to many young men, and functioned as judges and arbitrators. If anybody refused to accept their verdicts, the rest of the community would suspend dealings with him or her. All Gallic Druids were led by a single chief, serving for life and chosen by his fellows (sometimes after a civil war). Each year they all met in the territory of the Carnutes, the geographical centre of Gaul, to decide legal cases from all regions. They kept out of war, and so were excused both military service and payment of the taxes raised for it. In their schools young men were trained by learning many verses, and some took twenty years to complete their education. To preserve their teachings as secret they never wrote them down; but Caesar knew that the greatest was that human souls did not perish on death, but 'pass from one to another'. This gave Gallic warriors reckless courage. They also studied 'the stars and their movement, the size of the cosmos and the earth, the world of nature [and] the powers of deities'.

All this is confidently presented, as if from personal knowledge; and that is something that Caesar may reasonably be expected to have possessed. The great problem with it has been debated by modern historians, without conclusion, for over a hundred years: given the importance that he accords to them, the Druids ought to have featured prominently in his very full account of his conquest of Gaul. They are, however, completely invisible in it, appearing only in a self-contained section on native customs which he interjects into his narrative. It is possible that he did not feel the need to comment on the particular role that they played in the resistance to him, or that he was actually quoting an earlier writer who recorded a situation that had ceased to exist by his time. On the other hand, it is also possible that he was misrepresenting the Druids, making them appear far more powerful, sophisticated and menacing than they actually were, and far more similar to the Roman priesthood. Suspicion that something is wrong in Caesar's account is strengthened by a comment left by his great contemporary and rival, Cicero, that he had met a Gallic Druid who was visiting Rome. This man, Divitiacus, was indeed learned in the ways of the natural world and the art of predicting the future. The same person actually features prominently in Caesar's account of his campaigns, there called Diviciacus; but he appears not as a Druid but as a powerful chieftain and active warlord, doing just the sorts of thing from which Caesar seems to say that most Druids held aloof.

Wise Druids also feature in three works of historical geography produced in the century after Caesar's time, between 40 BCE and 50 CE. All were the work of authors who relied for their information on earlier writings, now disappeared. The first was Diodorus Siculus, who repeated the story that the Gauls believed 'the Pythagorean doctrine' that souls 'are immortal and live again for a fixed number of years in another body'. He divided the learned men of their society into bards, soothsayers and Druids, the latter being deeply respected philosophers and theologians. They were held in such respect that armies about to join battle would desist if Druids came between them to halt the conflict. He was followed by Strabo, who divided Gallic society into bards, *vates*, who were experts in divination and natural science, and Druids, who studied 'moral philosophy' as well as the workings of nature. He added that Gauls in general believed that 'men's souls, and also the universe, are indestructible'. He repeated Diodorus's story about the power of Druids to stop wars. The third writer was Pomponius Mela, who asserted that they claimed to know 'the size and shape of the world, the movements of the heavens and the will of the deities' and restated Caesar's story about how their education could last up to two decades. He likewise added that only one of their teachings was generally known: 'that souls are eternal and that there is another life in the world below'. Because of this belief, they burned or buried with the dead those objects that they were expected to need most in the next world, and sometimes even deferred the completion of business and the payment of debts until the people concerned remet after death. Some threw themselves onto funeral pyres, to be burned to death alongside the body and so accompany its owner to a new life.

We have no evidence concerning how trustworthy any of this information is. It has been suggested that Strabo was just adding a few extra details to a mixture of Caesar and Diodorus, and Pomponius just rehashing Caesar with a few imaginative flourishes; which would make two out of the three virtually worthless. More commonly it had been argued that Diodorus and Strabo both used the lost book of a Greek scholar called Posidonius, who visited south-eastern Gaul before Caesar's time. This idea has generated arguments over how honest and perceptive Posidonius himself was, and how typical that corner of Gaul was of the rest; but, if true, the data at least comes from first-hand observation. The problem is that none of the references to Druids occur in passages that are clearly attributed to Posidonius.

After this clutch of texts from the hundred years between the late first century BCE and the early first century CE, there is only one more detailed reference to Druidic wisdom. This is a hostile one, made by the Roman poet Lucan in the mid first century. It mocked Druids for claiming a unique knowledge of the divine world and teaching 'that the same body has a spirit elsewhere' and 'that death … is but the mid point of a long life'. After that we have only the brief admiring comments of the Greek authors, all probably reliant on earlier and vanished sources, and three references to female Druids written by Roman historians in the fourth century. These are actually the only absolutely certain appearances of Druidesses in the whole of ancient literature, and they always perform the same function: to predict accurately the future greatness of men who subsequently become emperors. All these alleged incidents are set in third-century Gaul, and the women concerned seem to be individuals of low social status distinguished by the gift of prophecy. What we can make of this is, again, unclear. These texts may be an indication that women had always been Druids, or else that they had become them as a result of the disintegration of the old Druidic brotherhood after the Roman conquest, so that the term 'Druid' became devalued and extended to cover anybody – female or male – who carried out any of its functions, including predictions.

All this body of evidence leaves us pretty sure that Druids were the recognised specialists in religion and learning among the peoples of north-western Europe just before the Romans entered the region. It is also fairly certain that they taught, and shared with the rest of those peoples, what was for the age an unusually strong belief in the survival of the individual human soul and personality. What is horribly unclear is what form that survival took, and anything else about their religious doctrines and scientific knowledge. The comparison with Pythagorean teachings actually confuses more than it reveals. It seems (though is not absolutely certain) that this school of Greek philosophy taught that souls were reborn on this earth in new mortal bodies, human or animal. Such a concept would fit both what Diodorus says, and perhaps the more ambivalent phrase used by Caesar. It is, however, blatantly at odds with what Valerius Maximus, Lucan and Pomponius state, which is that Gauls believed that human beings reincarnated after death in a parallel world. These are very different ideas, and the evidence of archaeology is that the Gallic tribes frequently buried personal possessions with the dead; a custom that might be interpreted as more compatible with the second belief, which was shared by many ancient peoples. We are left wondering, therefore, whether Druids taught a distinctive doctrine or just (along with the rest of their society) held a common one with unusual confidence and an unusually literal sense of the practical implications.

Some authors have believed that the deficiencies of the ancient texts as sources for Druid wisdom can to some extent be remedied by use of medieval Irish literature. This certainly has the virtue of having been produced by a native society which had itself included Druids, but there is a general and a specific problem in using it for this purpose. The former is that it was all written after the conversion of the Irish to Christianity, and therefore represents a retrospective portrait of a pagan society which had disappeared at least a hundred, and in most cases a few hundred, years before. Until fairly recently this was not regarded as a huge difficulty in itself, as the written sources were believed to have embodied orally transmitted stories and traditions that were indeed centuries old. Since the 1980s this belief has been comprehensively challenged, using the evidence both of textual analysis and of archaeology. There is now a very widespread, though not completely accepted, opinion that the authors of the surviving texts were attempting to recreate a pre-Christian past of which they often knew little. As a result, the passages referring to Druids – which are certainly more numerous than those found in the Greek and Roman works – may be either authentically remembered data or the product of fantasy.

The specific problem is that, whatever the fundamental truth of the information, much of it is clearly fantastic. The Greek and Roman texts, however truthful in reality, were almost always purporting to convey hard fact. The Irish equivalents consist mostly of heroic tales, not concerned with reality in the modern sense of the word. Thus the chief function of the Druids in them is to work magic, in the sense of achieving changes in the natural world by the use of supernatural means. In other words, they curse and blight humans and lands, raise storms and fogs, cause glamour and delusion, confer invisibility, transform people into animal shape or into stone, subdue and bind them with incantations, fly up into the air, and raise spiritual barriers to halt physical attackers. The Irish words *druidecht* or *draideacht* (or variants of them), literally meaning 'druidcraft', feature as a general term for magic. This means that in many of the texts a Druid is simply anybody who is working an act of magic, irrespective of what she or he is for the rest of the time. A minority of sources do seem to portray them as a distinct class of specialist, but the particular features of this class are never defined. It exists most obviously in relation to royal courts, where the classic function of the people called Druids is to divine the course of future events or explain the meaning of current events. As most traditional societies had specialists in this sort of skill, it is easy to believe that Irish Druids were indeed expert in it. The problem is whether any of the specific methods employed by those in the medieval stories are authentic or the inventions of the authors, trying to imagine how ancient pagans would have behaved.

The sources do contain one super-Druid, Cathbad or Cathub. He features in the Ulster cycle of heroic tales as arbitrating between the rulers of the province, teaching hundreds of pupils, and having the right to speak first in a tribal assembly, before the king himself. This is a figure who matches the classical descriptions of the Gallic Druids. Kim McCone, however, has suggested that Cathbad was invented by medieval churchmen anxious to exalt their own power as (by implication) his successors. Certainly some of the tales show him as having no inherent position of authority, but having started his career as a rogue warlord of unusual ruthlessness who fought his way to his hugely influential position by combining the usual martial skills with an exceptional talent for magic. As in the case of the Irish sources in general, it is only possible to use his career as evidence for ancient Druidry by selecting preferred features of it and ignoring or dismissing tremendous difficulties regarding the overall trustworthiness of the texts.

Irish literature, in any case, hardly featured in considerations of Druidry until the nineteenth century, except in its own homeland: for most Europeans, including the British, it was physically and linguistically inaccessible. Those engaged in the great revival of the image of the Druid as a heroic national ancestor, between the fifteenth and eighteenth centuries, were left with the scraps of classical text. In this context, the Druids had three tremendous weaknesses for anybody who wanted to hail them as repositories and teachers of knowledge: they had left no writings at all; they could not be visualised because there was not a single ancient picture of one; and there were no physical remains at all – such as temples or tombs – which could reliably be associated with them. As such they were appallingly insubstantial figures for those who wished to work with their memory. The authors of the sixteenth century accordingly rose to this challenge with a number of different strategies. One was that exemplified and led by Annius of Viterbo (or his informant): simply to cook up the evidence needed to fill the gap in the actual records.

A second was to misinterpret genuine data. The German nationalist poet Conrad Celtis described how when he had stayed with a friend at a monastery near Regensburg in Bavaria, he had found six stone statues built into the cloister wall. Each wore a mantle in the Greek style, with hoods covering their heads, and very long beards. Their feet were bare, their expressions severe, and each carried a book and staff of the design associated particularly with the Cynic school of Greek philosophy. All this might suggest that they were indeed representations of Greek philosophers, whether they had been carved in ancient times or in the middle ages. Celtis, however, decided immediately that they were ancient portraits of Druids, and informed the world of his find. Scholars across western Europe then repeated his belief: as the statues themselves have disappeared long ago, it is impossible to investigate it. Another false train was laid by the greatest of Elizabethan English historians, William Camden. He set out to provide documentary evidence for the claim, made by German and French writers, that the Druids had predisposed their peoples to receive the Christian faith. In the specific case of Britain, he cited the ancient Christian writers Tertullian and Origen as making just this statement. Neither in fact did. Tertullian, even in Camden's quotation, just said that Britain had Christians in it by his (late Roman) time. Origen actually said the same thing as Tertullian; but Camden misread him to declare that, before the coming of Christianity, the ancient British already believed in one god. Again, this error was to have a long influence on scholarship.

The Scots made their own contribution to this process of myth-making. Then, as now, the British Isles were littered with monuments left by their Neolithic and Bronze Age inhabitants, including circles, avenues, rows and chambers of great stones. In England and Wales these were generally regarded either as natural or as the work of historic peoples such as the Romans, the post-Roman British or the Danes. In one region of Scotland, they took a very distinctive, and visually striking, form, to which twentieth-century archaeologists have given the name of recumbent stone circles. These consist of rings of upright megaliths, with a single huge stone lying flat, and flanked by two unusually impressive uprights, in the southern half of the circle. The flat stone looks very much like an altar, which is indeed quite probably what it was, and it is accordingly easy to interpret these monuments as temples; moreover, they occur in the immediate hinterland of Aberdeen, which contained one of Scotland's most dynamic sixteenth-century universities. It was that associated with the scholar Hector Boece, who included in his national history the suggestion that they had been heathen temples and the setting for rites like those of the ancient Egyptians. The translator of his book into Scots verse, William Stewart, was more direct: he stated firmly that they had been the holy places of the Druids. This provided the ancient British priests with an imposing physical presence in the Scottish landscape.

It was, however, one that was ignored by the other British peoples, while growing suspicion concerning the work of Annius, and irritation concerning Camden's misreading of Origen, only reinforced a sense that nothing of use could be known about Druid wisdom. Writers from John Caius in the mid sixteenth century to John Milton in the mid seventeenth credited them with being the founders of the English tradition of learning, but could say nothing more than that. This situation was to alter from the mid seventeenth century onward, so that all of the three missing elements in the reimagining of wise Druids – the writings, the pictures of them, and the monuments – were apparently supplied. It was, however, a slow process, requiring another hundred years to become truly effective.

One major contribution to the change commenced with a young man called Henry Jacob, who became one of the first English experts in the new science of philology, the study of the nature and relationship of words. Based at Oxford University, he used sophisticated linguistic analysis to prove such things as that Hercules and Joshua had been the same person. He added in passing that philology proved that the Druids had been taught the true religion of the Hebrew patriarchs by Abraham himself, and had then brought it to Britain. Poor Jacob then went completely and permanently mad, but his ideas were stolen, and published years later, by a fellow don at his college, Edmund Dickinson. The book, which came out in 1655, was duly imitated by other Oxford philologists in the next quarter of a century. They used a massive amount of linguistic learning to develop its point that the Druids were pupils and heirs of Abraham, so opening up an apparent route to them straight out of the Old Testament, which avoided all the fictitious kings of Annius and Boece. In the process they gave them a new dignity and importance.

They also, however, had to reckon with the problem of how these properly instructed Druids got from Palestine to Britain at such a remote period, and here a mechanism was provided by another philologist, the Frenchman Samuel Bochart. He had formed the opinion that Phoenician was the language at the root of most of those recorded in Europe, as the Phoenicians themselves had been the greatest sailors and colonists of the ancient world, before the Greeks. They had certainly traded all over the Mediterranean and founded colonies as far west as Spain. It took only a little imagination on Bochart's part to get them up the coast to Britain, and some of his English readers began to suggest that these ancient navigators had brought religious teachings as well as their language. The most influential was a London lawyer called Aylett Sammes, who published a history of ancient Britain in 1676. In his view, the Phoenicians had introduced the first bards to Britain, carrying with them the doctrine of the immortality of the soul; the Druids proper followed them some while later. Just as the arguments of the philologists were utterly wrong, being based on a misunderstanding of the actual relationships between languages, so were the statements concerning the Phoenicians. Three and a half centuries of investigation have failed to produce a single piece of good evidence that, great voyagers though they were, they ever got to Britain. None the less, that claim was to be made, usually as if it were proven fact, until the twentieth century: it was just too useful to be dropped easily.

Sammes, moreover, simultaneously disposed of another of the main problems regarding Druids. A large part of the selling point of his book was that it was decorated with illustrations, based on the best available authorities and models. One was of a Druid, and was taken directly from the description that Celtis had left of the statues in Bavaria, which Sammes read in the work of an English scholar. It showed a wise-looking old man with the beard, hooded robe and staff that had been recorded by the German poet, and was so striking that it was to be copied repeatedly in work after work. It fixed, apparently for all time, the dominant image of the ancient Druids in the British pictorial tradition, and was – like most conventions – the more effective for the fact that its (dubious) origins were soon forgotten.

If what was to become the discipline of philology seemed to break through one section of the barriers around knowledge of Druidry, what was to become that of archaeology broke through another. This process commenced in January 1649, as Cromwell and his comrades in the English Revolution set about the trial and execution of King Charles 1 and the abolition of the monarchy and House of Lords. A group of Wiltshire royalists met at Marlborough to discuss possible reactions to the crisis. In the end, they decided that the most sensible one was to do absolutely nothing and go home. Their discussions, however, took several days, and on one of those, being nobles and gentry, they decided to go hunting hares on the neighbouring downlands. The chase took them through the village of Avebury, where one of their number dropped out to look at the great standing stones that he saw there. The locals, it seemed, shared the general opinion that they were natural. To the huntsman, a young squire called John Aubrey, they seemed to form circles and an avenue. In later years he went back there to study them and became convinced that he was looking at a huge ancient monument. This story is known to virtually every archaeologist in Britain, and across much of the rest of the world too; it is one of the favourite tales from the heroic age in which the concept of archaeology was born. What happened next, however, is less well known, or not known at all.

When the monarchy and House of Lords returned together, in the 1660s, Aubrey became a member of the new Royal Society, founded to promote British science. He introduced it to his discovery at Avebury, and in doing so drew the attention of two Scottish members, who told him about the stone circles of their own country; which, of course, had by then been associated with Druids for a hundred and forty years. This seems to have opened Aubrey's eyes to the existence of a huge, hitherto unsuspected, complex of megalithic monuments scattered across the British Isles, the range of which meant that they could logically only be prehistoric. He realised that Stonehenge, hitherto thought to be unique and to be of Roman or later date, was only the most remarkable of these. More cautiously, he thought that the Druids, the only prehistoric British priests of whom there was evidence, had probably designed them as temples. In 1665 he drafted a book to argue this case. He had, in fact, produced an intellectual hand-grenade, well-argued and well-illustrated, but having written it he lost his nerve and decided that he needed more evidence. The hard truth is that Aubrey was incapable of finishing a book in the normal sense of the word. What he could do was compulsively jot down notes on a range of different subjects. In 1665 he had written a best seller by accident, but then began to tinker with it. Thirty years later he had succeeded in turning his brilliant, tight polemic into a shapeless mass of jottings, filling two volumes, which no publisher would touch.

That is where things might have rested had Oxford University not come to his rescue. It was his old university, and, as bad luck and general unworldliness turned him into a permanent bankrupt, dependent on friends for board and lodging, it became one of the places in which he hung out, chatting about his ideas. One of those who heard him was a brilliant young don called Edmund Gibson, who decided in 1692 to edit a completely revised and enlarged edition of Camden's classic Elizabethan guide to the history and monuments of Britain, *Britannia*. Gibson's plan was to incorporate all the discoveries that had been made in the course of the seventeenth century. To do so he assembled a team of young Oxford scholars to do the job. He also hired various consultants, one of whom was the Irish radical John Toland. Another was the now aged Aubrey, who once again received an impetus to have faith in his theory of a Druidic megalith-building culture from a Scotsman. This was John Garden, another professor at Aberdeen University, with those helpful recumbent-stone circles on his doorstep, who arged forcefully to Aubrey that his ideas were correct. Some of Gibson's young men were persuaded in turn by the old gentleman's revelation of the extent and importance of Britain's prehistoric monuments and the likelihood that they could be attributed to the Druids. They made an effort to get Aubrey's own book published at last, but failed because he had rendered it unpublishable. What they did instead was to advertise his ideas to the public in the revised *Britannia*, which appeared in 1695. It was a great success, becoming a standard reference work for educated readers, and carried in it the hypothesis that the legacy of the Druids was rooted in the landscape of England, Scotland, Wales and Ireland alike, expressed through magnificent structures of which the modern British could be proud and which they could now study properly.

It was, however, still just a hypothesis, and too novel to be rapidly accepted. Perhaps in time greater familiarity would have won acceptance for it, reinforced by the writings of Toland, which appeared after his death in 1726 and accepted and enhanced Aubrey's ideas. None the less, by the 1730s the connection between Druids and megaliths was still not generally recognised. This is where the work of William Stukeley proved to be decisive. A string of reasons have been propounded to explain the extent of his impact, and here four personal characteristics can be added, which between them enabled him to carry out the work which ensured him his success. One was his deep love of structure, form and design. It was this that tempted him away from the family career of a lawyer to become a doctor as a young man, and it also led him to the study of ancient monuments. He enjoyed equally the dissection of dead bodies, the excavation of prehistoric burial mounds, the surveying of stone circles, the sketching of buildings and the contemplation of the stars. Behind all this was a yearning to understand the meaning of things from the way in which they were constructed: the underlying message and purpose in their composition. This made a fit with his second characteristic: that he was a born artist. He was always compulsively drawing things, whether people, landscapes or monuments, or combinations of all three. Both were linked in turn to the third trait, his instinctive religiosity. For

Stukeley the universe brimmed with spirit, and he was at once convinced that the universe must have a Creator, and fascinated by questions regarding the nature of this being and of the divine plan for what had been created. It was this aspect of his nature which was to cause him to give up medicine at the onset of middle age and take holy orders. His fourth quality is much more general in humanity: a yearning for fame, in his case as scholar and scientist.

In a sense, he became John Aubrey's last and best pupil, because in 1718 he was lent a transcript of Aubrey's unpublished book. The impact on him can be seen in one of his notebooks. This, begun as a collection of medical data, became a repository for whole sections copied out of Aubrey's text, and then went on to include further information on megaliths. Stukeley was a person prone to passions, enthusiasms and conversion experiences: and this was one of his greatest moments of all three. He immediately commenced his own explorations of prehistoric sites, which became the earliest systematic fieldwork of its kind. In 1740 and 1743 he published much of it in his two famous books on Stonehenge and Avebury, which – as suggested before – put the Druids firmly on the mental map of the British. For the next hundred years it was generally accepted that most prehistoric ritual monuments in the British Isles had been their temples, including all the most spectacular. What he had established by his books was a fundamental truth: that the megalithic structures of these islands were the work of the pre-Roman native British. Furthermore, he provided a classification of them into different types, and names for various aspects of individual sites, that have become permanent aspects of the study of prehistory. To these observations, he tacked Aylett Sammes's scheme of ancient religious history, whereby Phoenician colonists and missionaries had brought the faith of Abraham to Britain, where it became Druidry. As such, to Stukeley, it remained the best of all ancient pagan religions, preserving much of the original divine revelation to the Hebrew patriarchs and looking forward to Christianity. He used the layout of the ritual landscape of Avebury to argue that its Druidic architects believed in the Trinity, and added that they had extensive foreknowledge of Christ's mission, including his birth from a virgin and his crucifixion. Until his time, scholars had rued the complete absence of records containing Druidic teachings. Stukeley's response was that ancient monuments were themselves texts, which could be decoded, using geometry and numerology, to reveal the messages that they embodied as symbols.

His impact was uneven. His basic argument, that British megalithic monuments were prehistoric, became generally accepted for all time. His associated one, that they were the work of the Druids, became orthodoxy for the next century. What relatively few people found convincing was his own interpretation of their Christian message, which relied on a much greater stretching of the evidence. Instead, he inspired others to do their own work at prehistoric sites and draw their own conclusions concerning the messages that the Druids had embedded in them. Both the extent and the limits of his influence are illustrated by two important case studies. The first concerns one of Georgian Britain's greatest architects, John Wood. Like Stukeley, Wood was fiercely ambitious and devoutly religious: his particular aims were to further his own career as a designer and contructor of impressive buildings, to beautify and glorify his own city of Bath, and to establish that the whole European tradition of architecture was derived through the Greek and Roman world from the tabernacle of Moses, as described in the Old Testament. The tabernacle was supposed to have been made according to the specifications of Jehovah himself. It followed that architects like Wood himself, who worked within the classical tradition, were divinely inspired and carrying out the cosmic plan of the Almighty himself: no small claim.

Before 1740 Wood was already becoming interested in Druids, having read Toland's posthumously-published writings on them. It was the publication of Stukeley's *Stonehenge* that threw him into a fever of jealousy and competitive activity. He immediately set about his own surveys of that monument and others, and a stream of publications, between 1741 and 1747, intended to prove that his own west country was the main seat of ancient Druidry and that megalithic circles and avenues were indeed expositions of the truly revealed religion of the Hebrew patriarchs. The revelation that he read in them, however, differed significantly from Stukeley's, whose work he attacked: among other features, Wood's vision depended much more on a polarity between cosmic powers of male and female, and good and evil. As a theorist, Wood had little impact outside his own region, but as an architect he could go one better. His enduring masterpiece is the circular range of stately houses at Bath, pierced by streets and enclosing an open space with marvellous acoustics, known as the Circus. Timothy Mowl and Brian Earnshaw have made an interpretation of its symbolic significance which seems to have won wide acceptance: that it incorporates the mystical sequence of numbers that he claimed to have discovered in megalithic structures and to represent the divine plan. He had, in effect, erected a Druidical college of the sort that he had dreamed to have existed in ancient times. In its symbolism it functions as the first Druidic temple to have been erected in the British Isles since the end of antiquity; it may actually be the first stone one ever built and, in its grandeur and complexity, the greatest.

The second example of Stukeley's impact is provided by the career of the Cornish clergyman William Borlase. He was an unusually intelligent, dynamic and inquisitive individual who found himself bored by the life of a country rector, serving the parish of Ludgvan on a slope of that granite upland, full of prehistoric remains, which forms the westernmost peninsula of Britain. He began to take an interest in these antiquities as an outlet for his energies, but could find no framework for an understanding of them until Stukeley published his books. These convinced him that most of the monuments that he was exploring were Druidical, and he commenced a systematic survey of them across Cornwall, sweating across moorland and heath and through furze, briar, bracken and boulders until he had amassed a huge compendium of information. This he published in 1754, as *Antiquites, Historical and Monumental, of the County of Cornwall*, which revealed to the world of scholarship, for the first time, the richness of the Cornish prehistoric heritage. Like Stukeley's books, it was gorgeously illustrated, with drawings of sites and artefacts, and included extended discussions both of different classes of monument and of the beliefs of the Druids. Indeed, he went beyond Stukeley in suggesting that features of the landscape which geologists have since proved to be completely natural, such as basins hollowed in slabs of granite and striking outcrops of rock, had also been involved in Druid worship. This greatly extended the range of phenomena which could now be linked to the ancient priests and scholars, encouraging people to find traces of them in areas that had few or no prehistoric remains. Borlase also set an example to be followed by other local antiquarians, in uncovering lost sacred landscapes in their own counties and districts, which was eagerly followed for almost two hundred years. His interpretation of Druidic religion was, however, almost completely different from those of Stukeley and Wood.

For now, it is important to make the point that, within fifteen years of the publication of Stukeley's two books, it was already becoming obvious that ancient monuments were not texts that could be read in the manner of written evidence. While the latter had its own tremendous difficulties of interpretation, the symbolism encoded in physical structures – if it was indeed there at all – was even more difficult to prove beyond doubt and to raise above the level of individual speculation. While that speculation continued unabated after the mid eighteenth century, and indeed persists to the present day, inevitably attention to some extent soon wandered back to written sources. The problems and limitations of the Greek, Roman and Irish references to Druids have been discussed above; but there remained one other possible body of source material, in the medieval Welsh bardic literature. To a scrupulous or timid scholar, it was also the most unpromising. Whereas the texts in the other languages certainly do deal with Druids, in however unsatisfactory a manner, the Welsh set may not do so at all. They make occasional references to a kind of individual called a *dryw* and a sort of people called *derwydon*. These could quite credibly be translated as 'Druid' and 'Druids' respectively, but also as other things. The *derwydon* were exclusively prophets, thus fulfilling one important function of the ancient holy men but none of the others. If they were, indeed, Druids, then the word may have been adopted from medieval Irish literature rather than surviving from pagan times.

Most writers who have drawn on Welsh sources for insight into Druidic wisdom have not, however, used these terms as more than supporting evidence. Instead they have drawn on the body of mystical Welsh poetry associated with the legendary bard Taliesin. This has now been attributed to a range of possible dates between the eleventh and fourteenth centuries, but was formerly thought to be much older. There are two major difficulties with these texts, both of which are rooted in the loss of a proper understanding of the narrative conventions and symbolic system of the old bards. One is that the difference between Middle and Modern Welsh is great enough to make the literal meaning of many passages difficult to establish. To take a famous example, a passage of medieval verse was translated by one expert in 1803 as lines from a Druidic hymn:

> O son of the compacted wood, the shock overtakes me!
> We all attend on Adonai, on the area of Pwmpai

It became in the work of another, in 1858, a satire on monks:

> Like wood-cuckoos in noise they will be,
> Every one of the idiots, banging on the ground.

In 1918 a third expert, declaring that both of the above two versions were equally misleading, concluded that the text, like many others, was genuinely obscure.

Even if it were possible to translate the meaning of the actual words in a fashion acceptable to everybody, the second problem would immediately kick in; that their significance is almost always lost. Medieval bardic verse was heavily allusive, making constant reference to characters, objects and incidents that were familiar to its original audience from older poems and stories but have long been forgotten and do not feature – or are not explained – in any surviving sources. So, if the first translation above had been perfectly correct, and universally accepted, we would still have no certain knowledge of the nature of the 'compacted wood', or of Adonai, or of the area of Pwmpai. If these considerations present a more or less insuperable barrier to the scrupulous or timid, however, they provide a more or less irresistible temptation to those who love speculative scholarship, and may find an almost infinite source of evidence for their own theories in lines that can be read in so many differing fashions.

When Evan Evans made his suggestion, in 1764, that the Taliesin poems might contain 'Druidical Cabbala', he could suggest no means by which it might be understood if it was there at all. This was, of course, an open invitation to Iolo Morganwg to provide his own solution to the challenge. He deployed both of the methods outlined above. Like Stukeley and Wood, he thought that megalithic monuments could function as texts, making the stone circle the standard meeting-place of his 'traditional' Bardic Gorsedd and investing its individual stones with particular symbolism. Like Evans, he thought that the genuine medieval verse, especially that credited to Taliesin, should be interpreted as containing Druid teachings. He proceeded to interpret portions of it freely to support his ideas. The core of his material for the enterprise, however, was forged by himself, both in the form of prose treatises and of triads. The outline of his system was complete by 1792, though he continued to elaborate it until his death. It depended on the concept of a benevolent, all-powerful and all-knowing god, who had created the whole world with three diverging rays of light and three musical notes or three letters that made up his own divine name. This being directed that all living things should attempt to rise through three circles of existence. The lowest, Annwn, was where life was created. The next, Abred, was that of the material world. The third, Gwynvyd, was that of perfection and bliss, and the highest that might be attained. There was a fourth beyond these, Ceugant, but it was occupied by the deity alone. Forms of life represented a moral and physical staircase, with the most ferocious forms of animal at the bottom and the finest human beings at the top. Individuals moved up or down it by a process of reincarnation, so that well-behaved animals could be reborn as humans, and humans who indulged traits such as pride, falsehood and cruelty could be reborn as animals. Abred was thus a place of free will and probation, in which beings could, in extreme cases, pollute themselves with evil so thoroughly that they sank back to the amoral and bestial chaos of Annwn, or purify themselves of it so completely that they could ascend, finally, to Gwynvyd, where death, suffering and evil were all unknown.

Iolo had thus created a cosmology that preserved the basic theological structure of Christianity but did away with a wrathful God and eternal damnation and added reincarnation as the mechanism for salvation. By doing so he pretended to have elucidated the cryptic and confusing references to a Druidic belief in the survival of the soul from one body to another found in the Greek and Roman writers. He had actually blended Christian doctrine with Hindu and Buddhist concepts of cycles of rebirth, and indeed he explicitly noted the similarity. He explained it, however, in terms of an original revelation from the creator to humanity, creating a patriarchal religion of which those of the Hebrews, Brahmins and Druids were all derivations. In that sense, his Druidry represented a parallel Old Testament, and he made the comparison the more complete by declaring that the One God had incarnated himself as Christ in order to encourage and assist the entry of beings to Gwynvyd. The addition of this revelation to the pagan Druid teachings created, according to Iolo's pseudo-history, a Christian Druidry that flourished in Britain until the fifth century, when the Roman Catholic Church began to corrupt and absorb it. The remnants of it in the Welsh Bardic tradition thus represented a resistance movement to a new kind of vicious Roman imperialism, which had succeeded in transmitting the old teachings (through Iolo) to the present.

Iolo also had plenty to say about Druidic organisation, which in his version represented an elaboration of the threefold division found in Strabo, between bards, vates and Druids. Although bards can certainly be found in medieval Welsh literature, and Druids arguably can, there is no equivalent of the word *vates*. Iolo therefore copied a mistake made by the earlier Welsh scholar Henry Rowlands and used the term 'Ovydd' as one. This was made possible because in Strabo's original Greek text a figure like an 'O' is put before the word 'vates' as a pronunciation guide (that the 'v' should be spoken like a 'w'). The word 'vates' thus becomes 'Ovates', a word which became in Iolo's teachings the English equivalent of 'Ovydd'. 'Ovydd' itself is certainly found in medieval Welsh works, but as the Cymric equivalent of the name of the Roman poet Ovid. By this series of errors, Iolo got his three divisions of an ancient bardic order, responsible between them for all learning and religion in ancient Britain. They were divisions, not grades, for Iolo's libertarian leanings were too strong for him to want his imagined system to be a hierarchy; nor, for the same reason, did it have a chief of the sort that Caesar had represented in Gaul.

As Iolo explained it, all three were members of the Gorsedd, but with differing areas of competence. Bards had been responsible for the performing arts and worn blue robes. Ovates wore green and were individuals who had made achievements in learning. Druids wore white and were responsible for education and religious ceremonies: after the conversion, they were Christian ministers. All were dedicated to learning, justice, liberty, truth, reason, equality and vegetarianism, and to pacifism, avoiding, abhorring and attempting to stop wars. These moral imperatives were embodied in scores of triads that Iolo composed. His Bards, Ovates and Druids always met in daylight and in the open air, so that all might see what they did, and a chief Bard presided over each meeting; in his own *gorseddau* this was naturally Iolo himself. If a Druid presided, he could take the title of Archdruid, but only for that meeting, and at all gatherings decisions had to be taken by vote. Their great festivals were the solstices and equinoxes, with lesser meetings at new and full moons to instruct disciples; as part of a religion that associated its deity with light. Iolo gave to the big feasts the Welsh names of Alban Arthan (midwinter), Alban Eiler (spring), Alban Hefin (summer) and Alban Elfed (autumn). The symbol of their faith consisted of three lines diverging and descending from a common point, which he called 'the mystic sign' and held to be a representation of the divine act of creation. It was, in fact, a common mason's mark, one which would have been very familiar to him as the family trade, and the one that he most commonly followed, was that of stonemasonry.

Iolo's ideas had a tremendous impact both in Wales and England, although readers were natually varied and selective in their reception of them. Anybody who knew anything about real medieval bardic poetry found the idea that bards were pacifists, vegetarians and egalitarians preposterous. His concept of the circles of existence and his moral triads were most influential: some authors professed to see proof of the doctrine of reincarnation through the circles in the designs on Iron Age coins or the layout of prehistoric monuments. The first half of the nineteenth century was the high summer of Druidry in the English and Welsh imagination, in which it dominated most people's vision of their island's prehistory. Those who concentrated upon its teachings did so by mixing three component features together, according to taste: Iolo's ideas, megaliths and the true religion of the Book of Genesis. This was the more easily done in that the first of those automatically incorporated the others, and the last two were also naturally intertwined. The megalithic monuments most familiar to most British people of the age were not those in their own land – not even Stonehenge – but those of ancient Palestine, as recorded in the Old Testament. Stone pillars, solitary or in groups, were set up by Jacob, Moses and Joshua as memorials to great events, and by Absalom as a grave marker. The fact that the ancient Israelites had erected standing stones made it still easier to believe that the Druidic religion had derived from the same source. What authors of the period between 1800 and 1850 had to decide for themselves, and over which they differed in more than a hundred books, articles and poems, was how much it had decayed from the original divine revelation given to the patriarchs such as Noah and Abraham, of what it had actually consisted, and with how much solid learning, about the physical world, it had been associated. It was also a matter for personal taste whether or not Druidic wisdom had survived the Roman period to become the essential component of a specifically British variety of Christianity, which was suppressed by Roman Catholicism but looked forward to the Protestant Reformation, as Iolo had suggested.

From the 1850s, interest in the subject began to wane rapidly because of a number of converging forces. One was the appearance of sustained scholarly investigation of old Welsh literature during that decade. It immediately raised doubts both as to the reliability of Iolo's material and as to the dating of the genuine texts on which the quest for surviving Druidical thought had depended. Hitherto they had been assumed to have been composed in the fifth and sixth centuries, by the very early bards or mythological figures with whom they were associated. Now it was suggested that they were actually much later, from the twelfth to fourteenth centuries; which of course much reduced the likelihood that they were reliable repositories of ancient tradition. This issue was disputed for over a hundred years until the definitive edition of the Book of Taliesin was produced by Sir Ifor Williams in 1960. Williams suggested that some of the work credited to that poet was indeed from the sixth century, but the rest – which included all the possible religious references – was much later. More recently, it has been argued, on linguistic grounds, that even the verses which Williams had attributed to the sixth century could not have been composed before the year 1000 at the very earliest. It remains possible that there is native pre-Christian tradition embedded in this later literature, but – in the nature of things – this is almost certainly now impossible to prove. Even the initial, early Victorian onslaught on this possibility was enough to weaken confidence in the use of these sources as evidence for Druidic beliefs.

A second development was a school of thought that maintained that Britain's megalithic monuments were not prehistoric at all, but had been erected by the natives during the post-Roman period under the influence of foreign ideas. Opinion as to the nature of the latter varied – Buddhism and Scandinavian paganism were favourites – as did that on whether Druids were still involved. All writers in this group were agreed that, being so late and novel, these remains could not reflect an ancestral and pre-Christian tradition. They marshalled between them a great deal of erudition, deploying the undoubted facts that no ancient author ever associated Druids with stone temples or ever noticed impressive native monuments in Britain. The most influential of them was the architectural historian James Fergusson, but they received strong support from the surveying work carried out at Stonehenge by the future father of modern British Egyptology, Sir Flinders Petrie. This school of thought, which appeared in the 1830s, and gathered momentum in the 1850s, held its own until the end of the century, when sufficient archaeological data began to accumulate to disprove it.

The fact that Fergusson was a Scot may have been highly significant, because his nation waged a collective war on the identification of megalithic structures with Druids throughout the nineteenth century. It had, of course, been the Scots who were the first British people to adopt them as heroic ancestors and to link them with stone circles. After the English took them up, enthusiasm for them north of the border started to wane – Macpherson pushed them to the margins of his epics. Once the Welsh had claimed them, it almost disappeared. There were still a few Victorian Scots who admired and defended them, but they were much outnumbered by those who were either indifferent or actively hostile. In creative literature, the situation was characterised by leading Scottish authors at opposite ends of the century. In 1819, the greatest one of his age, Sir Walter Scott, portrayed the stone circles of Orkney in his novel *The Pirate* at a time when enthusiasm for all things Druidical was at its height in England and Wales. He remarked tepidly that some attributed them to the Druids and others to Goths or Scandinavians, but nobody could be sure (and, he implied, it did not matter). The 1890s lay at the epicentre of the career of William Sharp, who wrote both in his own name and (with much more success) in the character of a Hebridean woman called Fiona Macleod. As William, he reviled Druids, portraying them in one poem as crucifying Christian missionaries. As Fiona, he ignored them, even when – as in his famous play based on the Irish legend of Etain, *The Immortal Hour* – he might easily have given them some lines.

Scottish scholarship followed suit. In the 1850s and 1860s two authors led an all-out attack on the importance ascribed to Druids in British prehistory. John

Stuart opened it by noting, correctly, that excavation indicated that the prehistoric stone chambers commonly known to the scientific world by the Breton name of dolmens, which had been identified as Druid altars, had in fact been burial places. He went on to add that burials had also been found in the recumbent stone circles, which had started the whole association, and to conclude that all megalithic structures were actually tombs and cemeteries, not temples. He picked up the observation that no classical author had linked them to Druids, dismissing the latter as of no consequence to the prehistorian. He was seconded by Sir Daniel Wilson. Wilson admitted that the human remains found in stone circles might have been added to them later (a supposition which has turned out to be broadly true), but still argued that as so little of certainty could ever be known about the Druids, they should be removed from discussions of British prehistory. By 1871 a Scottish minister could state that the attribution of stone circles to them was rejected by 'nearly all the great archaeologists of the present day', even though they had no alternative explanation for the monuments. The following year one of those archaeologists, Sir James Simpson, classed stories about Druids with those concerning sea-serpents and mermaids. In 1886 the reigning keeper of Scotland's national museum, Joseph Anderson, declared that they were now firmly consigned to a history of 'unscientific interest' and 'quasi-historical relations'. He thought that the similarity between the design of prehistoric chambered tombs all over Britain indicated that they had been made by the same people with the same ideas: he just no longer wanted those people to have been the Druids.

In this the Scots were slightly in advance of, and helping to lead, scholarly opinion in the rest of Britain. What propelled that most effectively were the huge intellectual changes taking place in Victorian society around the year 1860, which drew in turn on ideas that had matured in Denmark and France. It is possible to make an argument that the knowledge of European prehistory takes a quantum leap at every point at which the Danes have a hard time. In the early seventeenth century they sustained a series of humiliating military defeats by the rising kingdom of Sweden, which had taken independence from them a few generations before. What followed was a huge cultural effort to restore national pride by defining Danish identity more clearly than before. One consequence was the first comprehensive survey of megalithic monuments undertaken in a particular nation, which influenced the reworking of John Aubrey's book on those of Britain. In the early nineteenth century the great powers of Europe punished the Danes for having been too loyal to Napoleon by stripping them of their greatest remaining overseas possession, Norway, awarding it to Sweden. This blow provoked another effort to bolster a sense of enduring nationhood, part of which centred on the national museum opened at Copenhagen in 1819. Its first curator, Christian Jurgensen Thomsen, set out its galleries according to a hypothesis that had been floated in the previous century, that prehistoric Europe had passed successively through ages in which stone, bronze and iron tools were used. In the 1830s and 1840s he propagated this idea with the help of his assistant, later his successor, Jens Jacob Asmussen Worsaae, who was probably the world's first professional archaeologist. Worsaae applied the three-age system to monuments as well as artefacts, testing it by excavation. Their books on the subject were translated into English at the end of the 1840s. They only became revolutionary, however, when coupled with French discoveries, especially those publicised by Jacques Boucher de Crévecoeur de Perthes from his private museum in the northern town of Abbeville. These showed that ancient human stone tools were clearly associated with the bones of extinct animals. In 1859 England's Royal Society accepted this evidence, and the two streams of thought, Danish and French, combined to make a permanent breakthrough in attitudes to prehistory. They showed that humans had undergone a very long and slow development before the beginning of historical times, which indeed began to look like a brief and rapid postscript to that story. They demonstrated that this development could be divided into periods associated with particular lifestyles and tools, which could be studied in detail from the evidence yielded by excavation. Finally, they suggested that the account of the human past provided in the Book of Genesis, hitherto regarded as (at the least) an indispensable component of any discussion of human origins, was effectively worthless for the purpose.

Most of this new information was brought back to Britain by English scholars who travelled on the Continent, but some of it was supplied directly by a Scandinavian cultural missionary, Professor Sven Nilsson. The first scholar to apply the three-age model systematically to the European past, he lectured in London in 1865 on its relevance to British monuments. A major component of his argument was an attack on the idea that the Druids had any place in the subject. He reported, correctly, that Scandinavia, a region that had never been associated with Druids, had many dolmens of a kind similar to those of the British Isles. Accordingly, he argued that prehistoric megalithic structures were the work of a different, and older, people, though he could still not quite break free of the older frameworks of interpretation, because he then identified these people as the Phoenicians. His greatest supporter and promoter in Britain was also the person who first introduced the new ideas about the European past comprehensively to a British audience. This was Sir John Lubbock, heir to a baronetcy and a banking fortune, who went on to a career in politics which eventually took him to the House of Lords as Lord Avebury. In 1865, the year in which Nilsson addressed Britain's Ethnological Society (of which Sir John was president), Lubbock published *Pre-Historic Times*, one of the landmarks of Victorian scholarship. It related the three-age division to British prehistory, and elaborated it by dividing the Stone Age into the Old, or Palaeolithic, and the New, or Neolithic. He assigned the megalithic monuments of western Europe to the Neolithic and Bronze Ages, bluntly dismissing the Druids as irrelevant to them and also dismissing (more gently and with respect expressed to Nilsson) any Phoenician contribution to British prehistory.

Lubbock's scheme was swiftly adopted by British intellectuals in the major national scholarly networks. By 1872 he could already claim that 'few now regard Stonehenge as a Druidical temple'. In 1880 the leading expert in the excavation of Palaeolithic sites in Britain, William Boyd Dawkins, managed to write a general survey of the island's prehistory without ever mentioning the Druids. From the 1870s onward it became the norm for authors who published fresh studies of megalithic chambers, circles and rows to avoid an attribution of them to any specific people or else to assign them vaguely to the New Stone or Bronze Ages as Lubbock had done. There were as yet no reliable dating methods – in 1899 the pioneer of folklore studies, Edward Clodd, assumed that the Bronze Age was somewhere around 250 BCE – and as yet no positive proof that megalithic structures actually did derive from the ages concerned. That was only provided in

1915, when a committee of the British Association, set up for the purpose, finally reported that excavations at Avebury and other sites had linked the construction of the monuments to objects from the Neolithic. What was clear was that the British scholarly establishment no longer wished them to be Druidic. In 1892 one prominent authority on stone circles, A. L. Lewis, remarked that any suggestion that they might be was now 'resented with a ferocity which seemed to embody almost as much racial antipathy as antiquarian zeal'.

It had taken almost a hundred years for the English and Welsh in general to accept the idea that megalithic monuments were built by Druids; it was to take about as long for them to lose it. Four years after Lewis wrote his remarks about scholarly ferocity, the latter was exemplified by the author of a new textbook on prehistory, H. N. Hutchinson, who commented that the Druidical explanation of megaliths 'has been abandoned – though, unfortunately, it lingers on in popular guidebooks'. He went on to lament that fact that 'it is a thousand pities that, in the face of so much striking evidence … schoolmasters and others should persist in putting the Druid as the first actor on the stage of human events in Great Britain'. Local authors, indeed, persisted in attributing stone rings to the Druids until the 1930s, no doubt aided by the fact that not until the 1920s did the Ordnance Survey expunge the term 'Druidical Circle' as the name for such structures on its very popular maps. Even in my own childhood, in the 1950s and 1960s, the idea that megalithic structures were not the work of the Druids was still regarded as novel and exciting among those who taught me; so insubstantial did the Neolithic and Bronze Age British seem by comparison.

Indeed, there *was* no reason why Druids could not have been incorporated into the new scheme of prehistory, had those who promoted it really wanted this to be done. Changes in technology and lifestyle, which were all that the three-age (after Lubbock, the four-age) system actually signified, need not have meant changes in religious belief or personnel. There were thinkers – respected and in other matters influential people – in Britain around 1900 who pointed out that this might be so. One was Arthur Evans, Keeper of Oxford's Ashmolean Museum and the future discoverer of the Minoan civilisation. In 1889, writing of Stonehenge, he suggested that 'we may yet find ourselves once more in Druid company, but we must at least arrive there by the methods imposed by modern science'. Three years later, A. L. Lewis, in the article quoted above, pointed out as temperately that it appeared that stone circles were ceremonial monuments, clearly associated in some cases with the movements of the sun, and very hard to date; he was correct on all three counts. He went on to suggest that it was possible, though not proven, that use of them had carried over from the Bronze Age, when some were certainly constructed, to the succeeding Iron Age, and that the Druids – recorded in ancient times as observers of heavenly bodies – had been involved with them throughout. Eminent scholars in other fields, such as the philologist Sir John Rhys and the folklorist Sir Lawrence Gomme, were likewise prepared to suggest that the people of the British Iron Age had taken on religious ideas from earlier periods.

Why were the practitioners of the emerging discipline of archaeology so resistant to this suggestion? There seem to have been three reasons. The first and most general was that those attacking the old identification of prehistoric monuments with Druids were in the classic position of revisionists assaulting an intellectual orthodoxy. To succeed in this enterprise would automatically establish them as the new leading authorities in a branch of knowledge, disempowering and replacing their predecessors. It is a pattern known since ancient times in the politics of scholarship. Probably more important, the Druids also fell foul of two of the most important concepts of the late Victorian age: progress and race. The view of human history implanted by traditional Christianity was essentially one of degeneration, temporarily reversed by moments of renewal. It depended on the notion of an original perfect world and pure religion, created and revealed by a good god and then corrupted by a cosmic power of evil, using the sinful nature of humanity as its principal tool. This process was inherent in the nature of the earth, though interrupted at times by divine interventions such as Noah's Flood, the revelation to Moses, the incarnation of Christ and (depending on one's religious politics) perhaps the Protestant Reformation or Catholic Counter-Reformation. The world was, however, ultimately doomed to destruction and a final divine judgement. Such a view of nature, and of history, was dramatically challenged by the discovery of the huge age of the planet and of the evolution of life upon it, of which humanity was itself a recent manifestation. This discovery was the result of the emerging new sciences of geology and palaeontology, the study of rocks and of the fossils within them. It was under way in the 1840s, and its victory became more or less complete in the 1860s. The result was not an eviction of Christian religious doctrine from science but the rapid substitution of a new version of it: the belief that the benevolent and all-powerful god had built into his creation a natural desire for development and improvement. The result was a constant upward evolution of species, of which humanity was the ultimate result and contemporary European civilisation the highest manifestation to date among humans.

Sir John Lubbock, the person who introduced the new concept of prehistory to many of the British, was one of the strongest proponents of this belief in progress through natural competition and selection. His true father-figure during his youth had been Charles Darwin, the scientist most closely associated with the discovery of the evolution of species, a model which Lubbock applied vigorously to prehistoric humanity. In Lubbock's view, human development had been a more or less straightforward one from the lowest barbarism to civilisation. Prehistoric Britain had therefore to have been a dreadful place. It was populated by savages, and to Lubbock 'the true savage is neither free nor noble; he is a slave to his own wants, his own passions; imperfectly protected from the weather, he suffers from the cold by night and the heat of the sun by day; ignorant of agriculture, living by the chase, and improvident in success, hunger always stares him in the face, and often drives him to the dreadful alternative of cannibalism or death'. To do him justice, Lubbock's nightmarish vision of the past was used to propel a generous vision of the future, which he laboured to create. He gave much energy to assisting the education and social advancement of working-class Londoners, argued strongly against racial prejudice, did more than anyone else to establish Bank Holidays as new, state-enforced, periods of rest for workers, and was influential in the enactment of the first laws to protect prehistoric monuments from destruction. His scheme of things, and that of his many followers and imitators, however, had no room for wise Druids, who threatened to spoil his picture of an Iron Age Britain characterised by a barbarism and ignorance only dignified by some advances in material culture which elevated it over the even lower forms of human society that had preceded it.

In many ways, the wise Druids had been the victims of their own earlier success. They had been assimilated too thoroughly by too many writers to the Book of Genesis, with its model of a pure and original patriarchal religion, linked to a high morality and an acute understanding of a divine creation, which the new archaeology was out to refute in its entirety. To provide an example of the kind of author whom Lubbock and his fellows were out to discredit, one need turn only to Samuel Lysons, rector of Rodmarton in Gloucestershire and a noted proto-archaeologist. In the same year that Lubbock published *Pre-Historic Times*, 1865, Lysons brought out *Our British Ancestors: Who and What Were They?* This book began by declaring that the Bible was the highest measure of truth in history and archaeology and by ridiculing Darwin and the three-age system. It then went on to make a full-blooded reinstatement of the Druids as practitioners of a wise and benevolent religion derived from Japhet, son of Noah, acting as instruments to prepare the British for Christianity and being gifted with a prodigious knowledge of mechanics, medicine and other sciences. Lysons also defended with equal vigour the belief that they had constructed megalithic monuments, and used his own excavation of one of the most remarkable in his county, the chambered long barrow of Windmill Tump, to illustrate his point. He represented its architectural features, one by one, as conforming to the customs of the Israelites of the Book of Exodus and the practice of a faith that despised idolatry and sin and called for purification through penitence. With friends and defenders such as this, the Druids were natural enemies for proponents of a secularised, long-term prehistory marked by the slow development of technology and society.

They were further marginalised by the new preoccupation with distinctions between races within the human species. In its origins, this was bound up with the development of the European concept of nationhood, from the late eighteenth century, to one based more firmly on the collective will and identity of the mass of people within a particular state. These people were expected to be bonded by certain common characteristics, of which language, culture and a shared heroic past were most important. Increasingly, however, these qualities were blended with the notion of a common genetic inheritance. It was a notion greatly strengthened by the new doctrine of evolution, which destroyed the Christian belief (however attenuated or ignored in practice) in the fundamental unity of humanity as descendants of Adam and leaders on earth of a divine scheme of creation. As the new doctrine drew attention to distinctions and relationships between species, so it invited a comparable tendency to view the human race as divided into subspecies with their own characteristics. The starker implications of such a view for authors increasingly concerned with natural competition and selection were emphasised by the contemporary expansion of European colonial settlement. In parts of all the other inhabited continents of the world, European settlers were engaged in conquering, exploiting, displacing and sometimes destroying indigenous peoples of different races and less advanced technologies.

It was very tempting to think of Europe's own prehistory in the same fashion, and such a concept was built into the three-age system from its adoption. The Danes Thomsen and Worsaae had argued that each of the three ages had been introduced to their country by a fresh wave of foreign invaders, of a higher material culture than the natives, whom they had driven out or absorbed. This picture was transplanted to Britain along with the same divisions of prehistory by Lubbock and his successors. The human skulls found in ancient graves, having been measured and classified, were used to support a theory, which became restated as more and more certain fact as it moved away from the evidence, that each phase of the remote British past had been associated with a different racial group. Farming and pottery, the hallmarks of the Neolithic, had been introduced by a long-headed people who had driven out the hunting folk of the Palaeolithic. These built the dolmens and other megalithic chambers that had formerly been regarded as altars, platforms or sepulchres of the Druids. They were overcome in turn by a round-headed race who introduced bronze and built the stone circles and rows, and who were overcome in turn by a still more advanced tribal folk who ushered in the Iron Age, and were known variously by the end of the nineteenth century as Indo-Europeans, Aryans and Celts. There was a tendency by that time for the successive waves of invader to be associated with superior physical traits as well as more advanced technologies: bluntly, from the New Stone Age onward, they got ever taller, stronger, blonder and lighter-skinned. According to this scheme, the Druids could only have been the priests of the last arrivals, the Aryans or Celts, and so worth only a glance at the end of any survey of British or European prehistory.

This double model, of progress produced by successive invasions, remained dominant in British archaeology for most of the twentieth century, and slowly made its way into the public imagination. This latter process was made even slower by a number of cross-currents. One was represented by the continuing appearance of literature produced by writers either innocently or wilfully ignorant of the changes in scholarly opinion. A naval officer turned clergyman, Lawrence Roberts, published a short book called *Druidism in Britain*, aimed at ordinary readers. It synthesised a number of nineteenth-century works, especially *Barddas*, to repeat the message that Druids had been bearers of the true patriarchal religion of the ancient Hebrews, shipped to Britain by the Phoenicians to prepare it for the Christian Gospel. His grasp of even outdated sources was slender – he referred to 'Robert Stukeley' as a great authority – but his book had still gone through four editions by 1934. Twenty years later the vicar of Glastonbury published one which assumed that Druids, equipped with Iolo's theology, had built the megalithic monuments of Britain. Its argument was that they had then received Christianity, and converted the whole of western Europe from their base in his parish; and it had been through seven editions by 1955.

Another cross-current came from the world of scholarship itself. The initial interest in Druidic wisdom in Britain had been fostered by two embryonic disciplines – philology and archaeology – at a period when they were still new enough to make colourful and creative mistakes. Now a third emerged: archaeoastronomy, the study of the astronomical alignments of ancient sites. It was represented by one of the greatest of Edwardian astronomers, Sir Norman Lockyer, who made a series of interventions in history and prehistory. He began in 1901 by using the plan of Stonehenge, in relation to the movements of the stars, to calculate its exact date of construction. This enterprise was based explicitly on the idea that the Druids had been the inheritors of a long accumulation of knowledge concerning the heavens. Lockyer came up with 1680 BCE for the erection of the main stone circle. Modern dating methods based on radiocarbon reveal that he was almost a thousand years out. He went on in 1906 to publish a book that used the alignments of ancient buildings to resurrect the old belief in an ancient wisdom brought from Palestine to Britain by the Phoenicians and culminating in the Druids. In his secularised version, however, it was sun-worship and not the religion of the Old Testament that was carried. Finally, in the following year, he declared that the alignment of stones in the Welsh Gorsedd circles, as prescribed by Iolo, was an accurate map of the stars over Britain in the second millennium BCE. Therefore, he declared to the Welsh, 'it makes the Gorsedd I take it just about the oldest thing that we have on the planet connected with any human activity'. Its officers were (briefly) thrilled enough to initiate him with the Bardic of Gwyddon Prydain, the Magician of Britain. The work of archaeologists and historians has proved him to have been, in these last two cases, even more wildly wrong than in the first; but for decades the prestige of his name as a scientist gave his view much credibility amongst the public. It is a classic example of what can happen when a pioneer of one branch of knowledge meddles self-confidently in others.

The strongest potential cross-current, however, came from the leaders of British archaeology themselves. If one single work served to sever the connection between Druids and megaliths in the popular imagination, it seems to have been Richard Atkinson's book on Stonehenge, published in 1956. This was based on the excavations that he had undertaken at the monument with Stuart Piggott over the preceding few years, and which were designed, in part, to answer key questions about the construction of it. Atkinson declared roundly that 'there is no evidence whatever for connecting Stonehenge with the Druids', using the Victorian arguments that no ancient author had portrayed them as worshipping in human-made temples and that they belonged to a Celtic culture that had only reached Britain in the late Iron Age. He added that they had 'been the subject of so much ludicrous and unfounded speculation, that archaeologists in general have come to regard them as almost unmentionable in polite society'. Finally, he declared that Druids and the monument were so inseparable in the popular imagination that 'I have no illusions that anything I may say, however, forcibly, will do much to break the connection'. He was wrong; as I have suggested, my own impression is that such strong language, in what was supposed to be a definitive book written in an accessible manner, did a great deal to accomplish just that. An attentive reader, however, may have noted possible weak points among such a deployment of invective. He noted that Roman debris found on the site was so abundant that people of that period might have visited it as 'devotees', and that there was 'at least equivocal' evidence that the Romans had wrecked the stones as part of a campaign against Druids.

His professional colleagues were more willing to cut ancient Druidry some slack. In 1927, Sir Thomas Kendrick, of the British Museum, raised the possibility that the Druids had rebuilt Stonehenge in its present form, and been responsible also for some of the ancient timber ceremonial sites nearby, such as the recently-discovered 'Woodhenge'. The excavator of Woodhenge, Maud Cunnington, formed with her husband R. H. Cunnington part of a group within the powerful Wiltshire Archaeological Society known to its opponents as 'the Devizes School', which declared that the bulk of the existing structure at Stonehenge was indeed Iron Age. They presented these arguments through the 1930s, and in 1941 they were reinforced by a rising star of archaeology who was to be Atkinson's partner and friend, Stuart Piggott. He suggested both that Iron Age people had used the site and that 'the old Bronze Age tradition' of religion had persisted all the way through till the conversion to Christianity, leaving some of its lore in medieval romances.

No sooner had Atkinson published his book than other, equally respected, experts in prehistoric Britain began to undermine his statements regarding Druids. In the following year Christopher Hawkes, posing the question 'Are not the Druids the nameless priests of the old megalithic religion Celticised?', suggested that indeed they were, practising a faith which blended the goddess of the Neolithic inhabitants with the sky-god of their Bronze Age conquerors. Finally, in 1972 Glyn Daniel, the leading archaeologist of Cambridge University, put on record that 'I have no doubt myself that a knowledge of some facts about megaliths and the faith of the megalith builders survived through the Roman period and the Migration period into the Christian middle ages'. He added, in case of any possible lack of clarity, that the 'Druids of protohistory may quite well be the priesthood of the earlier megalithic religion', and that it could even be that, 'having scoffed in a superior way' at Aubrey and Stukeley, 'we are now restoring the Druids of history to the megaliths of prehistory'. It seemed that, having finally defeated the old belief in a religion brought to Britain from the biblical patriarchs, archaeologists were now ready to salvage the Druids from it and incorporate them into their own model of earlier prehistory.

It was not to be. The 'new' or 'processual' archaeology that pushed aside that of Daniel and his generation in the 1970s was interested in the construction of social and economic models rather than of spiritual systems. As the view of British history based on races and invasions collapsed with the abandonment of the European colonial empires – when such an image of the past became embarrassing – it was replaced by one of separate prehistorical cultures characterised by lifestyle packages. Like late twentieth-century consumers (of course) ancient people were now seen as taking on new possessions, customs and beliefs by importing them from neighbours with whom they interacted culturally. This concept of prehistory tended to stress the self-contained nature of the different periods that succeeded each other, and the lack of ideological continuity between them, although the motor for change was now social development rather than the appearance of new tribes. Two pieces of research, in particular, emphasised the imaginative distance between the time of the Druids and the preceding ages. One was the definitive study of the development and dating of Stonehenge, published by English Heritage in 1995, which firmly reassigned to the Bronze Age features at Stonehenge which many previous experts had considered to be Iron Age. It also emphasised the small quantity of material at or around the monument from that later period, both absolutely and in comparison with that left both from earlier prehistory and by the Romans. The amount was so small, in fact, that (so the study argued) it could be attributed to 'tourist' visits. The other publication was made by Richard Bradley in 1981. He surveyed the evidence from across southern England and found that from the later Bronze Age onwards farmers had begun to destroy Neolithic and early Bronze Age ritual monuments in a way never known earlier. This argued for a new sense of disassociation from them, and a loss of respect for them; and he could not find one single case in his sample of a continuity of use of one of these monuments into the Iron Age. These landmark studies fit into a general pattern of data that suggests a major rift in Britain between the religious systems of the second and first millennia BCE.

Nor did Druids get much help from the flourishing market in alternative views of prehistory that developed in the late twentieth century, partly in reaction to the full professionalisation of archaeology and partly as an attempt to adapt traditional religious views of the past to a post-Christian society. This was largely because they focused on the Neolithic, the period onto which the earlier view of the wise Druids' time, as the one of megalithic monuments, close observation of the heavens, personal liberty and collective harmony with nature, had now been displaced. In 1969 John Michell published *The View Over Atlantis*, which introduced British society fully to the concept of straight lines called leys, running across the landscape and charged with a magnetic energy arising from the earth. This, in his view, had been harnessed by a scientific elite who had visited almost every corner of the globe and planted a network of megalithic structures around it to channel this energy for the benefit of humanity. This was in fact a projection of mid-twentieth-century 'big science' onto the old belief in a former universal true religion, which had decayed because of the unworthiness of later generations. As part of it, Michell paid tribute to Aubrey, Stukeley and Lockyer as inspired predecessors, and gave fresh impetus to the myth that Iolo Morganwg had drawn his picture of Druidic belief from genuine sources. None the less, Michell downgraded the Druids to latecomers who had never fully understood the great old knowledge that they had inherited. In his view, the early Christian churches had actually comprehended it better, and the Druids had yielded to them easily because they recognised Christianity as 'a more glorious expression of their own tradition, now degenerate'. Likewise, one of Michell's most prominent admirers, Paul Screeton, dismissed the Druids as 'elitist and corrupted'. He added that they had inherited the ley system, 'but my guess is that they understood it less than we do'.

They did no better out of the other great tradition to emerge as an alternative to orthodox prehistory in the late twentieth century: the archaeological dimension to the Goddess movement. Whereas ley-hunting was in origin quintessentially English, the Goddess was an American phenomenon, though with a significant impact on Europe. Once again it reasserted an old model, because it declared belief in the practice at the opening of prehistory of a benevolent religion dedicated to a single all-wise deity, covering the whole of the European and Mediterranean worlds but with an epicentre in the Near East. It adapted the early nineteenth-century concept in three different ways. First, the lost golden age was identified with the Palaeolithic and Neolithic, which now occupied the symbolic space of the Book of Genesis. Secondly, its epicentre was in Turkey and the Balkans, rather than Palestine. Thirdly (and most important), it had a female deity and a female-centred society. As in the earlier belief-system, this good religious and social system was corrupted into the polytheistic paganism and flawed societies that existed by the time history dawned. In this case, however, rather than an inherent pessimism regarding human nature, the late Victorian model of invasions by new peoples was called in to explain the corruption. The matriarchal view of remote prehistory had even less time for Druids than the ley-hunters, as they appeared too clearly to be a male-dominated priesthood produced by the kind of cultures that had destroyed the Neolithic golden age. Between the combined influences of ley-hunting and matriarchal feminism, those writers who wished both to resurrect the formerly dominant belief in a universal old and good religion, and to preserve in it a heroic rôle for Druids, were very few and isolated, and distinguished mainly by their lingering attachment to Christianity.

Nor has archaeology succeeded in turning up a single object that can be linked without controversy to Druidic wisdom. The one most commonly proposed for this purpose has been the Coligny calendar, a collection of bronze fragments found in south-eastern France in 1897 among the ruins of a temple. It dates from the late second century CE, more than two hundred years after the Roman conquest of the area, and is written in Roman script. It is also, however, in the native, Gallic, language, and represents a system of marking time found nowhere else, so may fairly (though not absolutely surely) be thought to embody pre-Roman ideas. As such, it has taken its place ever since in discussions of Druidic belief. It was, however, found in 153 pieces, making up between them less than half of the original text. The beginning and end are missing, and only two months are completely present out of a probable total of more than sixty. The notations use a system of abbreviation that has no universally agreed interpretation in itself. Nor is there any agreement on whether the surviving fragments include the opening of the year, and therefore none on where, in the year, any of the months shown on the pieces can be located.

All this means that different commentators have always had ample opportunity to come up with sharply contrasting views. A sample of three of the most recent may serve to illustrate the confusion. In 1992 an American academic,

Garrett Olmstead, announced that the calendar contained a scheme of 'pure mathematical beauty and precision', which ensured that 'Gaulish Druids could predict, hundreds of years into the future, lunar and solar positions to within one day in 455 years!' It proved that they were great philosophers and scientists, producing 'the most accurate solstice predictor in the ancient world'. In 1998 another American, Stephen McCluskey, declared that the calendar represented a botched attempt to reconcile solar and lunar systems that created a year which was on average almost two days out. He concluded that such a way of reckoning time would have needed constant adjustment, and that the reason why the Druids were recorded as constantly studying the heavens was that they had been too scientically inept to produce a calendar which did not need regular correction. Finally, it is worth keeping in mind the suggestion made by a distinguished French scholar in 1988 that, in its names for months, its way of ordering them, and its division of the year into two parts, the Coligny calendar is similar to some used by the ancient Greeks, and may simply have represented a local version of a Greek model. It must be clear from just these few citations, out of several possible, that the fragments can be used to support almost any view of ancient Druidry that a commentator wishes to propose, or none.

The wise Druids have therefore returned in the general British imagination during the course of the twentieth century to the limbo which they occupied during the sixteenth and seventeenth. They emerged from it for about a hundred years in between because they were linked to megalithic monuments and the Bible, and when those links were snapped they drifted back into obscurity. Just as in the case of the patriotic Druids, however, something that was a national phenomenon can have a second life as a sectional one, something that was an orthodoxy can become a sectarian belief, and something that was once exoteric can live on as an esoteric tradition. The wise Druids were to do all those things.

The Green Druids

Green Druids lived and taught in wild and beautiful natural places, away from the distractions, temptations and discomforts of civilisation. They drew their undoubted wisdom from this close relationship with the natural world and their resulting understanding of it. All of it was precious to them, but especially trees, among which they delighted in particular to live, worship and debate. They provide one of the most perfect images in the European historical imagination of the way in which the human quest for knowledge and power can be reconciled and partnered with the framework of the earth's own environment.

These Druids are also based on ancient texts, in this case a small group of Roman writings from the first century CE. First off the mark was the geographer Pomponius Mela, probably writing in the 40s, who said simply that Gallic Druids met in secret, in caves or remote valleys. About twenty years later, the poet Lucan commented that their rites were carried on in the depths of forests. Much more information was supplied, apparently in the 70s, by the natural historian Pliny. In his most famous passage he declared that their most sacred tree was the oak, and their most sacred plant the mistletoe when it was found growing on an oak tree (botanically, a very rare event). In Pliny's account, they worshipped in groves of oak and required a branch of it to be present at any of their ceremonies. From this he proposed that the very name 'Druid' *could* derive from the Greek word for that tree. This possibility has been debated by philologists for hundreds of years, and remains an open one, although the name could also come from an Indo-European root word indicating wisdom or knowledge. The matter will probably never be resolved.

Pliny also added the only full description of a probable Druidic rite to come down to us from the ancient world. This occurred among the tribes of Gaul when mistletoe actually was found growing on an oak. Then the Druids gathered it, if possible on the sixth day after a new moon. Having made preparations for a banquet and sacrifice beneath the tree, they led two white bulls thither. Clad in a white robe, the officiating priest climbed the oak and cut the mistletoe with a gold sickle, so that it fell into a white cloak spread out ready for it. The 'victims' (presumably the bulls) were then killed, with a prayer to a god that the plant would be as effective as possible. Druids believed, added Pliny, that, administered in a drink, it made barren animals fertile and was proof against poison; they called it 'the all-healing'. He added that they also thought that the *selago* plant warded off evil and that its smoke cured eye disease; it was gathered while wearing a white robe and with bare feet, and carrying no iron objects. They also valued the *samulos* plant, as a cure for ailments of cattle, and cut it with the left hand, while fasting. Finally, they treasured objects like small, hard-shelled, pocked apples, which they believed to be a form of egg formed from the juices secreted by groups of snakes. These were supposed to have the power to influence magistrates and rulers. It is not absolutely certain what *selago*, *samulos* or the 'eggs' were.

Two problems have long been noted with these texts. The first is familiar: that none of their authors seem to have been writing from first-hand experience, all being dependent on material which may or may not have been accurate in any or every detail. All, moreover, were themselves hostile to Druids. The second problem is that none of the writers on Druids in the preceding century, such as Caesar, Diodorus and Strabo, seem to have associated them especially with wild places: rather, they located them at the centre of their societies. It is possible that the association was always present, but at least equally so that a century of increasing Roman persecution had driven them into practising their rites and holding their schools in caves, forests and secluded valleys. Tacitus had certainly written of sacred groves on Anglesey, when the Romans first arrived there, but these were also planted around many Greek and Roman shrines and need not imply an especially close mystical relationship with trees. If they were as obviously connected with oaks as Pliny insisted, then it is curious that no other writer mentions this.

None the less, the sources were there for anybody who wished to make use of

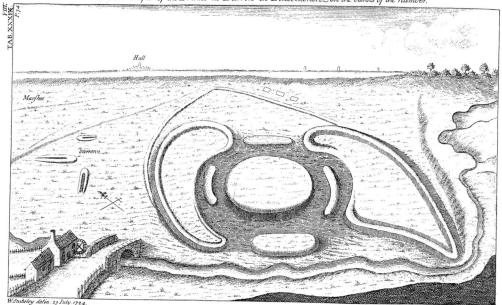

TAB. XXXIX. VIII P.74

The alate Temple of the Druids at Barrow in Lincolnshire, on the banks of the humber.

Hull

Marshes

barrows

W. Stukeley delin. 23 July 1724.

Above: 15. William Stukeley was in many respects a superb field archaeologist, but like most pioneers of knowledge he got things wrong. Here is his plan of a medieval motte and bailey castle in Lincolnshire, which he mistook for a Druidic temple, and which he made the type specimen of a whole non-existent class of monument.

16. Stukeley's reconstruction of Stonehenge, as he imagined it being in Druidic times. Inaccurate in details, it is still superior to previous attempts, and reflects Stukeley's own sense of the majesty and sacred nature of the monument.

Above: 17. Druidry as garden ornament, on the grand scale. A Neolithic tomb from Jersey, dug up and presented by the islanders to the English governor, and reassembled as a 'Druid's Circle' in the grounds of his mansion in Buckinghamshire in the 1780s. As illustrated in John Britton's *The Beauties of England and Wales*, in 1801.

18. The most elaborate 'Druidic' folly of all: the temple of the zodiac, representing an imagined Druidic monument, erected by a local gentleman a Swinton, Yorkshire, in about 1800. From a drawing by Barbara Jones.

Above: 19. A lithograph by N. Whittock, showing a restored Stonehenge based on Stukeley's ideas. The dignity and reverence of the scene certainly echoes Stukeley, but it could also be read as a swipe at ceremonial religion, above all Roman Catholicism; and the bound prisoner on the left looks ominous.

20. Robert Cruickshanks's famous drawing of Iolo Morganwg in his later years, seated in the chair in which his asthma forced him to sleep upright, and holding a paper with his 'mystic sign' of Druidry at the top. It perfectly captures his pulsating nervous energy.

21. The celebrated representation of an Archdruid in Samuel Meyrick and Charles Smith's *The Costume of the Original Inhabitants of the British Islands* (1815). Every detail is carefully taken from respected texts, notably Stukeley, and prehistoric objects found in bogs and graves.

22. Meyrick and Smith provide their imagined portrait of a pair of 'ordinary' Druids. The details mix sculptures of the Roman period from Gaul, more individual prehistoric artefacts, and Iolo Morganwg's invented system of Druidical grades.

23. Two more of Iolo's grades, the Bard and Ovate, are shown here by Meyrick and Smith, with a 'Druidical cross' imagined by Stukeley in the background.

24. Druidesses are rarely depicted in art, reflecting their scarcity in the ancient sources, but Meyrick and Smith made a brave attempt to give them their due, using Roman art to reconstruct their conjectural costumes.

25. Finally, Meyrick and Smith provide their own reconstruction of Druid ceremonies at Stonehenge, leaning heavily on Stukeley.

26. A Druid meekly converting to Christianity on the appearance of a stern-looking missionary, from Charles Hulbert's Victorian history of British religion. The picture expresses the view first expressed in Elizabethan times, that the British in general, and their Druidic religion in particular, were peculiarly well-disposed towards Christianity.

27. Reassembled fragments of the Coligny Calendar, the artefact that has been most commonly used to prove (or disprove) the wisdom of the Druids in recent times.

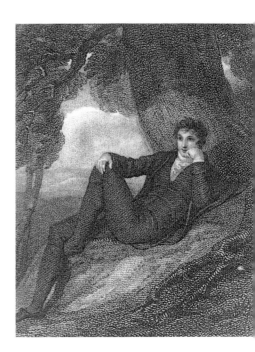

28. A design by the great architect Inigo Jones, for a play in 1638, shows a free spirit of nature, crowned with leaves, simply dressed and barefoot. This was one of the period's vague associations of Druids, as personifications of the land.

29. The early Romantic poet in his classic habitat: Thomas Wharton posed as a child of the natural world, musing beneath a tree and presumably listening to its wisdom, in the portrait that accompanies his collected works.

30. Pliny's image of the Druid as mistletoe-gatherer, migrating between woods and megaliths, engraved to accompany some of William Mason's verses.

31. Ancient Britons at home in a forest wonderland, in Edward King's *Munimenta Antiqua* (1799). The party of warriors, however, respectful, seem to have startled a group of Druids enjoying a string concert.

33. A re-enactment of Pliny's mistletoe-gathering ceremony, without bulls but with added maidens, staged at a pageant at Builth Wells, 1909, as one manifestation of the modern Welsh love-affair with Druids.

32. A Druidic seminar in the woods, imagined for George Craik and Charles Macfarlane's "Pictorial History of England" in 1849.

34. A pair of ancient Britons, created by the visiting artist Lucis de Heere in 1575. The spears, shields, nudity and paint are taken from (hostile) Greek and Roman sources, but their heads are modelled on contemporary Gaelic Irishmen, and in addition the whole composition owes much to European concepts of native Americans. Thus ancient stereotypes of savages were used to reinforce sixteenth-century justifications for the conquest of indigenous peoples. It was hard for many people to think kindly of Druids, as part of a society portrayed with such disgust.

35. Things get no better in John Speed's *Historie of Great Britain* (1611). This ancient British tribesman, drawn by an artist called de Bry, is a compendium of ancient and early modern clichés of savagery.

36. The seminal image of the wicker man, as a mechanism for the sacrifice of human beings. Derived from the ancient writings of Caesar and Strabo, and put into visual form for the first time in Aylett Sammes's history of Britain, in 1676.

37. This illustration from one of the earliest volumes of the journal *Archaeologia*, in 1773, shows how John Toland's interpretation of 'rocking stones' as Druid monuments had become accepted. It had the virtue of enabling areas which were short of megaliths, such as parts of upland Yorkshire and Glamorgan, to substitute these naturally-formed stones instead. The manic expression of the Druid in the picture also fits Toland's fantasy that the stones were used as mechanisms for corrupt judgements in legal cases.

them, and they were pressed into service as Druids began to seize the imagination of the British in general during the 1740s. This adoption of the Druids as patriotic and wise ancestors coincided neatly with the first stirrings in Britain of what was to become known to cultural historians as the Romantic Movement. These depended partly on a new belief that there was an inherent wisdom and virtue, as well as a beauty, poetry and numinous divinity, in wild nature. Those who held it urged civilised peoples to seek out natural places, apparently unaffected by human activity, in order to renew their acquaintance with them as sources of cosmic knowledge and artistic and intellectual inspiration. The fact that the ancient Druids had habitually seemed to do exactly that made them easy objects for admiration by those who adopted these ideas.

The first great Romantic writer in Britain was the poet James Thomson, who has been cited earlier as a forerunner of the cult of the patriotic Druid. In the poem that embodied that cult, 'Liberty', his ancient Britons are all forest-dwellers, and their natural freedom is associated with their wild homeland. In Alexander Pope's subsequent draft for the poem 'Brutus', his Druids feature as flower children, gentle worshippers of sun and fire who offer fruit and blossom to their deities. William Collins's 'Ode to Liberty' had its Druids carry on their rites in a woodland shrine to freedom, and when his friend Thomson died suddenly in 1749, he hailed him at the opening and closing of a poem of tribute as a Druid himself. This was, by implication, simply because Thomson had been a poet who loved woods: the Druids had become the spiritual ancestors of modern British nature poetry. Ten years later, in William Mason's 'Caractacus', the chief Druid of Anglesey was a seer living in a cave, with his colleagues occupying other caverns in the cliffs to left and right of him. They all gathered at night, in a grove consecrated by springs of vervain dipped in dew, and dedicated their ceremonies to peace and sanctity, and the honouring of the celestial spirits who presided over the rugged landscape of north-west Wales:

> The airy tribe that on yon mountain dwell,
> Even on majestic Snowdon: they, who never
> Deign visit mortal men, save on some cause
> Of highest import, but sublimely shrined,
> On its hoar top in domes of crystalline ice

Hold converse with those spirits that possess
The sky's pure sapphire, nearest heaven itself.

In the last full year of Mason's life, 1796, a fellow author associated him with
the beauty of English woodlands, and fantasised that Druids could still live on
somewhere in their depths. When Mason died, he got the Thomson treatment,
with compound interest: a poet called for his burial beneath 'a central oak's
mysterious shade', and dreamed of Druids, bards and 'dark-robed priestesses of
the grove' (out of the pages of Tacitus) attending the rites.

These writers were accompanied by others working in the same vein. Two
of the most influential were the Oxford don Joseph Warton and his younger
brother Thomas. In 1745 Thomas wrote an ode to express the belief that Druids
had first discovered the value of philosophy while musing in 'oaken bowers'. In
the next year Joseph honoured a hollow oak, standing beside a classic English
village, as possibly once the dwelling of 'a holy Druid'. Ten years later he declared
(rather ungratefully, given his position) that wild and natural scenery stimulated
the imagination better than any university, and celebrated it 'as the supposed
habitation of Druids, bards and wizards'. By the last decades of the eighteenth
century, even poets who had never shown an interest in Druids needed to be
associated with them by admirers: two admirers of Oliver Goldsmith suggested
that the ancient nature-priests had retreated into fairyland, where they could
'hear the rules of love' in enchanted woods and spy on modern masters of nature
poetry like Goldsmith.

Like the patriotic Druids, the green Druids reached their apogee in the later
Georgian period. In 1792 the author of an anonymous poem could hail them as
the gentlest priests in the ancient world, each one a 'foe to blood'. He portrayed
them processing to Stonehenge to make offerings of woodland fruit, ewe's milk,
honey and wild grains, with female Druids among them wearing hoods bound
with fillets and carrying oak branches. Once among the stones, their chief made
a speech extolling the blessings of peace. To another poet, four years later, it was
inconceivable that a people as honourable and civilised as the Romans would
have wiped out holy men as sweet and pious as Druids were now thought to be.
So, he rewrote history, having them flourish all through the Roman occupation
to be destroyed finally by the savage Anglo-Saxons.

All this adulation made it inevitable that sooner or later somebody would produce 'Druids: The Musical', and it was done sooner – in 1774 – by John Fisher. His show, *The Masque of the Druids*, was all the rage at Covent Garden in the succeeding winter, setting the ancient holy men in a woodland paradise over which the goddess Venus reigned and through which nymphs capered. Their religion was shown as one of celebration of the bounty and happiness of the natural life, and the Druids pranced around like shepherds in classical pastoral fantasies:

> Holy Druids from your consecrated woods,
> Rocky cliffs and silver floods,
> From their margins fringed with flowers,
> Hither move, foresake your bowers,
> Strewed with hallowed oaken leaves,
> Decked with flags and sedgy sheaves,
> To yon bright dome straight repair,
> But leave behind you all your care.

In view of all this it was equally inevitable that statues of Druids would join those of goddesses, gods, dryads, naiads, tritons and all the other cast of characters to populate the grottoes, temples, groves, ponds, terraces, rivulets and general Sublime Prospects with which late Georgian landowners struggled to turn their parks into never-never lands. By 1780 Druids were peering out from the shrubbery in the grounds of stately homes across England and Wales, though only Sir Richard Hill, owner of Hawkstone Park, Shropshire, seems to have taken the extra step of installing a live one. By 1802 he had persuaded an anonymous retainer to take up residence in the grotto that was (and is) one of the spectacular follies constructed on his land. The brief of this individual was to dress up in vestments every time that he heard visitors approaching and appear in the chapel of the grotto, bowing to its altar, in order to impress, delight or terrify them.

They were, moreover, still associated with more stirring landscapes and emotions than those of the soft lowland English woods. A Cornish schoolboy called Richard Polwhele frequented the high bare ridge of Carn Brea, overlooking what in his time were the booming miners' towns of Redruth and Camborne. The summit is covered with prehistoric remains, and they fired young Polwhele's imagination as he saw the guardian spirit of the place remembering its former glories:

> Still she sees the Druid train
> (Revered Chorus) sweep the lyre!
> Still she hears the thrilling strain:
> Glows her heart with holy fire.
> Richly robed the hoary sage
> Still the mystic rites performs;
> Silvered o'er his brow with age!
> Still his frame devotion warms.

The first poem entirely devoted to Druids was the work of a Scot, John Ogilvie, who was minister of Midmar where the fertile farmlands of Aberdeenshire roll up to the massive slope of the Highland Line. His thoughts were concentrated by the sight of one of the recumbent stone circles that have featured so prominently in Scottish attitudes to Druidry. Indeed, he could hardly avoid this experience, because it stood next to his church. In 1787 he published 'The Fane of the Druids', with enough success to bring out a sequel two years later. It showed them as devotees of peace, education and the one true god, led by a silver-haired chief robed in white. His home was a dell grown with oaks and poplars, and he combined a saintly asceticism with a kindly understanding of human nature: in short, the perfect Scottish pastor. The society around him was that of the classical Arcadia, a primeval paradise of innocence and joy. He concluded by declaring that such happiness was only found now among primitive peoples in remote parts of the world, such as the natives of Tahiti and India. In this, he was tapping into one of the other major literary themes of his age: a revived enthusiasm for the ancient concept of the noble savage, a being uncontaminated by the corruptions and oppressions of civilised life and free to enjoy a natural and untroubled existence. This was in most respects an obvious outgrowth of Romanticism, but it pressed into its service the discovery by European explorers of hitherto uncontacted native peoples in remote parts of the globe. In the words of the pioneering scholar of the subject, Hoxie Fairchild, 'by 1799 no traveller with an eye to publication would deal very harshly with savages'. The inhabitants of Polynesia and of ancient Britain were equal beneficiaries of this fashion.

The absolutely guaranteed result was that they would suffer equally as it waned, which it had begun to do sharply by the 1820s. This was for four interlinked reasons. The first was simply that the natives of places such as Tahiti had been overidealised. As more detailed information was received about their customs and beliefs, an inevitable reaction set in against the view of their existence as that of a primitive golden age. None the less, the earlier portraits of them had been deliberately rose-tinted for a home market that wanted to think well of them, and the urge to exchange rose tints for pens dipped in venom was propelled by a change in that market itself. This was caused by the second and third factor in the shift. The former consisted of the growing European technological superiority over traditional peoples, provided by what used to be called the Industrial Revolution, and the resulting dramatic expansion of colonial empires. As more and more non-European tribes and states came under European rule, there was a powerful incentive to justify conquest by undertaking to civilise and improve, as well as to exploit, the societies thus being taken over. This linked with the third factor, the Evangelical Revival in British Christianity, with both established and nonconformist churches making missionary efforts to reach both the marginalised members of their own societies and traditional peoples in other parts of the world. All these developments boded ill for any celebration of the virtues of pre-civilised peoples, whether ancient or (so far) surviving, and a couple of decades later the theory of evolution by natural selection came along to reinforce them. Sir John Lubbock's withering verdict on primitive societies may stand as characteristic of what had happened.

It is small wonder that green Druids and noble savages faded together into the background of British culture in the first half of the nineteenth century, leaving wise Druids, who were initially more compatible with the new attitudes, to flourish for a few decades longer. Victorians and Edwardians who still wanted to celebrate the pleasures of a simple rural life – and there were an increasing number of those – found their inspiration in Greek and Roman texts. These peopled the countryside with spiritual beings who begged none of the difficult questions now raised about primitive peoples, and Pan replaced the Druid as the dominant symbolic figure of those seeking a green and pleasant land. Some of the old associations lingered in a marginal form. Poets celebrating woods, and especially oak trees, continued all through the nineteenth century to mention their linkage to Druids, but to emphasise their great age and traditional nature as part of the landscape; the Druids themselves were generally now off the stage.

At the same time the Romantic Movement itself shrugged them off. In the era of the French Revolution its (subsequently) most celebrated British authors acquired a more radical edge, deployed against conventional social and religious attitudes. All were English poets, and it seems that they found that the Druids themselves had become too familiar and conventional: too bound up with patriotism and Christianity. In the case of the great Romantics, as in that of the archaeologists of the later nineteenth century, the ancient holy men (and women) had apparently become victims of their own success. At any rate, Coleridge ignored them and Byron dismissed them:

> The Druid's groves are gone – so much the better:
> Stonehenge is not – but what the devil is it?

Shelley was not interested in them either, Wordsworth thought them nightmarish, and Keats found their presumed monuments depressing in a more humdrum way:

> like a dismal cirque
> Of Druid stones, upon a forlorn moor,
> When the chill rain begins at shut of eve …

Although relatively few poets continued to work with a concept of Druids as nature-lovers, they continued to appear throughout the nineteenth century. Keats and Byron had published their dismissals in the 1820s; at the beginning of that decade, a minor author called Edward Quillinan brought out a 'Hymn to Nature', hailing Her as

> Goddess of the green retreats,
> Thee my boundless worship greets!
> Every hill and every dell
> Has for me a Druid cell,
> Every leafy fane of thine
> Holds for me a holy shrine.

Near the end of the decade a different Wordsworth, Christopher, studying at Trinity College, Cambridge, entered a competition for the best poem concerning Druids. He narrowly beat Thomas Hankinson's patriotic Druidry (quoted in the first chapter of this book) to first place, with an evocation of them as priests of the natural world:

> All hail, ye saintly band, whose souls aspire
> With vows that burn, and feed the holier fire.
> What though your hearths no spicy sweets exhale,
> Nor scented incense loads the languid gale;
> Nor marble halls are yours, nor sculptured stone,
> To lure the great Creator from his throne.

This Wordsworth went on to concentrate on different saintly bands, for he became a bishop and never returned to writing about Druids. In the 1830s, however, another poet of the third rank, William Stanley Roscoe, published a celebration of them on the more famous Wordsworth's own home turf of the Lake District. He called to the guardian spirit of the woods around Rydal Hall as follows:

> O thou that rul'st this wild of wood,
> Lord of the forest and the flood,
> Whose sullen voice is heard to roam
> By fits amid the leafy gloom,
> Where erst the rolling orb of night
> Gleamed on the Druid's hallowed rite,
> Spirit, we hold thy oak-crowned shrine,
> And altars as of yore divine.

What is significant about this sequence of verse is that it signals a shift of attitude between the eighteenth and nineteenth centuries which was to have important implications for the treatment of Druidry, and of ancient paganism in general, in modern British culture. The Georgian poets had been celebrating a lost world of innocence and freedom, which taught the lesson that close personal communion with nature could reveal profound truths. Those of the following period were starting to slip into the language of people who to some extent imaginatively shared the Druidic religion of nature, which in that sense might be continued or revived. During the rest of the century, while interest in patriotic Druidry almost disappeared and that in the Druids as scientists, engineers and priests of formal religion began to wane, writings on 'green' Druids slightly increased. They never again became a major genre of British letters, but they represented a consistent minor one.

A selection of texts illustrates the range of treatments possible within it. In 1851 Esther Le Hardy published an epic poem set on the island of Jersey, *Agabus*, in which the natural world is to Druids 'the leafy page of God' and their creed a pagan equivalent to the Christian hymn 'All Things Bright and Beautiful'. A youngster is instructed by one in the following terms:

> Sweet child! That thy young heart may know,
> By seeing how the flowers grow
> Without man's help, or even care,
> That God is good, and everywhere.

The poem ends tragically, and significantly, with the gentle old Druid and brave old Druidess, who are the central characters, being murdered by invading Christian warriors with Germanic names. In 1880 a scientist called John Eliot Howard lectured to the Philosophical Society of Great Britain that Druidry had consisted of pantheism, the unity of all nature with deity, which seemed to him 'the highest effort of the natural mind in religion'. His opinion was based on Iolo Morganwg's forgeries, given a green tinge, and he himself was uncertain of his own relationship with the creed he was describing. On the one hand, he suggested that, unlike Christianity, 'it has no remedial feature for the hour of adversity, no consolation against the darkness of the grave'. On the other, he admitted that he so far shared the Druids' attitudes that 'I should prefer the breezy air of the Wiltshire downs to the atmosphere of Westminster Abbey'.

Howard's was a rare example of a prose work dealing with the issue. Mostly, as before, it was put into poetry, where feelings could be conveyed less explicitly or analytically. In 1857 the curate of a London parish dedicated some verses to the president of the nation's main scientific institution, of which Howard was to be a fellow, the Royal Society. He praised the Druids as ancestors of modern scientists:

> Dost *thou* seek that truth-based knowledge
> Man demands to make him sage?
> Here then learn to study, stranger,
> The vast universe thy college,
> And thy book *her* varied page.

Thus far the message is conventional enough, but it develops into an apparent symbolic endorsement of Druidic solar worship:

> Full orbed God's truth rises, routing
> Ignorance, darkness, Goth and Hun,
> Nations telegraph to nations,
> Sects conflicting, all are shouting,
> Men! It is the Sun! the Sun!

Another minor poet, writing a sonnet about a 'Druid' stone on the Cumberland coast in 1887, could find sanctity there still:

> If Seascale's copse and oaks of Drigg have waned
> And pearls no longer at thy feet are laid,
> From Esk to Duddon by the votary brought;
> Still to thy stone of help is reverence chained,
> With sense of lonely watching, and the thought
> Of silent faith – here vows anew are made.

Another, writing twenty years before, had repeatedly expressed similar sentiments. This was Robert Leighton, whose intense love of woods gave him a proportionate empathy with the old priests thought to have worshipped there. His affection for them persisted, even when he left the shelter of the lowland trees and trekked out to the tall stone circle at Stenness in Orkney:

> O Druid! We are one; I feel thy thoughts
> Now climbing up to God. The *form* of thought
> Goes with the age – the thought is for all time
> As stones, grass, sun the same.

A third poet, in 1886, felt the same impulse to worship at a megalith:

> Well might the Druid old bow down with awe,
> And deem thee, when thy uncouth form he saw,

An altar cut by nature's hand in stone,
That her God might be worshipped thereupon
More largely and in more majestic ways
Than on those lesser ones which mortals raise ...
And though thou who wast, ages gone,
An awful altar, now art but a stone,
Yet let my song to God our Maker be
As solemn fire to rise once more with thee.

The nineteenth century also produced a different sort of association between Druid and natural world, first proposed by a Scottish minister in 1803. This was that the ancient nature-priests, retreating deeper into the woods and hills in the face of Roman and then Christian persecution, had long survived there as a secret society and were the origin of the later belief in fairies. In this theory, they had kidnapped healthy baby children from mainstream human society in order to replenish their numbers, so giving rise to the tradition of changelings. The idea that Druids were behind traditions of the fairy folk was taken up by other Scottish writers, and passed from them into French scholarship, which gave it still greater currency. It outlasted the nineteenth century, still flourishing in the early years of the twentieth.

As the Victorian period gave way to the Edwardian, hints began to appear that the nature-worship of the Druids had been earthy in more ways than the literal. This correspondingly made it more exciting, if also more disquieting. Walter Chalmers Smith wrote in 1902 of five beloved old pine trees whom he called 'Druid sisters', adding that

They were like living things to me, with thoughts and memories
And passions of the women in the untamed Druid times;
I heard them sing their skalds at night unto the raving seas,
And moan their rugged lyke-wakes in the ancient runic rhymes.

Susan Mitchell, publishing in 1912, thought those who kissed under the mistletoe were 'Love's Druids', and advised

Beware O girl and boy,
Who, in a sudden joy
Have here adventured on enchanted ground,

Unto the wheels of life ye shall be bound,
The wizard wheels that whirl and whirl around.
Breathing her magic in the mistletoe
The Druid earth hides laughing in the snow,
And from her glowing fire
Lights the taper of our desire.

The appearance of Druids as pantheists in British literature diminished with the outbreak of the First World War, which destroyed most of the cultural fashions of the preceding century. One of these was the taste for sentimental nature poetry within which Druidry had played a residual, but consistent, part. Two dramatic productions from the period between the world wars serve, however, to show how the ecological aspects of ancient Druidry could continue to surface within other literary contexts. One was Rutland Boughton's opera *The Immortal Hour*, first staged at Glastonbury in 1920. Its libretto was based on the play by William Sharp, writing under the name of Fiona Macleod, but featured additions of Boughton's own. One of these was a procession of Druids singing a liturgy. Gone is the pantheist God associated with Druidry by the Victorians; instead the Druids call upon the pagan deities of ancient Ireland, with their separate attributes, headed by 'sky-set Lu who leads the host of stars'. They also salute the powers of nature, in a blessing that has the tone of genuine invocation:

By the voice in the corries where the Pole-Star danceth,
By the voice on the summits the dead feet know,
By the soft wet cry where the Heat-Star troubleth,
By the plaining and moaning of the sigh of rainbows.
By the four white winds of the world
Whose father the golden sun is,
Whose mother the wheeling moon is,
The North and the South and the East and the West,
By the four good winds of the world
That Man knoweth, that One dreadeth, that Lu blesseth,
Be all well on mountain, moorland and lea,
On loch face and lochlan and river,
One shore and shallow and sea.

In 1939 a Welsh author, Alvin Langdon Coburn, produced a play for children called *Fairy Gold*, with an Archdruid as the hero of the story, as a wise man pitted against an evil witch. Served by the spirits of the four elements, he declares that 'All the world is my concern. The world and its loveliness is my deep concern. The beauty of the dawn and the stars at eventide. The silver shimmer of the waves, the rustle of the wind in autumn leaves, the smell of new rich earth turned by the plough, fire's warmth in winter's cold: all these are my delight. Yet beyond all these there is a deeper, richer joy, as when the soul sweeps upwards on its flight to its true home.' His partners in religion are the priestesses of Ceridwen, a deity portrayed as the great goddess of the natural world, who herself manifests in the play at a prehistoric dolmen. She speaks of 'the love of God', and of the gift of justice, love and inspiration to girls initiated into her mysteries, and promises the coming of a golden age in which humans can reclaim the ancient Druidic wisdom. The play ends with the redemption of the witch, who turns into a priestess of the goddess.

The green Druids had thus moved through a series of transformations. To the Roman authors who first represented them, they were mysterious and rather suspicious characters who hid out in wild places and taught herblore. The eighteenth-century British made them into devotees of the wisdom of nature and priests of a primeval paradise of innocent joy. In the nineteenth century, they became (for some) teachers of a pantheist religion which retained allure and truth, investing their holy places with a lingering power. The twentieth century began to put back individual goddesses and gods, and elemental spirits, as representative forces of that benevolent natural world that Druids understood and served. The final part of the process (to date) was to revive this presumed Druidic religion of nature itself.

4

The Demonic Druids

Demonic Druids were the priests of a religion of gloom and gore, demanding for its regular practice the lives of large numbers of human beings. They represent the unacceptable face of religiosity, turning glorification of the divine into a means of degrading the human spirit. Their rule was founded on fear and cruelty, and the terror inspired by their predatory faith only served to reinforce their own power over their people. The result was a vicious circle of tyranny and brutality, ended by the twin forces of Roman civilisation and Christianity, whose victory over it marked one of the major advances in the condition of European humanity.

These Druids are certainly found prominently in ancient sources, consisting of a succession of texts produced in the Roman Empire between the last century BCE and the opening of the second CE. They do not represent a different body of material from those that portray Druids as patriots or scholars, or as dwelling in close harmony with the natural world; instead they overlap, sometimes completely, with these. Modern writers who drew on classical sources for visions of 'green' Druidry, in particular, had to do so selectively, for the original intention of the authors whom they quoted was not to admire Druids for living in wild places but to make this one aspect of their general savagery. Nor is there any boundary between writers who credited them with a capacity for philosophy and science and those who thought them murderous barbarians; instead, the most detailed of the surviving accounts integrated both, to produce Druids who had a capacity for metaphysical speculation but also practised human sacrifice. There was, however, a significant distinction in the way in which the two different aspects of Druidry were portrayed: whereas ancient writers tended to be hazy as to the nature of Druidic wisdom, when it came to Druidic barbarism, they were all too appallingly precise.

The first was Caesar, in his account of his conquest of Gaul. He stated that one of the duties of Gallic Druids was 'the due performance of sacrifices', including those of human beings. Such acts were made, or vowed to be made, by people in mortal danger, either from disease or violence, who believed that by offering deities the life of another person in their place they would be spared themselves. On special occasions, he added, mass human sacrifices were offered, by building colossal figures of woven twigs and filling them with living people before setting them on fire. The individuals selected to die were preferably those convicted of serious crimes, but, if none of those were available, innocent victims had to be claimed. Caesar was followed in chronological order by Diodorus Siculus, who claimed that the most important form of divination carried out by the Gauls was to stab a man in the chest and observe his death-throes to see the patterns formed by his limbs and the trail of his blood. He added that no sacrifice was performed without the assistance of a 'philosopher', apparently meaning a Druid, and that criminals were executed by being impaled in groups and prisoners of war were burned to death as an offering to deities at the beginning of harvest. He was followed in turn by Strabo, who repeated the information that convicted criminals were sacrificed, and that the Druids thought that, the larger the number of people offered in this manner, the better the harvest would be. He also repeated and augmented other information found in the two earlier writers: that the presence of a Druid was necessary for any sacrifice and that the rites took the form of stabbing (with divination from the victim's death-throes), shooting with arrows, impaling (within shrines) or burning to death in a colossal figure of straw and wood, together with cattle and wild animals. Strabo added that the Romans had abolished these cruel practices.

It should be emphasised here that the custom of human sacrifice was certainly carried out by some cultures in human history, among whom it is documented either by internal records or by observation by reliable outsiders, or both. Classic examples were found in Central America, among the Mexica (the people formerly known more familiarly as Aztecs) and Maya, as well as other cultures, and in several Polynesian island groups. The Central American cases make good parallels for what authors like Caesar said about the Druids, as they had priesthoods who made a sophisticated study of the stars as well as claiming human lives. Human sacrifice has, however, been a relatively rare phenomenon, abhorred by most societies: since Greek and Roman times civilised Europeans have used it as one of the classic traits that indicate savagery or barbarism. In the context of the Druids, it should be noted that the practice was alleged against a wide variety of other cultures in ancient Europe and the Near East, including the Germans, Scandinavians, Syrians, Phoenicians and Palestinians. Given that it tends, where it occurs, to be a regional tradition, this may be significant. The fundamental problem is that none of these peoples have left records of it themselves: it was, rather, something of which they were accused by their enemies or outsiders, principally Greeks, Romans and Hebrews. The Romans had already deployed it as a charge against their most dangerous opponents during their rise to power in the Mediterranean, the Carthaginians. In recent years archaeologists specialising in Carthaginian culture have conduted a lively and inconclusive debate over this, some claiming to have proved the truth of the Roman allegations from material evidence, while others believe that the same evidence represents much more innocent religious practices which were misunderstood or misrepresented by the Romans.

It is important also to distinguish human sacrifice from two other phenomena. Most human societies have used capital punishment for serious crimes, and most have invested the execution of criminals with a large element of (often elaborate) ritual and commonly of religion, down to the prayers usually read to a condemned person on a modern European scaffold. Likewise, many societies have put to death prisoners of war, often also in a ritualised manner. Homer's heroes operated within a world in which most of the male population of a captured town was routinely slaughtered. The greatest of all, Achilles, killed twelve young noblemen captured in battle upon the funeral pyre of his friend Patroclus. Readers of the Old Testament will be aware that warfare in ancient Canaan was just as brutal, including that waged by the Israelites with the full encouragement of their god Jehovah. The Romans used their arenas as settings for the destruction of both criminals and war prisoners, in highly theatrical displays. On occasion, also, they had formerly killed prisoners ritually in order to satisfy certain omens: this had happened as late as 97 BCE. The only reason why the Greeks of the classical period, and the Romans, discontinued the earlier custom of wholesale butchery of males in a defeated population was that they found an economic use for large numbers of male slaves. To outsiders, these three forms of activity – human sacrifice, execution of criminals, and murder of prisoners of war – could look remarkably similar, but there is a chasm between the first and the other two. The crucial determinant of a culture that sacrifices human beings is that it has hungry gods: that the shedding of human blood is regarded as essential for the proper practice of religion. This is the significance of Caesar's claim that innocent victims had to be found if the supply of criminals had run out: he was indicating clearly that the Gauls sacrificed human beings in the true sense of the term.

Was he correct? The details of the accounts left by Caesar, Diodorus and Strabo slide between two models. In the one, human sacrifice is an irregular event among the Gauls, held in a personal or collective emergency, and involving victims who are already marked to die as criminals. In the other, such sacrifices are expected to bring a good harvest, and if no (or insufficient) criminals are available, then completely innocent people must be offered. This is a situation in which only a little misunderstanding or misrepresentation could create a major shift of perception. Here it is necessary to emphasise, once again, the sheer unreliability of the sources. As already discussed, Caesar's account of the Druids is anomalous in his history of his campaigns in Gaul and fits badly with some other contemporary evidence. He certainly had the strongest possible motive for misrepresenting native customs in order to portray the Gauls as peoples deserving of conquest. More important is the point, made earlier, that nobody can tell how good was the quality of the information on which all three writers depended, collectively or individually, and in default of such information no final judgement can be made upon it.

Certainly the idea that the Druids were concerned with human sacrifice, and therefore to be condemned and suppressed, became a theme of Roman literature, expressed most forcefully after they had vanished from Roman territory. Writing in the early second century CE, the historian Suetonius recorded that the Emperor Augustus, Caesar's successor as leader of the Roman state, had tried to prevent the Gallic ruling class from becoming Druids by declaring that nobody could be both a Druid and Roman citizen. Suetonius added that the third emperor to rule after Augustus, Claudius, had banned altogether 'the barbarous and inhuman religion of the Druids in Gaul'. Pliny, writing in the 70s and so closer to the event, said that the ban actually occurred earlier, under Augustus's successor, Tiberius. Pliny added that the world owed a huge debt to Rome for ending 'this monstrous cult, whereby to slaughter a man was an act of great piety, and to eat his flesh most beneficial'. It may be noted that no other writer went as far as to accuse Druids of cannibalism. Pliny also had a juicy titbit of gossip about the British: that at their religious festivals the married women paraded naked, with their skin dyed black with the juice of a herb. Scholars have long noted that the contents of his book, the *Natural History*, veer between scientific fact and preposterous fantasy. Nobody can now tell where on that spectrum this piece of information should belong.

Classicists still argue over whether the Romans wiped out Druidry because it was indeed concerned with horrific rites; or whether they did so, and then blackened its name, because it was a barrier to the assimilation of the Gauls to their rule. Certainly, by the middle of the first century CE, Roman writers found Druids to be good bogeymen. The poet Lucan lambasts them in his epic poem, the *Pharsalia*, as having formerly been leaders of 'barbarous ceremonies' and 'sinister practices'. At another point in the poem, he describes a sacred grove that had allegedly existed near Marseilles at the time, a hundred years before, when Caesar was besieging the city. Marseilles was actually a Greek colony and was under siege as part of a Roman civil war. The grove got in the way of Caesar's intended siege works, so he ordered it felled. As his men hesitated to touch the sacred trees, he struck the first axe blow himself, and, as he sustained no harm, the soldiers then followed his command. The episode is intended to display his tough-minded courage. Lucan could not resist embellishing it with a description of the grove itself: 'interlacing boughs enclosed a space of darkness and cold shadows, and banished the sunlight far above … gods were worshipped there with savage rites, the altars were heaped with hideous offerings, and every tree was sprinkled with human blood'. No birds or beasts dared enter it, and not even the wind, but the branches moved of their own accord and water fell from 'dark springs'. 'The images of the gods, grim and rude' were uncouth blocks formed of felled tree trunks. 'Legend also tells', added Lucan, that 'yew trees fell and rose again, phantom flames appeared among its trunks, and serpents glided between them'. No humans ever entered it except its priest.

Anybody who has read the *Pharsalia* knows that Lucan had an imagination that later generations would term Gothic: elsewhere in the poem we encounter a loathesome witch who can drag the moon down from the sky. There is very little doubt that here he is using that imagination to spice up the episode, and also perhaps to distract attention from the fact that Caesar had committed sacrilege by destroying a (presumably Greek) sacred grove. Despite this, this passage has been quoted down the centuries, out of context, as if it were an objective piece of ethnography, providing a clear portrait of Druidic religion.

Finally we have Tacitus's famous description of the attack on Anglesey, quoted in full before and ending in the charge that the people of the island 'had believed it, indeed, a duty to drench their altars in the blood of prisoners and to consult their deities through human entrails'. The difficulties with this passage have been discussed, and its possible significance lies at any point along a spectrum between two extremes. The fact that it bears such a close resemblance to what was said about Druids by Diodorus and Strabo (or a common source to both) may mean that there was, indeed, a uniform and horrific Druidic tradition that stretched all the way from the Mediterranean to the Irish Sea. At the other extreme, this same resemblance could mean that the sentence was an embellishment based on the (celebrated) work of the two geographers, put in to add drama to the episode. It may be noted that Tacitus speaks of prisoners of war as the victims, rather than the native population, but, in a source of such questionable basic reliability, this may not be very significant.

All in all, is prudent to suggest that the ancient sources do not provide information trustworthy enough for any firm conclusions to be drawn regarding the place of human sacrifice in ancient Druidry. What has really mattered has been their cultural impact, for they provide a damning portrait of Druids in texts which have long been among the most widely read to survive from the ancient world and the most commonly translated. For those who wanted to move beyond the classical curriculum, and make use of Irish literature, there were more unpleasant images in store. The classic role of a Druid in the life of a medieval Irish saint was as an evil pagan magician, who is defeated by the hero of the hagiography, using the power of the true god, and so is either killed or converted. In the words of the editor of Irish saints' lives, Charles Plummer, 'they meet us at every turn as the chief, if not the only, opponents of the new faith'. They appear as such in the earliest Irish literature and play the same part into the seventeenth century, falling foul of a succession of Christian holy men of whom the first and greatest was Patrick himself. They are his main opponents in Muirchú's life of the saint, which was written in the late seventh century and as such is one of the oldest surviving Irish texts. It describes how Patrick confronted the high king Loegaire, whom he found surrounded by different kinds of magicians and soothsayers to whom Muirchú gave various Latin brand names. Of these, the *magi* were those commonly translated by scholars as Druids. They were certainly the most important and the most hostile to Patrick, who defeated them with a series of miracles in the course of which their two leaders perished. Muirchú makes plain, however, that he is not merely, or even primarily, recounting a native tradition but seeking to assimilate Patrick to the great figures of Christian literature. He expressly compares Loegaire to the biblical king Nebuchadnezzar, who kept court magicians, and Patrick's duel with one of them to St Peter's contest with Simon Magus. Another parallel, this time implicit, is with Elijah opposing the priests of Baal. Significantly, we possess two actual letters written by the historical Patrick about the nature of his mission, over two centuries before Muirchú's time. They never mention Druids, nor dramatic confrontations at Tara: his problems are all with local kings or hostile fellow Christians.

Irish literature also has one unequivocal, and famous, reference to human sacrifice in Druidical times. It appears in the *Metrical Dindshenchas* of the twelfth-century Book of Leinster, a series of traditions recorded about particular places. One of these places is Maigh Slecht, a plain now in County Cavan, and the verses concerned describe how thirteen idols once stood there, the greatest of which was called Cromm Cruiach. It adds that every year a third of the children of Ireland were killed as offerings to this image, in the hope of getting good harvests of corn and milk in return. This story appears in turn to have been based upon one in the *Tripartite Life of Patrick*, written at some point between the eighth and eleventh centuries and celebrated among scholars as the latest and most fantastic of the early medieval biographies of the saint. This describes how Patrick found on Maigh Slecht the chief idol of Ireland, an image of gold and silver called Cenn Cruaich, accompanied by twelve other idols of brass. He expelled the demons that inhabited them and drove the idols into the ground. There is no mention of sacrifices. This sounds, then, like a medieval Christian fantasy, developing over time and apparently mixing together Old Testament accounts of the idols of the Babylonian kings and of child sacrifice with Diodorus or Strabo. The one note of realism in it is the description of the remains of the sanctuary that accompanies the story in the *Tripartite Life*, which was said to be still in existence at the time when the text was written, with the idols buried up to their heads in earth and a mark left by St Patrick's staff visible on top of the biggest. It seems likely that a genuine pagan sanctuary had existed on the spot – perhaps of standing stones – which was linked to the lurid fable recounted in the *Tripartite Life*.

During the sixteenth and seventeenth centuries, when the Germans, French and Scots were all taking up Druids as admired ancestors, English authors often trotted out the hostile ancient texts, or impressions ultimately based on them, as reasons for failing to follow their example. They still found an imaginative use for Druidry, but as an example of wrong attitudes or behaviour. Two spiritual phenomena in particular worried the Tudor English – corrupt religion and witchcraft – and Druids could be assimilated to both. The first person actually to publish a text in English that dealt with them was the Protestant evangelist John Bale, in 1546. He mixed together various medieval and Renaissance pseudo-histories, the Old Testament and Pliny to present a unique portrait of them as priests who had arrived in Britain from Athens, proclaiming the faith of a single god, and had set themselves up as chaste hermits dwelling in forests. This show of piety was, however, merely a pretence to win the respect and allegiance of the native British. Once they had been put in charge of the latter's religion, they enriched themselves from it, feasting on sacrificed livestock and keeping whores whom they decked with jewels. They could therefore function as a prime example of the worst kind of priest, at a time when Bale was striving for the reformation of the English Church.

The theme of corruption appeared on a grander scale in the bumper history of the British Isles produced by Ralph Holinshed's team of writers in 1577. The sections on Druids were the work of another strenuous evangelical Protestant, William Harrison. In his version of their story, which conflated the pseudo-histories of Annius of Viterbo and Hector Boece with the ancient authors, they had been instituted by descendants of Noah to propagate and maintain the true faith revealed to the Hebrew patriarchs. Gradually, however, they adopted worse and worse beliefs and habits, until they became the overpowerful, bloody-handed idolators portrayed in the hostile Greek and Roman texts. Christianity then arrived as the Romans abolished them, rescuing the British from falling prey to the even worse excesses of polytheism and superstition associated with Roman paganism. The notion that truly revealed religion decays naturally among human beings, because of the inherent imperfections of human nature after the Fall, is rooted in the Old Testament. Indeed, one of the chief objections that Victorian liberals were to have to the biblical version of history was its deep pessimism with regard to human beings. On the other hand, it embodied an optimistic view of divine nature, which ensured that true faith was periodically restored by processes of reformation and purification. Protestantism had a vested interest in emphasising those processes, and Harrison's Druids therefore represented a dress rehearsal for the clergy of the medieval western church: godly and devout products of a genuine religious revelation who had gradually turned to error and ungodliness over many generations, until their replacement by a restored version of the true religion became imperative.

At a popular level, in the era of the English witch trials, there seems to have been a strong impression that the Druids had literally been demonic, ranking alongside witches as practitioners of a malevolent magic inspired by Satan. The Elizabethan playwright Thomas Nashe lampooned them as evil sorcerers 'lousy' with attendant devils: 'had they but put their finger and thumb into their neck, they would have plucked out a whole nest of them'. In 1612 a pamphlet describing a witch trial in Northamptonshire railed against those who still doubted the reality of witchcraft, holding up among other evidence 'the ancient records of the witches called Druids'. Interestingly, both Nashe and the pamphleteer thought that the Druids had operated out of a base in the Isle of Man, accepting the Scottish identification of Tacitus's Mona; which made them foreign as well as malevolent.

In general, though not as an absolute rule, those English Protestants who were most hostile to Druids tended to belong to the radical and evangelical end of the religious spectrum, concerned with Scripture, preaching and a personal relationship with the deity as a prerequisite for salvation. Conversely, there was a tendency (though no more) for authors who favoured them to be Roman Catholics or to belong to those parts of the Church of England that emphasised sacraments, ceremony and hierarchy, and had some fellow feeling for a well-trained established clergy. Although the general British adoption of Druids as heroic forebears, which came in the mid eighteenth century, had other causes, it must have been aided by the fact that mainstream English religion had calmed down considerably by then and its evangelical wing had long lost power. As part of the same process, the belief in witchcraft was evaporating among the ruling elites. None the less, there was still a potential for even radically new ideas to appropriate hostile images of Druidry, as is illustrated by the work of John Toland.

Toland was one of the most notorious freethinkers of his time, who steadfastly rejected all forms of established religion and professional clergy. In the prospectus for a book on Druids that he hawked round in 1718, he turned them into classic prototypes of the 'priestcraft' that he hated so vehemently. By studying the way in which they had starved their flocks of knowledge, terrorised them with the threat of excommunication and taken their wealth, he believed that people would be better able to reject clerical power and pretension in the present. This radicalism was too much for its time and was probably the main reason why Toland never found a sponsor for the work. None the less, his three letters making up the prospectus were published soon after his death. Collectively they became one of the favourite texts on Druidry read by the British over the next century and a half: five new editions of them appeared in the years 1810–15 alone. A particularly good example of Toland's influence lies in his assocation of megalithic monuments with Druidic religion. Having been convinced of this by Aubrey, he was ahead of the intellectual field; and, once Stukeley made the connection an orthodoxy, Toland posthumously supplied some particular linkages that caught the British imagination.

The greatest of these did not concern genuine prehistoric monuments at all, but a natural phenomenon: boulders that the action of weathering or glaciation has left balanced on top of others, so they can be rocked from side to side. In Cornwall, where they were especially common, they have acquired the generic name of 'logan' stone. Geologists are now certain that they are wholly the work of natural forces, but eighteeth-century scholars were inclined to credit them to human hands. As megaliths of all kinds became regarded as Druidic, logan stones were included with a variety of other natural formations as monuments of the ancient religion. In the case of rocking stones, Toland's loathing of priests drove him to a particularly potent fantasy. He proposed that they had been put there by Druids to manipulate the system of justice, so that an accused person would be invited to rock the stone, only to find it immobilised by a lever secretly activated by one of the cunning priests. As soon as the wretched person withdrew, the lever was withdrawn and the stone again rocked easily, making the guilt of the accused apparently attested by divine authority. Alternatively, Druids could use the same system to acquit a guilty person of whom they approved. In Toland's words, 'by this pretended miracle, they condemned of perjury or acquitted, as their interest and affection led them'. As rocking stones were never constructed by any sort of human being, we can be pretty sure that Toland was wrong; but then he never had the slightest evidence to support his conjecture. It was a flight of imagination propelled by violent prejudice. Yet his image of the rocking stone as an instrument of Druidical injustice was to reappear steadily in English publications, both of fiction and non-fiction, for three hundred years to come.

During the eighteenth century, as the British imagination embraced the Druids as wise, learned, pious and patriotic national ancestors, engaged with the truths of the natural world, hostile references to them dwindled to a minority of the writings that concerned them. A number of strategies were developed by their defenders to minimise the accounts of Druidic atrocity in the ancient texts. One was just to ignore them. Another was to say that they may well have been true, but only of Gallic Druids; in other words it was possible to believe anything bad of the French. Another was to dismiss the authors of those texts as agents of Roman imperialist propaganda, devoted to justifying the conquest of the peoples whom Druids had served. A more sophisticated version of this pointed to the weaknesses of the texts themselves as evidence. In addition, some authors suggested that the Greeks and Romans had mistaken the ritualised execution of criminals for human sacrifice.

At the same time, the production of works hostile to Druids never ceased, even at the apex of national enthusiasm for them. There were various reasons for this. One was that many Georgians retained an admiration for Greek and Roman civilisation that outweighed anything to which they could be inspired by ancient Britain; they were far more accustomed to seeing the ancient world through the eyes of a Caesar or a Tacitus than in any other fashion. Another was that, to many devout Christians, Druids remained indisputably pagan, and none of the attempts by Stukeley and others to argue this away carried enough conviction. The new association of them with megaliths just caused them to visualise dolmens as altars smoking with blood, or to view standing stones as idols, not as miracles of engineering or markers of Pythagorean geometry. A third source of hostility was that already manifested by Toland, a detestation of priesthoods in general. As the philosophers of what became known as the eighteenth-century Enlightenment frequently displayed varying degrees of anticlericalism, they sometimes found it convenient to make Druids into the pre-Christian version of the evils that they condemned in churchmen. Towards the end of the century, moreover, Romanticism sprouted a side channel, into the movement known subsequently as Gothic. This found a new excitement, and creative inspiration, in phenomena traditionally regarded as morbid: death, darkness, the irrational, the occult, and the more frightening or disturbing aspects of the natural world. To workers in this idiom, ancient priests who carried on ghastly rites by night in impressively gloomy natural places (with or without decorative megaliths) could be too great a temptation as subjects to resist.

Disapproving images of Druidry, therefore, continued to appear throughout the eighteenth century, multiplying as the British became more concerned with Druids in general. Some of the most influential were provided by William Borlase, the Cornish parson who integrated Druidry into the first great county study of prehistoric monuments. To his view of ancient religion he brought the full traditional Old Testament disapproval of the 'abomination of the heathen'; he instinctually regarded all pagans as dreadful, and Druids were as bad as the rest. To him they had induced, instead of 'the true fear of God, a gloomy kind of awe, and religious dread' and 'instead of the true purity of heart, a false superficial purity ... consisting of ablutions, white garments, outward sprinklings and lustrations'. By a process of imaginative extrapolation, he provided detailed reconstructions of Druidical rites, including minute descriptions of what each class of celebrant wore. In his imagination, they took place at noon or midnight, and consisted of the kindling of candles and torches from a sacred fire, the sprinkling of celebrants with holy water, and prayers, libations, and blood sacrifices. This country clergyman became the first British writer to make much of Pliny's naked women, claiming that they were exposed before the young men in order to deaden the sensibilities of the latter to the horrific scenes of ritual murder taking place. No ancient author had suggested that there had been anything remotely orgiastic about Druidic ceremonies, but to Borlase it was obvious that, as these were pagans, 'after sacrifice, luxury and debauch ensued'. He added an endorsement of Toland's idea that rocking stones had been used to convict or acquit criminals as the Druids had wished. In this manner, a particularly lurid impression of ancient Druidry was built into the book that served for many as the model for a survey of local monuments.

If Borlase's view was inspired by a puritanical piety (to dig no deeper), almost the opposite impulse caused one of the greatest British philosophers of the century to take an equally dim view seven years later. This was the Scotsman David Hume, who, among much else, anticipated and encouraged the Victorian doctrine of human progress in both material and moral spheres. Against the prevalent, biblical, orthodoxy that all human religion consisted of a degeneration from an original, true and divinely-revealed, form, he argued for an increasing element of truth and sophistication in religiosity. While flattering to the present, this promised little generosity to ancient forms of religious activity, and, in addition, the Druids fell foul of Hume's dislike of powerful clergy. As a result, when the final volume of his *History of England* appeared in 1761, it declared resoundingly that 'no species of superstition was ever more terrible than that of the Druids'. In Hume's imagination, they cowed their followers with threats of excommunication and of rebirth in forms of lower animals, kept ordinary people ignorant by confining their teachings to their own ranks, and hoarded wealth. He declared that they were idolators of the worst kind who sacrificed human beings, and praised the Romans (whom he much admired) for having got rid of them. Also in this tradition was Joseph Strutt, writing in 1779, who declared that ancient priests in general had been characterised by 'pretended miracles and mysterious doctrines' designed to overawe the common people. 'But', he thundered, 'all the ancient records of the known world cannot furnish a more striking view of the prevalence of superstition in the people, or the arbitrary government of the priests, than we shall find among the deluded British.'

Poets, in keeping with the different nature of their medium, voiced similar sentiments in still more heightened language. One of the earliest to do so was the Bristol writer Thomas Chatterton, who travelled a few miles south from his city in 1769 to visit the large complex of prehistoric stone circles and avenues at the village of Stanton Drew. Stukeley and Wood had made these famous as a great centre of Druidical worship, but whereas they had looked at the huge stones dozing in the meadows above the River Chew, and seen marvellous patterns of Pythagorean geometry and astronomy, Chatterton wrote

> Joyless I hail the solemn gloom
> Joyless I view the pillars vast and rude
> Where, erst the foot of superstition trod
> In smoking blood imbrued
> And rising from the tomb
> Mistaken homage to an unknown God ...
> All hail ye solemn horrors of this scene
> The blasted oak, the dusky green,
> Ye dreary altars by whose side
> The Druid priest in crimson dyed
> The solemn dirges sung,
> And drove the golden knife,
> Into the palpitating heart of life

Admittedly, Chatterton was not in the best of moods on the day of his visit; he had just been jilted by his girlfriend. Admittedly, also, he eventually committed suicide. None the less, his verses stand at the opening of a succession of others, concerned with the sacrificial propensities of Druids, that cascaded through the next hundred and fifty years. Chatterton's were, indeed, relatively restrained.

Hitherto, hostile images of Druidry had generally credited its practitioners with some dignity, as cold and calculating leaders of a bad religion. By the last three decades of the eighteenth century, they were turning into homicidal maniacs, displaying advanced forms of murderous psychosis; or, if you like, devils in human form. The portrait published of them by Michael Wodhull in 1772, in what is otherwise a tribute to the vanishing beauties of English woodlands, differs from the norm only by adding halitosis to the list of their unpleasant characteristics:

> Though in your holy grotts retired
> The subtle priests with venomed breath
> The thirst of homicide inspired
> And urged the lingering rage of death:
> To their polluted altars led
> Where erst the captive youth had bled
> Victim of hellish cruelty ...

Although these negative images represented a minority of the work published on Druids during the late Georgian period, the enormous growth of writings on Druids in general meant that there were actually more of them circulating than ever before. By the time that the young William Wordsworth began to write poetry, they had literally become the stuff of nightmares:

> At noon I hied to gloomy glades,
> Religious woods and midnight shades,
> Where brooding superstition frowned
> A cold and awful horror round,
> While with black arm and bending head
> She wove a stole of sable thread.
> And hark! The ringing harp I hear
> And lo! Her Druid sons appear.
> Why fix on me your glaring eyes?
> Why fix on me for sacrifice?

Images of Druids as savage and bloodthirsty priests only multiplied as the nineteenth century came in, and in the course of it they became dominant, as those of patriotic, wise or nature-loving holy men and women waned. This was because all the motives suggested above for hostility to Druidry to linger through

the Georgian period still existed, and more were added. The latter consisted of
the forces working against the positive images, which may be summed up here
as evangelism, imperialism and the theory of evolution. The Evangelical Revival
in British Christianity, the increasing extent of, and need for moral justification
of, Britain's tropical empire, and the concept of nature as a progression to higher
and higher forms, and of human existence as one from brutishness to civilisation,
were all inherently unfriendly to Druids. The first two had most impact in the
first half of the century. The third joined them for the second half.

The changing attitude to traditional peoples in the contemporary world
had a direct impact on those towards ancient Britain. Two areas of the globe in
particular were especially influential in this respect: Polynesia and India. The
natives of Tahiti, Hawai'i, Fiji and the Marquesas all engaged in human sacrifice
at the time of their discovery by Europeans, while between 1820 and 1850 the
British government of India orchestrated a series of well-publicised campaigns
against Hindu customs that it had come to regard as unacceptable. Four of these
in particular caught the imagination of contemporary authors: *sati* or suttee (the
burning of widows alive upon their husbands' funeral pyres); infanticide; human
sacrifice (especially the cult of *thagi* or Thuggee, in which travellers were ritually
murdered as offerings to the goddess Kali of Bindhachal); and suicides before the
image that the British called the Juggernaut. This was a huge statue of Krishna,
dragged at festival times through the city of Puri, beneath which devotees would
through themselves to be crushed to death. All of them rebounded on attitudes
to Druids.

The relationship between Druids and representations of traditional peoples,
was one of constant intellectual cross-pollination. In 1799 the antiquarian Edward
King, noting a report by Captain Cook of a rite of human sacrifice in Tahiti, used
it as an argument for believing the Roman reports of the same custom among
Druids. He added: 'And when we consider the vast improvements of the arts and
of the conveniences of life, which have attended our emerging from the dreadful
chains and fetters of those corrupt times ... we may become sincerely and
heartily thankful, to the only true and Almighty God.' King effectively wrote this
view into the plan of Stonehenge, for it was he who named the prone megalith
lying in the Avenue as it approaches the main circle, 'the Slaughter Stone'. The

channels worn into it by weather were likened by him to those designed to allow the blood of victims to run off an altar. As the name caught on, and was unthinkingly repeated, the reputations of both the monument and the Druids were further damned. The comparison between the latter and modern natives could also rebound in the other direction, for when the novelist Mary Russell Mitford described a human sacrifice in Tahiti, in 1811, she termed it 'the Druid rite'. More common were Indian parallels. The poet Stephen Prentis wrote of Stonehenge in 1843

> when thou
> Hadst superstitition redly written on thy brow,
> And wickered victims in their blazing cage
> Upheld with shrieks the glory of a creed,
> Whose crimson prop, in a benighted age,
> Was ignorance, that bade the wretches bleed
> And holocausting torture was the mead
> Of their fanaticism, murder-fraught.
> That faith is gone, but has the world indeed
> From blushing time a holier colour caught?
> Go ask the ensanguined car of modern Juggernaught!

Thirteen years later another poet, the Cumbrian parson George Newby, accused the Druids of

> sad superstition and more cruel by far
> Than crushed the wretch 'neath Juggernaut's cruel car.'

As for widow-burning, a series of wall-paintings were commissioned in 1841 as decorations for the central corridor of the newly-rebuilt Houses of Parliament, to illustrate the progress of Britain. They were in a series of three 'before and after' pairs; the middle one matched 'a Druidical sacrifice' with 'the suppression of suti'. Two decades later, a Cornish poet, John Harris, went an extra lap of imagination and accused the Druids themselves of having burned the widows of fallen warriors. In 1825 the author of an encyclopaedia, Thomas Fosbrooke, had made a catalogue of deplorable practices carried on among recent or contemporary tribal peoples – India and Polynesia again taking first place – to argue that their presence in the modern world made it easy to believe that all of them had been enacted by Druids. As the century went on, and colonial administrations reformed native customs, the comparison seems to have become ever less favourable to Druidry. In 1905 a folklorist, Charles Squire, declared confidently that Druids had committed human sacrifice 'upon a scale which would seem to have been unsurpassed in horror even by the most savage tribes of West Africa or Polynesia.'

Images of Druids as the priests of a savage and revolting religion were embedded in heavyweight histories such as Robert Southey's Tory one of British Christianity and Henry Lingard's Catholic one of England. They were equally prominent in lightweight equivalents such as Charles Dickens's *A Child's History of England*. Historical novelists, of course, made full use of their potential, as did dramatists.

Thomas Kitson Cromwell's *The Druid: A Tragedy* opened in 1832 with the following directions:

> 'Act 1, Scene 1. A circular arena, in the middle of a thick grove of oaks. – Within the area a double enclosure of vast pillars of stone, placed equidistantly, and surrounding a cromlech, or druidical altar. The inner enclosure consists of rough unhewn stones; but those of the outer circle are regularly shaped, superior in height, and have transverse masses at top, being trilithons – A rude stone chair, elevated on a flight of steps, behind the altar. – a gloomy twilight overspreads the scene. – Thunder.'

Cromwell went on to direct that the trees had to be 'age-ensilvered', 'like sheeted corpses', with their tops 'in gloom … murky as night'. The air, his characters' lines suggested, had 'a sulphurous taint', and even insects could not fly on it (thereby going one better than Lucan, whose Gallic grove had merely been uninhabitable by birds). Naturally, the main business of the place was human sacrifice, and the story ended with the archdruid ('the unbending, vindictive, almost fiend-like chief of a diabolical, politically ascendant priesthood') being struck dead by God Himself.

Joanna Bailey's tragedy *Ethelwald*, went one better still (in a sense) by featuring a cast of spirits, teeming about an archdruidess holding court in a gloomy cavern. The directions called for her to be robed in white and attended by similarly clad 'Mystics and Mystic Sisters'. They chant while moving in spirals, till 'a thick vapour ascends' and 'crowds of terrible spectres' enter.

Above all, evil Druids were exploited by poets. Few of the latter were as economical as the Yorkshireman John Walker Ord:

> On Eston's promontory
> Renowned in ancient story
> A reverend Druid stood –
> His locks were long and heavy
> His hands were red with blood

The Scotsman John Stuart Blackie, writing of Columba, one of the early Irish saints whose chief foes were pagan magicians, also came quickly to the point:

> For the Druids worshipped demons,
> Gods of earth and air and sky,
> Peopling land and peopling water
> With the glamour of a lie.

For the most part, readers were treated to descriptions of the lengthy adventures and horrible ends of victims who, whatever the precise means by which they were put to death in the tale, shared the common fate of being slowly crushed beneath hundreds of rhyming couplets. At times indignation clearly outran inspiration, as it did for the Devonshire poet Frederick Paas, in 1830:

> Upon the rough hewn altar's floor
> In thought I beheld the clotted gore,
> The hair and brains all scattered round,
> The hard, and firmly trodden ground,
> Often the scene of deadly struggle
> E'er the spirit left in the fatal gurgle.

These melodramas embodied another significant nineteenth-century development. No ancient source had stated that Druids ever sacrificed women or children. It is possible to infer that women might well have been among the criminals condemned to ritualised execution, and also (with less reason) that Caesar's reference to 'innocent' victims could be stretched to cover the young and the female; but both suggestions fall short of actual evidence. Despite this, during the nineteenth century it became accepted by many authors that, as one aspect of their demonic character, the Druids must have spared neither age nor sex. Another poet writing in Devon, and contemplating one of the prehistoric stone circles surviving on Dartmoor, could imagine how:

> O here the fair,
> The brave – the mother and her spotless babe
> The maid, blooming in vain – the wise, the good –
> Felon and captive – age and shuddering youth,
> In one vile holocaust, to fancied gods
> Pour'd out their souls in fire, amid the blast
> Which the loud trumpet flung – the deafening clash
> Of cymbal – and the frantic, frenzied yell
> Of an infuriate priesthood, drowning deep
> In one infernal burst of sounds, the shriek
> Of suffering humanity!

Many authors went beyond this, to fantasise that Druids must have had a particular enthusiasm for the ritual killing of young women (the 'virgin sacrifice' that became a theme of hostile modern depictions of Druidry) or of children. A novelist and historian, Agnes Strickland, turned them into menaces to youngsters on a level with wolves. Her story *The Druid's Retreat* (1876) was set in a late Roman Britain that had been almost freed of them, and her swipe at their memory is all the more effective for being made in passing: 'Children, who only three centuries before, would have shrunk in terror from the forests where the oaks waved their giant branches, now played fearlessly beneath their shade.' A playwright T. F. Wilkinson, who published *Iduna, Queen of Kent* in 1846, suggested that they had specialised in the destruction of babies, going on to describe how they hewed off the infant limbs, tore out the heart and entrails, and burned the little torsos on fires. Such passages confirm that at times Druids had become fair game for that sadism and prurience which represented two features of the Victorian literary imagination. It would be easy, by progressive quotation, to turn this chapter into a chamber of horrors. That invitation will be resisted, but the sheer number of publications in this genre, the manner in which they span the century, and the proportionate impact which they presumably had on readers, makes it necessary to pay further attention to them; and the tactic proposed here is to look in detail at a few selected works, to show what was possible to the literary imagination of the period.

The first, in chronological order, was a Staffordshire writer, T. G. Lomax, who published *A Complete History of the Druids* in 1810. Having made the usual horrified remaks about human sacrifice, he went on to say that 'they were so very cruel, that almost every week they not only murdered a great many upon their altars, but in their schools. Herphilus, one of their first doctors, taught anatomy over the bodies of living men at times to the number of seven hundreds.' No source references were provided to indicate on what Lomax had based this remarkable flight of fancy about ancient vivisection. Two years later, a doctor of divinity called William Hurd published a universal history of world religion, intended to illustrate the superiority of Christianity to all others. In contrast, he declared that the 'barbarous idolatry of the Druids, served only to harden their minds, and deprive the most tender parent of human feeling'. Among new information that he conveyed to his readers were the items that they had held women in common and that virgins were deflowered at a certain age by their own fathers. He also provided an account of a sacrifice. Hurd's Druids assembled under tall oaks, with their leader clad in fine linen, a mitre on his head and subordinate priests all around him. A prisoner of war was chained to one of the oaks, his back to the tree and naked except for a crown of flowers. Music played as the archdruid came forward and stabbed the man in the bowels. The people then danced and the Druids pretended to divine the future from his flow of blood as he died. In short, the scene was a mixture of Pliny, Diodorus Siculus and Regency British imagination; but it was presented by Hurd as historical fact, and that is how it was subsequently repeated by later writers.

Of the epic poetry generated by the subject, the most consistently colourful was probably Sandford Earle's *Eanthe*, published in 1830. His description of the Druidic New Year festival begins with Pliny's account of the gathering of mistletoe. When midnight comes in the grove, however,

> then the cheek
> Was flushed and high – the brow – the temples pale.
> The red wine cup was drained – and woman's shriek
> Of laughter wild was heard upon the gale,

With man's deep voice, as in lascivious round
Cheek pressed to cheek, and lip to lip, they wound
Through the mazy dance, with loosened hair
And naked breasts, and shoulders – bosom bare:
And slender arms in stronger arms entwin'd
And panting limbs on panting limbs reclin'd,
And fair young forms on manhood's glowing breast,
With burning sighs, half fainting, sunk to rest.
But let the veil be dropped, and darkness shroud,
Within its deep, impenetrable cloud,
Foul deeds like these, till ev'n their very name
Shall be forgotten, or linked with shame –
For not those orgies of the days of old
At whose bare name the shuddering heart grows cold,
Where naught that could of lewd debauchery boast,
Or sin or wickedness – was ever lost,
Out-did, in wild intemperance those feasts,
Led, ruled, encouraged by religion's priests.

It should be noted that, according to Earle, the Druidic New Year was the spring equinox (where the official year did begin in the ancient and medieval Julian calendar). His Druidic revellers were therefore clearly very hardy, enjoying themselves in a wood in the middle of a March night. Come the feast of Beltane in Earle's epic, at the opening of May, the human sacrifices could really get into their swing, starting with gutting selected victims on altars and sprinkling the congregation with their blood, and culminating with the wicker image mentioned by Caesar and Strabo:

But hush – Oh God of heav'n! What wild shrill cries,
And shrieks of agony, are those which rise,
Ascending far and high, above the din
Of those without, from those confined within
The living tomb? Oh! mortal cannot know
The shriek – the cry – in this extreme of woe,
Th' expiring victims give. The flames had now
Sprung from the sides, and wreath'd them round the brow
Of the huge figure, and the shriek that rose,

In hopeless agony and pain, from those,
Confined within its hot and burning womb,
As in a living and a fiery tomb,
Struck sudden wild and shrill upon the ear,
Above all other sounds. Oh! none could hear
These shrieks, and be unmoved; to that last cry
Of dying nature breath'd an agony,
So deeply wild, the gay and shouting crowd
Half turned away, yet, turning, shouted loud
And louder still, and clashed their cymbals high,
As if such sounds could drown the victim's cry,
Of mirth so false raise up one thought within
Their hearts, responding to the hollow din.

The heroine of the story manages to survive all this, only to be torn limb from limb by a crowd at Samhain, the festival that opens winter.

Victorian readers weary of poetic melodrama, and hungry for sober works of historical scholarship, would have been well advised not to start with Thomas Miller's history of the Anglo-Saxons. This appeared in 1852 and had gone through two more editions within four years. Its popularity was undoubtedly owed to its lush style. Druids were given a brief but vivid part in the first chapter, as Miller's enthusiasm for the early English demanded that a contrast be made between them and the native British, to the detriment of the latter, including their priests. He informed his readers that

There was a wild poetry about their heathenish creed, something gloomy, and grand, and supernatural in the dim, dreary old forests where their altars were raised: in the deep shadows which hung over their rude grey cromlechs, on which the sacred fire burned. We catch glimpses between the gnarled and twisted stems of those magnificent and aged oaks of the solemn-looking Druid, in his white robe of office, his flowing beard blown for a moment aside, and breaking the dark green of the underwood with the lower portion of his sweeping drapery, where he stands like a grave enchanter, his deep sunk and terrible eyes fixed upon the blue smoke as it curls upward amid the foliage – fixed yet only to appearance; for let a light and wandering expression pass over one single countenance in that assembled group, and those deep grey piercing eyes would be seen glaring in anger upon the culprit, and whether it were youth or maiden they would be banished from the sacrifice, and all held accursed who dared to commune with them.

Miller's Druids served 'brutal gods' with large-scale human sacrifice, while piling up treasures in their woodland lairs. They killed anybody who questioned their actions, contributed nothing to the good of society, and offered beautiful young women the choice of being sacrificed or becoming their partners in their dreadful rites. He went on, with an equal lack of hesitation, or accountability to sources, to describe how

> amid the drowsy rustling of the leaves and the melancholy murmuring of the waters which ever flowed around their wooded abodes, they taught the secrets of their cruel creed to those who for long years had aided in the administration of their horrible ceremonies, who without a blanched cheek or quailing heart had grown grey beneath the blaze of human sacrifices, and fired the wicker pile with an unshaken hand – these alone were the truly initiated.

The last in this short run of examples, fished out of an ocean of their kind, dates from 1861, when William Winwood Reade published what purported to be a revelation of the mysteries of the Druid religion. He drew on the concept of a pure patriarchal religion, which had been corrupted into one of idolatry and human sacrifice, but he represented one writer in a new, nineteenth-century, tendency to blame the Phoenicians, as swarthy easterners, for having corrupted the original faith rather than (as earlier authors had believed) carried it to Britain. He likewise adapted Iolo Morganwg's pseudohistory of the peopling of Britain to add a new component of racism to it. Like the other authors in this sequence, he went in for uninhibited fantasising delivered as plain fact. He declared that the Druids chose as victims for their deity 'the most innocent and beautiful of His creations – beautiful virgins and chaste youths – their eldest sons, their youngest daughters'. His visualisation of an act of human sacrifice was a compound of Diodorus, Lucan, Pliny, Iolo and Willam Hurd, with original touches of imagination:

> Such a one was led into a sacred forest watered by running streams. In the centre, a circular space surrounded by grey and gigantic stones. Then the birds ceased to sing, the wind was hushed; and the trees around extended their spectral arms which were soon to be sprinkled with human blood.
>
> Then the victim would sing the Song of Death.

The Druid would approach, arrayed in his judicial robes. He was dressed in white; the serpent's egg encased in gold was on his bosom; round his neck was the collar of judgement which would strangle him who delivered an unjust sentence; on his finger was the ring of divination; in his hand was a glittering blade.

They would crown the victim with oak leaves in sombre mockery. They would scatter branches of the oak upon the altar.

The voices of the blue-robed Bards would chant a solemn dirge, their harps would tone forth sinister notes.

Pale and stern the Druid would approach, his knife uplifted in the air.

He would stab him in the back. With mournful music on his lips He would fall weltering in blood, and in the throes of death.

The diviners would draw round, and would calmly augur from his struggles.

After which, fresh oak leaves would be cast upon the blood-polluted altar, and a death feast would be held near the corpse of the sacrificed.

Shortly after this, Reade went into a flight of pure personal fantasy:

It was one of their rites to procure a virgin and to strip her naked, as an emblem of the moon in an unclouded sky. They sought for the wondrous selago or golden herb … When they found it, the virgin traced a circle round it, and covering her hand in a white linen cloth which had never before been used, rooted it out with a point of her little finger – a symbol of the crescent moon. Then they washed it in a running spring, and having gathered green branches plunged into a river splashed the virgin, who was thus supposed to resemble the moon clouded with vapours. When they retired, the virgin walked backwards that the moon night not return upon its path in the plain of the heavens.

Pliny is presumably somewhere at the back of all this, with his accounts of naked British women at festivals, the importance of the new moon to the cutting of mistletoe, and of the gathering of the *selago* plant, but these elements are worked up into an original piece of fiction, which (as in the case of those of Lomax, Hurd and Miller) was presented to the reading public as historical fact. Towards the end of his book, Reade revealed the developments within contemporary British society which he believed to embody vestiges of Druidry and which he accordingly deplored: 'heathenish' Roman Catholicism, the Oxford Movement within the Church of England which threatened to bring back Catholic elements, and Freemasonry, which he thought a tradition of 'gluttons and wine-bibbers' who mirrored pagan rites.

Clearly, for the Victorians as for the Elizabethans, and for all periods between, Druids could act as a metaphor for any form of religion or spirituality of which an author disapproved. All that had changed was that traditional targets – Catholics, overmighty clerics, pagans and foreign religions – had been joined by Anglo-Catholics and Freemasons. Indeed, the negative image of the Druid was elastic enough to be applied to yet other exercises in condemnation. For the author of a novel called *The Ancient Britons*, published in 1851, as for the historian J. W. Willis Bund in 1897, the Druids' greatest presumed vice had been their opposition to the education of the masses, whom they preferred to keep in ignorance to increase their own power. In 1899 G. B. Carvill and Gervase Bailey staged a musical called *The Druids' Elect*, in which the Druids concerned turned out to be parodies of Spiritualist mediums, who were portrayed as charlatans. Their chorus went

> We carry on the priestcraft for this poor benighted race
> With a slow impressive manner and a sanctimonious face,
> From a sacrificial offering to the paying of accounts
> They always find the ready while we settle the amounts ...
> With raps and solemn music, and a tin of phosph'rous paint,
> We can raise the tortured spirit of some dear departed saint,
> With a hidden kinematoscope and twenty megaphones
> We can make the dreaded oracle give forth in measured tones.

Victorian scholars even found a way of restoring the connection between Druids and witchcraft which had lapsed during the seventeenth century, in a secularised and modernised form. In 1866 a Scot, John Forbes Leslie, suggested that early modern witchcraft had just been a continuation of Druidry, so that the murders, evil spells and animal sacrifices with which alleged witches had been charged in the sixteenth and seventeenth centuries could also be credited to Druids. In 1892 this was repeated by a leading folklorist, Sir Lawrence Gomme, who argued that the 'horrid rites' that early modern demonologists had imagined at witches' sabbats, including human sacrifice, had been real. They had, in his reading, been merely a continuation of those of Druidry, with women taking over the leading role from men. As specialists in the history of early modern demonology and witch trials now agree that the rites attributed to witches were pure fantasy, so, by extension, was this theory.

As with other forms of Victorian culture, the preoccupation with evil Druids continued without interruption through the Edwardian period, to falter at the great watershed represented by the First World War. After that traumatic collective experience, the mood of many writers among the British turned against various impulses characteristic of the preceding period, such as aggressive imperialism, religious evangelism and strenuous moral earnestness, all of which had inspired works dealing with demonic Druids. More important still may have been the possibility that the comparative peace and security of the century between 1815 and 1914 had given the British a taste for literature dealing with melodrama, horror and atrocity. The two world wars, and the political developments surrounding them, may have afforded sufficient examples of appalling events in real life to reduce such appetites. For whatever reason, images of evil Druidry went into sharp decline in the post-war period.

A few continued to appear and, of course, Victorian and Edwardian works in the genre continued to be read. In 1927 an amateur historian, Hadrian Allcroft, published the view that Druidry had never been a religion but was a political organisation designed to concentrate power in the hands of its members. He suggested that it had arisen shortly before Caesar's own time and had represented an infiltration of Gaul by German methods of political organisation; so the Druids had now become prototypes of the Nazis. Ten years later, a perfect throwback to Victorian literature appeared, Beth Coombe Harris's *In the Grip of the Druids*; a novel for children by an evangelical Christian spinster. It portrayed Druids as child-murdering tyrants, eventually slaughtered by noble Roman invaders who thus cleared the way for Christianity to convert the British. A foreword to it was contributed by a retired naval officer, who added the view (by no means evident from the text) that the book was a warning against the evils of the Roman Catholic Church. It apparently became a favourite prize in Sunday Schools. In the following year, 1938, T. B. Morris published a play, *Druid's Ring*, set in modern times at a farmhouse overshadowed by a hill crowned with a stone circle. Slowly, the malevolence inherent in the monument, because of its association with ancient blood sacrifice, seeps into the lives of the inhabitants and their fellow villagers, inflaming negative emotions to the point at which tragedy becomes inevitable.

These were, however, no more than droplets in comparison with the flood of publications that had come before. They reflected the general position of Druids in the mainstream British imagination between 1914 and 1950, as relics of an earlier period. In the late twentieth century, however, as comparative peace and security returned, and audiences began to hunger again for images of sensational violence, the demonic Druids made a comeback. Once again, the volume of material is large enough to make sampling necessary. In the historical novels of Henry Treece, during the 1950s, British society on the eve of the Roman conquest is characterised by large-scale human sacrifice in stone circles, with young people preferred as victims. This savage Druidic religion is portrayed as part of an unruly, superstitious and passionate Celtic world, contrasted with the order, decorum, rationality and civilisation of the Romans. In Freudian terms, the Celtic id is compared with the Roman ego. With lush prose, Treece evoked

> the threshing limbs under the great stones, the antlered men whose ghostly faces twitched among the dark forests, the white-robed wolves who annually carried away the first-born or mutilated the cattle with golden knives to bring rain … the black cock's entrails steaming omens before the chief's high table, the fresh blood hardening on some young widow's lintel, and the ruined and ravaged faces that peered out from the beehive slums as magnificent young lords cantered by with cloak floating and bright boar-spears flashing in their jewelled hands.

One other feature of Treece's imagined Druidry is of great significance: that his Druids had real magical powers, being able to communicate with birds and trees, and heal or blight human beings in uncanny ways. By contrast, no inherent power is credited to Christianity. The true opposition is between the forces of modernity, as represented by Rome, and a terrifying and titillating savagery of which Druidry is part.

In the 1960s came a 'B' movie, *The Viking Queen* (1968), which, despite its title, was actually about Boudica's rebellion. The opposition involved is Treece's one between glamorous (and sometimes noble) savagery, represented by the natives, and a Roman civilisation which is duller, and sometimes capable of treachery and rapacity on its own account, but at least more familiar to a modern audience. As in Treece's work, the element that tips sympathy towards the Romans is the Druidical religion of the British, which demands human sacrifice (within stone circles) in two forms: the burning alive of Roman prisoners, which is compatible with some of the ancient texts, and the apparently pointless butchery of British virgins, which owes everything to the nineteenth-century imagination. When the London Dungeon, the capital's museum of waxwork horrors, opened at the end of the decade, one of the prize exhibits was that of a Druid about to kill a naked young woman stretched out on an altar.

The 1970s brought another 'B' movie, but this time destined for cult status, *The Wicker Man* (1973), which – if the plot is taken seriously instead of being treated as a piece of glorious high camp – is a warning against the dangers of reviving paganism in a modern context. In the famous and shocking climax of the film, the anti-hero, a devout Presbyterian policeman, is burned alive as a sacrifice with various farm animals in a huge wicker image modelled on those described by Caesar and Strabo as being used for Druid rites. What the broad screen had begun, the small one continued in the remainder of the decade. The Goodies' near-fatal excursion into the homeland of murderous Welsh Druids was described in the first chapter of this book. Another television icon of the decade, the science fiction hero Doctor Who, had an encounter with 'The Stones of Blood' in 1978. In his incarnation as Tom Baker, he found himself pitted against, and defeating, a pagan religion of Druidical kind in modern Cornwall, manipulated by extra-terrestrials disguised as blood-hungry megaliths. In the same decade the veteran writer of historical novels, Rosemary Sutcliff, kept up the concept of an Iron Age British religion dependent on human sacrifice, both of prisoners of war and of people from the tribe itself, including (in emergencies) the chief.

The 1980s brought Edward Rutherford's best seller *Sarum*, an account of the intertwined fortunes of a set of families living in the Salisbury area over a period of six thousand years. In this scheme his Druids represented merely the last stage of a succession of prehistoric religions which made the sacrifice of human beings their central rite. The same decade brought Pat Mills's ancient Irish hero Sláine, battling his way through successive tales of swords and sorcery in the magazine *2000 AD*. The Druids in these sacrificed their own kings (after seven years, according to the Victorian mythology created by Sir James Frazer in *The Golden Bough*), prisoners of war, and the last person to turn up at a muster. For big rites, their line-up seemed to consist of a single male Druid and a circle of naked Druidesses, who may have come out of Pliny but had far more in common with modern pagan witchcraft, from which the series drew its presiding deities. These were, incidentally, the *good* Druids, dedicated to powers who aimed to renew life; there were also a set of evil equivalents who venerated the force of death and decay, 'Crom-Cruach' (from the *Tripartite Life of Patrick*).

The 1980s also gave the world the series of novels by Guy N. Smith, starring Mark Sabat as a modern warrior against 'the eternal principle of evil', as expressed through the occult forces of 'the Left Hand Path': a champion expert in both physical and spiritual combat and irresistable to women although apparently wholly ignorant of the concept of foreplay. The fourth in the sequence of books involved Druids, returned to modern England as representatives of 'a religion most thought long vanished, its otherworldly horror deep buried and forgotten save in the nightmares of the deranged'. Indeed, the phantom Druids succeed in doing a succession of people horribly to death (mostly by burning alive) before they are stopped; but, significantly, they are halted only by making a deal with them. The true villains of the story turn out to be corrupt members of the Church of England, who have provoked the ancient priests with their misdeeds, and the Druids are propitiated when Sabat himself beheads those responsible, one of them a bishop, at Stonehenge. The same decade saw the beginning of a longer and more celebrated series of novels, the comic fantasies of Terry Pratchett. In the second of these, first published in 1986, he made a characteristically deft and sophisticated satire out of three of the traditional images of Druidry – the 'green', the 'wise' and the 'demonic' – by mixing them together:

> like Druids everywhere they believed in the essential unity of all life, the healing power of plants, the natural rhythm of the seasons and the burning alive of anybody who didn't approach all this in the right frame of mind … senior Druids explained very pointedly that there was indeed room for informed argument, the cut and thrust of exciting scientific debate, and basically it lay on top of the next solstice bonfire.

In 1998 Barbara Erskine, a novelist in an older tradition, tried to remake a place for Christianity as the opponent of demonic Druids. Once again, the plot of her book hinges on the intervention in the modern world of a Druidic religion of fear, human sacrifice and all-powerful and vicious priests wielding genuine occult powers. While censure is given to modern Christian fundamentalism, represented by killjoy Scottish Presbyterianism, the forces of good are embodied in a Christian magic superior to Druidry and wielded by saints. By that year, however, the author who had turned out to be the most popular historical novelist of the decade, Bernard Cornwell, had completed his own trilogy of books about post-Roman Britain, retelling the Arthurian legend. He portrays a Britain still divided between Christianity and a paganism led by Druids. His Druidry is that of Henry Treece: a religion of fear and superstition, founded on human sacrifice, but also embodying heroic qualities and truths about the natural world, and disposing of real magical power. The novel contrast is with his version of Christianity, which turns out to be a religion with no intrinsic power at all, founded on sanctimony, hypocrisy and the repression of natural appetites and joys. It is clearly a set of stories for a post-Christian society, and shows, like many of the books, films and programmes above, how easily hostile images of Druidry may continue to flourish in one.

Given the length of time over which those images have been dispersed, and the sheer number of works embodying them, it is not surprising that in some places they seem to have sunk into folklore. When he collected local traditions in west Cornwall in the mid nineteenth century, Robert Hunt found a number concerning predatory giants, who had once lived within the ancient forts of the district. Those of Trencrom Hill were especially fearsome, dragging human captives back to their stronghold, where they sacrificed them on the flat rocks inside. It is tempting to associate these monsters with the Druids of whom Borlase had written a hundred years before, as occupying the same landscape and putting victims to death in the same manner. What is certain is that a recent collection of Glamorgan ghost stories includes a tradition concerning a cliff face at Castellnau near Llantrisant, over which the phantoms of Druids who once sacrificed there still try to lure unwary travellers at night. In this case the roots of the tale are equally plain, for Llantrisant and nearby Pontypridd were great centres in the nineteenth century both for the production of books about Druids and the recreation of Druidic rites.

In the early twenty-first century, a new purpose seems to be emerging for the propagation of negative images of Druidry. In 2002 Simon Scarrow published one of a sequence of novels about the Roman conquest of Britain, which seem likely to establish him as one of the most exciting current writers of historical fiction. Its villains are the 'Dark Moon' sect of Druids, who burn women and children alive in wicker images as offerings to its god, Cruach (from the *Tripartite Life of Patrick*, again), whom they believe will bring about the end of the world (and therefore, apparently, deserves encouragement). In an endnote, Scarrow admitted that these figures were fictional but held them to represent 'the extremist fringe that exists within any religious movement'. As such, he held them up as 'a corrective to [a] naïve and nostalgic re-invention of Druid culture' and 'a timely reminder of the extremities to which religious fanaticism can be taken'. This note is dated 12 September 2001, the day after the terrorist attacks on New York and Washington. In 2002, also, an expert in Romano-British archaeology, Guy de la Bédoyère, published his study of religion in that period which has been cited earlier in this book. In a passing comment, he declared that Druids must have had a great deal in common with extremist religious groups in general: 'ruling through ignorance and fear they went unchallenged', as the Taliban did in Afghanistan. So, it seems that having already been identified with so many other targets of dislike or disdain over the centuries, Druids are now being made to carry the can for Islamic fundamentalism.

Guy de la Bédoyère's career is of some significance here, because one particular, and probably very influential, recent source of hostile portrayals of Druids has consisted of the writings and museum displays produced by professional archaeologists. Once more, a selection of key texts has to be made from a relatively large body of material.

The earliest in sequence consists of the report on the objects recovered from Llyn Cerrig Bach, Anglesey, by Sir Cyril Fox in 1945. They had been found by workmen constructing an airfield, in a layer of earth dug out of the bed of what had been part of a nearby lake. When the earth was being spread across the future airfield, ninety metal artefacts, of many different kinds, and a mass of animal bones were discovered in it. The artefacts, and a few of the bones, were sent to Fox at the National Museum of Wales for inspection. The report that resulted became one of the landmarks of British Iron Age studies, as he carefully identified the likely origin points of each and revealed that they had lain across a huge area, from north-east Ireland to south-east England. Their likely date of manufacture covered the period between the early second century BCE and the early first century CE, and Fox demonstrated the length and complexity of the trading and exchange networks that a community in Anglesey had possessed by the latter time.

He also gave much thought to how the objects had ended up in the lake. Because their archaeological context had been destroyed, by the workmen who dug them out before realising that they were significant, certain major questions could never be answered; above all, that of whether they had been thrown into the lake as a single deposit or in successive actions over a period of time. In default of this information, Fox came up with four possible explanations. One was that the artefacts represented a rubbish dump, created by a nearby (and hitherto untraced) settlement. This would be consistent with the fact that many of them had been broken or damaged before deposition. On the other hand, some were in excellent working condition, notably chains that Fox interpreted as having been used to shackle prisoners or slaves together. There would have been no point in throwing those away. His second explanation, therefore, was that the hoard represented a rubbish heap on which certain valuable objects had been hidden by the natives, when the Romans captured the island, and never retrieved.

He himself preferred the two other hypotheses. One was that the settlement had been a community of Druids and that the victorious Romans had thrown all the objects associated with them into the lake, as contaminated by hideous rites. This view, of course, depended on accepting both Tacitus's account of the Roman landing on the island and his view of Druidry, but Fox did this without hesitation. He suggested that the 'slave-chains' had been 'the means of keeping safely and transporting the wretches doomed to ceremonial slaughter'. In his opinion the Druid 'cult was cruel enough in its Anglesey home, remote from Mediterranean influences, to provoke passionate hatred even for inanimate things associated directly or indirectly with its rites'. Here Fox outran Tacitus, but accepted antiquarian tradition, by assuming that Anglesey had been a particular 'home' for Druidry. His fourth explanation was that the hoard was a votive deposit of items, captured in war, to a god or a spirit of the lake. Here again he appealed to a classical text, this time Strabo, who had said that the tribes of Gaul offered metal objects to the spirits of pools, and he went on to state (again outrunning the evidence) that this was to be expected in 'a traditionally sacred spot like Mona'. He added that 'we cannot escape by this solution from the Druids: who but the local priest-seers would supervise such rites?'

Charles Scott-Fox has published a biography of Sir Cyril. This provides information that helps explain why Fox would have favoured those particular conclusions and held those attitudes. He had an enthusiasm for Greek and Roman literature, having joined a literary society to study it when in his early twenties, and had also become 'a dedicated Christian with a profound understanding of the Almighty' and a habit of quoting Scripture and using it to judge the morals of his own times. In reviewing his report, another celebrated archaeologist of his generation, Christopher Hawkes, called the reason for the deposition of the objects 'an absorbing problem', but added that 'it is impossible not to join Sir Cyril in connecting it with the famous Druids of this sacred land ... for read the puzzle how one will, the imagination cannot shut out the thought of the sack of the island's Druid groves by Suetonius Paulinus'.

Fox, in preparing his report, acted according to the highest standards of behaviour for an archaeologist of his time, and perhaps of any time. He laid out the evidence as he could understand it, and in doing so contributed greatly to our knowledge of communication and exchange systems in the Iron Age. He then provided a number of different explanations for the deposition of the finds, while making plain those which he himself favoured, as a subjective judgement. Likewise, Hawkes's review had a great deal of probity to it, acknowledging both the lack of a certain interpretation of the material and the overwhelming force that Tacitus's famous text had upon the imagination of people like Fox and himself. What is less defensible is the use made of Fox's report, almost immediately, by Christopher Hawkes's then wife, Jacquetta Hawkes, a former archaeologist turned popular writer. In a general survey of knowledge about prehistoric Britain, she declared that the Llyn Cerrig Bach hoard demonstrated that 'such bloodly and warlike times had a cruel and bloody religion'; which it plainly does not. Since then, until the present time, the find has featured regularly in textbooks on Iron Age archaeology, with the twin assumptions that Anglesey was a major centre of Druidry and that the hoard supports Tacitus's narrative in a classic example of material evidence substantiating that of literature. In fact, no ancient source makes the former statement, including Tacitus, and the second assumption is back to front: the material evidence has been interpreted overwhelmingly in the light of a passage of literature.

In the years since Fox wrote, the likelihood that the Llyn Cerrig Bach objects represent votive offerings, thrown into the lake as gifts to deities, a deity or spirits, has much increased. The animal bones sent to Fox have been carbon-dated to the fourth to second centuries BCE, suggesting that they were thrown in before the metalwork, and that the two together represent changing fashions in almost half a millennium of use of a sacred site. They also fit what has now been recognised as a pattern covering the whole of the British Isles and large areas of continental Europe, whereby large numbers of objects were ritually deposited in watery places – selected rivers, bogs, pools and springs – during the late Bronze Age and the Iron Age. In the British Isles almost all of them have been casually discovered by workmen employed in building, draining, dredging or peat-cutting projects (or, more recently, by metal detectors), and their archaeological context is lost; but in Britain there is one major exception. This is Francis Pryor's excavation at Flag Fen near Peterborough, where a major suburban development uncovered a prehistoric site which could be systematically explored to the highest standards of modern archaeology. The finds consisted of potttery, shale bracelets and three hundred pieces of metalwork, including very fine weapons and ornaments, most broken before deposition. They had been laid in a marsh between about 1200 and about 200 BCE, a period stretching from the late Bronze to the middle Iron Age, though most date from the central part of that period. Almost all of them had been placed on one side of a line of about two thousand big oak posts, driven into the marsh between an island and the nearby drylands. These had been 'consecrated' in turn by having loose human bones, a boar's tusk, a bracelet and skeletons of dogs laid around their bases. In his analyses of the site, Francis Pryor has considered various different interpretations of it as Fox did of Llyn Cerrig Bach, making a well-reasoned case that the most likely one is that it was used for religious purposes. What is most striking, in the present context, is the lack of any mention of the Druids in his analysis and the lack of any moral reflections on the nature of the religion concerned. The presence of human bones, in particular, has not provoked any suggestions of sacrifice. The reason for the contrast is twofold: that Francis Pryor is primarily an archaeologist of the Neolithic and Bronze Age, and they have different attitudes to those specialising in the Iron Age, and Tacitus never wrote about Druids in the Fens.

The second case study consists of Stuart Piggott's book, *The Druids*, published in 1968, which immediately became, and long remained, a best-seller. This success was understandable: it was produced by one of the leading figures of British archaeology, was lucidly and excitingly written, and was profusely illustrated, often with images never published before. It was not just based on an extensive knowledge of the archaeological evidence, but showed remarkable imagination and enterprise in bringing in concepts from cultural studies and examining modern as well as ancient representations of Druids. In earlier work, Piggott had already laid down four principles which promised an exceptionally sensitive and careful treatment of the subject. One consisted of the limitations of archaeology as a means of knowing the past: 'material evidence will give material results. You cannot, from archaeological evidence, inform yourself on man's ideas, beliefs, fears or aspirations … Perhaps all we can really perceive is the history of technology'. Secondly, he doubted the wisdom of judging previous ages in moral terms: 'If we start making value judgements about the past, from the point of view that technical development is an unquestioned good, we class [some past] societies as the failures. But this is just what we should not do. We should not expect to seek in history either a justification or an explanation of our own thoughts and actions.' The third principle consisted of the provisional nature of interpretation of archaeological evidence: 'I have had to adopt a more dogmatic phraseology than I should have liked, but it is impossible to qualify the reconstruction of events at almost every turn with some indication that they represent at best an approximation to a probability. The reader should therefore keep at the back of his mind the proviso that any interpretation of the sequence of

British (and indeed of European) prehistory must be thought of as representing the most likely explanation of a set of facts and observed phenomena *in the present state of our knowledge*' (his emphasis). His fourth principle was that the interpretation of archaeological data was inevitably conditioned by the prejudices of the person making the interpretation. In 1965, as he commenced work on his book on Druids, he published another in which he praised a cartoonist for prefacing a publication with a statement of his own class, religion, race, tastes and district of residence, and added that 'similar acts of self-revelation ... would contribute greatly to an understanding of scholarship'.

Almost needless to say, having praised such an endeavour, Piggott failed to carry it out himself. He had, however, made his own prejudices abundantly clear in his previous books. They clustered around a deeply pessimistic view of human nature: 'the basic theme of prehistory and history recurs as the instinct to dominate one's fellows, to defend what one deems one's own, to mate, to eat and avoid being eaten'. He regarded inequality, warfare, repression and a lust to wield power over others as inherent in our species, condemned the 'noble savage' as a myth, dissented from any view of the history of humanity as one of natural progress, and expressed his complete lack of sympathy with the optimism of either the American Declaration of Independence or the Communist Manifesto. This basic disdain for humanity fed into his view of prehistory, coupled with his own complete lack of religious belief and a proportionate lack of sympathy for those who professed any. So, to Piggott, the Upper Palaeolithic mind was 'concerned with the irrationalities of mimetic magic and a superstitious belief in unseen powers', Neolithic villagers in Orkney existed in 'a state of indescribable filth and disorder', 'the strong element of barbarity in Celtic religion must not be forgotten', 'stability of government and population ... was strange and alien to the Celtic mind', and 'with all their faults, the successive civilised communities of antiquity achieved an organisation of man's powers, and a control of his frailties, immensely superior to anything brought about by the barbarians'.

Given these views, there was really only one kind of book about Druids that Stuart Piggott could have written, and he duly produced it. Like many scholars, he accepted in principle the concept that a person's existing beliefs to a great extent determine the view that she or he takes of evidence, and then in practice treated his own prejudices as simply the obvious and sensible position that any right-thinking person should adopt. He began by making a remarkable misunderstanding of a key concept in cultural studies, the distinction between 'hard' and 'soft' primitivism made by Arthur Lovejoy and George Boas during the 1930s. As they had formulated it, both attitudes consisted of admiration of 'primitive' societies by civilised peoples, but the former emphasised the rigour, frugality and stoicism of savages and the latter the ease, plenty and idleness of their existence. In Piggott's misreading, 'hard primitivism' consisted of 'a realistic and often unflattering view' of 'barbarian culture', 'usually as a result of first-hand contact', and providing 'empirical and factual' descriptions. He turned 'soft primitivism' into an attitude in which 'distance in time or space lends enchantment to the view, and desirable qualities are not only sought for, but discovered and idealised'. To him, given his own view of human nature, what he called 'hard primitivism' had self-evidently to be the more objective and realistic attitude. He accordingly privileged those ancient texts that took a hostile view of Druids as inherently the more accurate, and downgraded those which expressed admiration for them as inherently less so, and matched the archaeological evidence to this assumption. Inevitably, he built up a picture of them that emphasised their more brutal and bloodthirsty attributes, downplaying the more positive qualities which had been credited to them, especially their learning. The result then became the standard scholarly work on the subject for most of the remainder of the century.

My third case study is of a physical object: Lindow Man. This is the name familiarly given to the head, upper torso, arms and part of the right leg of a man of high social status aged in his twenties, found in the peat bog of Lindow Moss, Cheshire, in August 1984. The peat had preserved all to a degree that made forensic analysis of the tissues possible. Three years later more of the legs and parts of the lower abdomen were recovered. The British Museum brought together a large team of experts to examine the body, which produced a report concluding that the skull of the man had been fractured by a heavy blow, and that his neck had been broken by a garotte, and his jugular vein had been severed with a sharp instrument. This represented, in total, a 'triple death' of such elaboration that the report drew the further conclusion that a major element of ritual had been involved in the killing. The body was first dated between the fifth and third centuries BCE, then more firmly to a period shortly before, during or after the Roman conquest of the region. This put it into an Iron Age society which had long been associated with human sacrifice, because of the classical texts. A further piece of evidence that possibly linked the body to Druids was the presence of mistletoe pollen in its stomach; Pliny had, after all, written of their veneration of this plant. As a result, Lindow Man has featured regularly ever since in works on Iron Age ritual and religion, as the best proof that the ancient British sacrificed human beings as Tacitus had said they did, and as other writers had said of the Gauls. He was arguably the most sensational find made by British archaeologists in the 1980s, as well as perhaps the most carefully investigated human body on record. He has become one of the prize exhibits of the British Museum, and the notice associated with the display of his remains repeats the interpretation of his death as a ritual killing, a phrase that most people seem to take as signifying human sacrifice. Ever since the original report on him was published by the museum, Lindow Man has been cited again and again, in context after context, as the physical proof that human beings were sacrificed in Iron Age Britain.

This interpretation is thoroughly insecure, however, for two reasons. One is its dating. The first radiocarbon tests on the corpse put it in the Roman or post-Roman period, and subsequent refinement of these suggested that it had been deposited near the beginning of the Roman occupation. The problem here is that human sacrifice was illegal in Roman Britain, as all over the Roman Empire. The allocation of the man's death to the pre-Roman Iron Age was achieved only by taking advantage of the fact that the possible range of radiocarbon dates extended back to a point shortly before the Romans arrived. In 1987 portions of a second body were found at Lindow Moss, while a head from a possible third one, dug up some years earlier, has been associated with the other remains. These other body parts have been radiocarbon-dated more firmly to the Romano-British period. Advocates of the theory of human sacrifice have therefore had to suggest that this practice was carried on in secret in the area by natives unwilling to accept the Roman ban on it. The difficulty here, of course, is that there is no unequivocal evidence that there was a native tradition of human sacrifice to carry on: the whole point of Lindow Man was that he was supposed to represent that evidence.

The other problem is that the analysis underlying the diagnosis of a 'triple death' is itself unsafe. The verdict was proposed by Iain West, a pathologist from a major London hospital. The body was also examined, soon after discovery, by another expert, Robert Connolly, an anatomist from Liverpool University, who reached a different conclusion. He believed that the man's neck had been broken by a blow, being one of a series that had also fractured the skull in two places. To him, the supposed garotte was simply a necklace, to hold a pendant or pendants which had been removed before he was put into the bog or had corroded away there. Its apparent tightness around the neck was due to the swelling of the neck tissues in the peat. Connolly thought that the gash over the jugular had been caused by damage to the body after it had been laid in the bog, perhaps by the peat-cutting machinery that had carved the corpse itself into pieces. If Connolly is correct, then the whole basis of the case for a ritualised killing disappears. The mistletoe pollen in the stomach amounted to just four grains, and, though it could be evidence that the man had eaten mistletoe berries, it could just as easily have been carried by insects onto the man's last meal. The other human remains found in the Moss are represented by too many fragments, the result of being broken up by peat-cutters, for a comparable diagnosis of cause of death to be possible.

In view of the popular status of Lindow Man, as the best evidence yet found for human sacrifice in Iron Age Britain, and of the questionable state of the data, I decided to provoke a debate over the matter in the *Times Literary Supplement* in January 2004. This summarised the problems with the accepted interpretation of the body and proposed instead that it was susceptible to use in a range of different possible pasts. He could have been a willing or a reluctant human sacrifice, a victim of violent crime thrown by his murderers into the bog, or a criminal himself, executed for his offences and buried in this remote place as part of his punishment. I hoped thus to make him an exemplar of a new, more open-ended kind of history and archaeology. My article, as I had hoped, drew a reply from J. D. Hill, one of the nation's leading archaeologists specialising in the Iron Age and the curator of the gallery in which Lindow Man was displayed. He reaffirmed his own faith in Iain West's diagnosis, as that of a practised pathologist, and put the Lindow bodies in the context of the large number of partial or complete human corpses recovered from wetlands in northern and western Europe, dating from the pre-Christian period of each region and showing signs, in many cases, of violent death. He also suggested that recent research had credited the possibility of a clandestine continuation of human sacrifice in Roman Britain, so that a redating of the remains need not rule out that as a cause of death. I replied in turn to him, pointing out that West had never before examined a body that had lain for almost two millennia in peat, and that recent legal cases (I had in mind those of child abuse and cot death) had revealed the danger of relying on one medical expert. I pointed out that the cause of death of the continental bog bodies was itself a matter of controversy (in particular over the means of distinguishing sacrifice from execution), and that the recent suggestion that human sacrifice had persisted in Roman Britain – made by Alison Taylor – was based on equally ambivalent evidence and had itself cited the Lindow body as proof that there was anything to persist. At this point the *Times* newspaper took an interest in the issue, quoting Hill as saying of Lindow Man that 'Even if the interpretation of a ritual killing is wrong, he's the best-preserved prehistoric or Roman Briton there is'. If his words were printed correctly, they seemed like a gallant acknowledgement of doubt in the matter, and there I let it rest. At the time of writing, however, the notice beside the display of the body in the British Museum remains completely unchanged.

The fourth case study consists of the excavations of the French archaeologist Jean-Louis Brunaux at Gournay-sur-Aronde and Ribemont-sur-Ancre in northern France during the late 1990s. At both places he uncovered large Iron Age rectangular temples of timber and mud brick. At Ribemont the bones of nearly a thousand young men had been broken, crushed and then burned in crematoria that had themselves been made of human skeletal remains. Around the outer wall, eighty headless male bodies had been displayed along with weapons of war. At Gournay about two thousand weapons and pieces of armour had been hung around the inner precinct or set up on the gateway. Brunaux himself concluded that these finds vindicated the reports of human sacrifice among the Gauls provided by Caesar, Diodorus and Strabo; he interpreted the remains as those of enemies who had been killed in battle or taken prisoner in it and then ritually slaughtered, whose bodies were then burned or displayed as offerings to deities. On the other hand, a British archaeologist, Martin Brown, has suggested that the sites might have been war memorials, to dead warriors of the tribe who were honoured by being cremated or displayed at holy places after their death, as a reward for their courage. The missing heads of the bodies on the wall at Ribemont would, according to this explanation, have been ritually committed to another revered spot, such as a river. The present state of the evidence makes either interpretation feasible: the former apparently proving the truth of the Graeco-Roman atrocity stories, the latter apparently showing how a native custom could be misunderstood or misrepresented by enemies.

The final case study to be considered consists of publications by Miranda Aldhouse-Green (formerly Miranda Green) and J. D. Hill, who has been mentioned in the discussion of Lindow Man. Both are among the finest scholars currently working on the Iron Age. The former has published many studies of ritual and religious behaviour in the pre-Roman and Roman periods of western Europe, while the latter has brought a further degree of sophistication to the interpretation of British Iron Age sites. Miranda Aldhouse-Green produced an article and a book in the years 1998 to 2001 that between them pooled all the evidence for human sacrifice in the late prehistory of western Europe, by setting the claims of ancient Greek and Roman, and medieval Christian, writers alongside the finds of human bodies that seemed to have suffered ritualised violence or been treated in other ways that set them apart from the norm. She acknowledged that 'almost all the archaeological evidence suggestive of ritual murder is capable of alternative interpretation', but believed that the sheer quantity of it, from different times and places, was persuasive, especially when supported by the literary testimony. Some of the data which she used was provided by J. D. Hill, who had made a careful study of material deposited on Iron Age sites in the southern English chalkland region. He decided that deposits of entire domestic animals, and of parts of animals, were probably the remains of sacrifices. He noted that human bodies were treated in the same way as those of animals, represented only a minority of the population, and did not reflect the normal attitudes to the dead represented by burials. His conclusion was that they were perhaps sacrifices too.

It must be stressed that the arguments which both have made are strong and well founded on evidence, and may well represent the truth. Against them can be deployed the obvious one – which Miranda Aldhouse-Green clearly recognised and J. D. Hill implied with his expressions of qualification ('probably', 'perhaps') – that the same evidence is susceptible of different interpretation. There is also, however, a less obvious one: that the current attitudes of specialists in the British Iron Age make a remarkable contrast, at the present time, with those in earlier periods of prehistory. Neolithic and early Bronze Age sites show many similarities in this context with those from later epochs: the presence of human bone in large quantity on ceremonial sites, the mixing or close proximity of human and animal remains on what seems to be an equal basis of treatment, burials that can represent only a minority of the population, unusual treatment of particular bodies, and so forth.

In the mid and late nineteenth century, when the theories of evolution and natural progression made a great impact on the imagination of scholars, and it was convenient for them to think of society as having progressed from savagery to barbarism to civilisation, these features were often interpreted as evidence for human sacrifice or even of cannibalism. Over the twentieth century, the attitudes of specialists have gradually softened, until such reading of the data has almost disappeared. Deposits of human bone on ceremonial and domestic sites are seen as the veneration of ancestors, or the representation of the human element in complete miniature recreations of the cosmos. The presence of animal bone treated in an equivalent manner is viewed as another component of that imagined cosmos, or as the presence of totemic beasts or personal spirit-guides, or an honouring of the particular species of livestock on which the economy most depended. The deliberate dismemberment of human corpses is interpreted as a burial rite designed to free the spirit most completely. Even finds that formerly had been taken as clear evidence of human sacrifice, such as that of a child's skeleton with a cleft skull as a foundation deposit at the late Neolithic temple popularly called Woodhenge, have been reinterpreted; in this particular case, it is argued that the child's skull could just as well have fallen apart naturally, as it was too young for the sutures to have bonded together. To state this is not necessarily to argue that the archaeologists of the New Stone and Bronze Ages are correct, and those who have drawn opposite conclusions from similar data for the Iron Age are wrong; the reverse may be true. The nature of the evidence makes it most unlikely that we shall ever know whether this is the case. What is clearly significant is the contrast of attitude. The most obvious explanation for it is that approaches to Iron Age archaeology are still coloured – in some cases at least – by the hostile Greek and Roman texts, while no equivalent writings exist for earlier periods.

The Fraternal Druids

Fraternal Druids belonged (and belong) to local groups called lodges, which were parts of national or international organisations called orders. They entered these lodges by paying a fee and usually also by undergoing an initiation ceremony. Once inside, they could rise to higher grades within the lodge, and perhaps come to hold office in the national order. The purposes of the orders have varied. Often the main one has been conviviality: the enjoyment of company, generally further enhanced by drink and sometimes by food, in an atmosphere made safe and familiar by the membership requirements. This has frequently been accompanied and sometimes replaced by mutual aid: the creation of a fund to provide financial aid for members who fall upon hard times because of illness, unemployment or other misfortunes or the families of those who die prematurely. Alongside these large organisations were others, consisting of a single group. Some of these had scores of members, representing the social elite of a locality and serving the needs of the whole community, while others consisted of no more than a dozen or two socially obscure individuals. What they had in common was the inspiring ideal of brotherhood. At times this extended to sisterhood as well. Although most of this sort of Druid have been male, and all were for the first few generations in which they existed, women have formed parallel organisations of their own or been given membership in those founded for or by men.

These Druids are thoroughly modern, and represent one aspect of the British love affair with clubs and societies, which was a feature of the period between the seventeenth and twentieth centuries. The main historian of it, Peter Clark, has estimated that in the course of the eighteenth century there may have been up to 25,000 such groups meeting in the English-speaking world. He has found over 130 different kinds of them in the British Isles during that century, including

social clubs, associations for self-improvement, alumni associations, artistic
bodies, book clubs, benefit clubs, gambling clubs, horticulture societies, literary
societies, masonic and pseudo-masonic orders, medical and musical societies,
neighbourhood clubs, philanthropic, political or professional societies, societies
to promote reform or prosecution, regional and ethnic societies, sporting clubs,
and scientific and learned societies. Like other forms of sociability, such as
assemblies, plays, balls, concerts and scientific lectures, they were mostly confined
to urban centres, although these included small country towns. They were not
a purely British phenomenon, but continental equivalents never achieved the
diversity, vitality and importance of those in Britain, because of the greater
persistence of older kinds of organisation (such as religious confraternities and
trade and youth guilds) and more suspicion on the part of governments. The
clubs and societies were essentially a new phenomenon: unlike the confraternities
– which Britain had lost at the Reformation – they had no religious aspect, and
unlike the guilds they had no regulatory function.

They were therefore essentially an invention of the pre-industrial era in this
island, spreading out from London under the impetus of fashion, competition,
commercialism and specialisation. They were linked to the opportunities and
challenges of what was by European standards an extraordinarily high rate of
urbanisation, along with improved living standards and increased social and
physical mobility.

A particularly successful variety of these voluntary associations was the
friendly society or benefit club, which was created to pool and administer regular
contributions from members as an insurance scheme against illness, unemployment and other accidents that could plunge people into poverty, and to ensure
members a decent burial. They combined this function with socialising. Their
popularity meant that they broke the general rule of voluntary societies by
flourishing in the countryside as well as in towns. By 1800 even official figures,
which must be underestimates as they depended on the willingness of such
groups to report themselves for registration, suggest that about 40 per cent of the
working population of London belonged to one, while in the Lancashire cotton-
making town of Oldham, half of the adult male inhabitants did. Nottingham
alone contained fifty-one such organisations, and it is estimated that there were

about 7200 of them in England by 1801. They were mostly comprised of artisans, but many included smallholders and labourers and some were middle-class and run by gentry and professional men. By the end of the eighteenth century they had become the most important means by which working people avoided becoming paupers.

It was absolutely inevitable that some of these clubs or societies should take the name of Druid, once Druids had become established firmly in the British imagination as admirable patriotic ancestors; which, as explained earlier, happened in the middle third of the eighteenth century. The first to do so was, appropriately enough, in Anglesey, the Welsh island that Tacitus had caused to become especially associated with Druids, and which had become a county in its own right. On 15 October 1772 eighteen of its wealthier inhabitants founded a Druidical Society, to promote the welfare of the island and its people. It became a tremendous success. At its peak, in the 1790s, it had up to a hundred members, including most of the local landowners and clergy from the Marquis of Anglesey downward. At that time it was paying out an average of thirty-four guineas per year from the funds subscribed by members, to give poor children apprenticeships, and to support hospitals in Chester and Liverpool and local agricultural societies. It made payments to people down on their luck, rewarded others who saved lives at sea, and gave prizes to farmers for introducing new kinds of crop and for making improvements on their land.

Ritual at the meetings was minimal, but the society acquired officers, a uniform and some ornaments. It was led by an Archdruid, who presided, a sub-Druid, who assisted him, Treasurers, a Secretary, and four Regulators to introduce new members to their seats. The uniform consisted of a dark blue coat, waistcoat and breeches, and red stockings. The coat had a blue velvet collar, with a yellow button showing a Druid's head, and every member wore a silver medal with an oak tree on one side and a Druid's head on the other. New members had to declare their willingness to attend monthly meetings and obey the society's rules. Ale and harpers were provided from the funds, to make the meetings still more enjoyable. After the first quarter of the nineteenth century interest in the society began to wane, and it was wound up gracefully in 1844, dividing its remaining funds between the hospitals and the Royal National Lifeboat Institution.

Nine years after the gentry of Anglesey had claimed the name, a humbler group of people gathered in a room at a London pub and founded another Druidical organisation that was to become both much greater and much more long-lived. No records, and few memories, of that event survived into the twentieth century. What did were two different, though compatible, traditions. One was that a group of friends, drawn from artisans and tradesmen, decided to formalise their meetings, and close them to outsiders, by giving themselves a collective name and admitting newcomers only if they were proposed and enrolled. The other was that the club was founded because one of the group died, leaving a mother who had been dependent on him. His chums decided to support her collectively, and to do so they established formal membership of their circle, with joint contributions to a common fund. Whatever did happen, it was remembered ever after that England's first modern Druidical society was founded, on 29 November 1781, at the King's Arms tavern on the corner of Oxford Street and Poland Street. It was also remembered that the moving spirit in the group, who persuaded it to take the name of Druids and became its first official leader or Archdruid, was called Henry Hurle. His identity can never be known with certainty, although the most likely candidate is a wealthy carpenter, surveyor and builder who lived in the City of London parish of St James Garlick Hithe and held all its main offices in succession.

Two years later, friends or contacts of the original set at the King's Arms asked if they could formally affiliate with them. It is a sign of how widely their connections spread that this other group was based on the opposite side of the City, in a tavern on the Ratcliffe Highway, Wapping, a district of merchants, dockers and sailors. Hurle's set responded by reconstituting themselves as a national society, with potential for limitless expansion. The model that they took for this was that of the most celebrated and influential form of voluntary organisation in the whole of Georgian Britain: Freemasonry. As constituted in 1717, this depended on a system of local groups called lodges, which answered ultimately to a Grand Lodge in London. Membership of every lodge was closed to anybody except persons recommended by existing members, who would be admitted with payment of fees, an initiation ceremony and the learning of passwords and signals common to all Freemasons. Imitating it, the King's Arms group became

Lodge No. 1 of the Ancient Order of Druids, and the equivalent of the Masons' Grand Lodge as the executive body of the order, to which new lodges had to apply for acceptance and registration, and which would make rules for all. By the next year a third lodge had been founded in rich and fashionable Westminster. It was later claimed that the famous radical Whig politician Charles James Fox became a member of that, in an attempt to cultivate support in the constituency. At the end of the decade lodges had sprung up in Ipswich and Bristol as well.

The new order had one clear selling point, apart from its charismatic name, and that was its dedication to music. Although members could read poetry and discuss a range of artistic and scientific subjects, the common activity of the lodges was to play musical instruments and to sing. This drew on the contemporary tendency to regard bards and Druids as identical, or as different divisions of the same ancient organisation. The meetings provided a haven for prosperous working people, and some of their social superiors, who enjoyed chamber and choral concerts and wished to perform as well as to listen. Some check was provided to the growth of the order in the 1790s by the government's suspicion of secret societies, provoked by fear that sympathisers with the French Revolution were plotting to stage a parallel uprising in Britain. As the Ancient Order was not formally a friendly society or benefit club, but a convivial society with optional charitable functions, it could not take advantage of legislation in 1793 that protected friendly societies that submitted to registration. Several of its lodges suspended meetings and some dissolved altogether, including that at Westminster. The order also underwent its first schism, when some members who had enlisted in military units for the war against the French brought their swords and pistols to meetings. The presiding officer asked them to leave these in an anteroom, whereupon some of them were sufficiently offended to resign and found a shortlived Grand Select Order of Druids. Despite all this, the order reached the end of the century with twenty-two lodges intact, including Grand Lodge itself; the furthest from London was in the ironworking district of Dudley, in the west midlands.

Once into the new century, more relaxed official attitudes allowed a fresh outburst of expansion, so that by 1831 the order had 193 lodges, with a total membership of over 200,000. They had been established as far away as America,

Canada and India, but the main expansion was into all parts of England, including the industrial areas of the midlands and the north. The lodges were concentrated in county towns, market towns and (above all) manufacturing centres. On the ground, local representatives of the order began to mount impressive displays of strength and confidence: in 1807 some seven thousand members, gathered for a meeting of all the midland lodges, paraded through the streets of Birmingham with banners and ribbons, watched by huge crowds. In 1832 the lodge at Dartford in Kent opened its own 'Druid school', for children of both sexes aged seven to thirteen.

By the 1820s the order defined its aims as being the present and future welfare of humanity; to keep alive the memory of the ancient Druids as a 'fraternal bond of philanthropy'; and to encourage responsible social and moral behaviour. Any discussion of religion or politics was forbidden (to reassure any lingering official suspicion), and anybody who divulged the special signs and passwords to outsiders would be expelled. In this respect it was, once again, following Freemasonry, as it did also in the basic form of initiation, in which the candidate was brought blindfolded into the lodge, promised obedience to its rules, and then treated to a 'charge' of instructions and ideals. The unique features of the order were its continuing commitment to conviviality with music as the heart of fellowship. The candidate for initiation had his head wreathed with evergreens, was shown mistletoe as the sacred symbol of Druidry, and taught the name of a mythical ancient founder, Togodubiline, whom the order had by now acquired. The initiation ceremony was punctuated with hearty choruses about the bonds of friendship and the patriotic connotations of the oak. That for the chairing of an officer went (to the tune of 'Hail the Conquering Hero Comes'):

> Bring the wreath and bind his hair,
> Which with honour he may wear!
> May his hours in pleasures fly,
> Friends and Druids ever nigh!
> Sing, Bards, sing, with heart and voice!
> Hail, all hail, our happy choice!

All this expansion produced new difficulties and tensions. In 1813 a Methodist published an attack on the order as being designed 'to promote alehouse conviviality, to revive ancient heathenism, and to plunge those who live in the nineteenth century into all the ignorance and barbarism of pagan Britain'. By that date many dissenting chapels, as well as those on Methodist circuits, shared those attitudes sufficiently to exclude members of the order from attendance. On the other hand, the obvious success of the AOD was starting to encourage imitation and competition. In 1824 an Independent Order of Ancient Druids was founded, and, although it subsequently failed, it was revived in 1843. Five years later, the pointedly-named Loyal Order of Druids appeared, and lasted. This was directly inspired by Iolo Morganwg's pseudohistory, theology and Gorsedd ceremonies. It was open to all Britons who believed in some kind of Supreme Being and existed primarily as a friendly society, with charity its main aim. Its officers, general rules and emphasis on music were taken from the AOD, though it had some trappings of its own; its Grand Arch(druid) wore a white robe, for purity, a belt, for truth, and a gold image of the sun, for leadership. It also had its own distinctive burial service, attended by members in black or blue clothes, with white stockings, gloves, sashes, aprons and collars and read by a Brother in a black gown after the officiating clergyman had read his Church's burial rite. The public were excluded from this, and the words of the liturgy emphasised the levelling nature of death and the eternal reward for virtue given to humans of any social station. Evergreens were then thrown into the grave by all there. An address was included in the book of ceremonies, to apologise to non-members (including the minister) who were being ushered away from the grave at this point. It emphasised that the order was not a religious body but a charitable and fraternal one; yet, none the less, it well illustrates the way in which, by this date, voluntary societies were starting to take on some of the emotional and philosophical role of religious bodies in a post-Christian framework.

Neither of these forms of challenge proved dangerous to the Ancient Order, which continued to expand at the same rate. Much more consequential were the strains produced by its own rapid growth. By 1810 some of the wealthier and more genteel members were starting to object to the need to consort with their social inferiors on equal terms, so an inner ring was created to the order, again on the Masonic model, to give those who sought it an elevated status. This was the Royal Arch Chapter, entry to which was restricted by the need for approval by all existing members. By the 1820s only eight lodges had adopted this chapter, but they were naturally among the oldest, richest and most important, including the Grand Lodge itself. The latter retained, under the constitition of 1783, ultimate absolute power over all the others, and levied a regular tribute of financial payments on them. Its style of meeting had become steadily grander and more opulent; a veteran member was to recall in 1833 how since the year 1808 he had seen it grow 'from the humblest meeting to the most splendid society in London'. By the 1820s a new tier of government had been established with the institution of provincial Grand Lodges, but this merely elaborated a hierarchy in which supreme power was still concentrated in the original lodge at London. This situation was likely to produce tension in itself, but it was more swiftly and seriously inflamed by a major conflict over policy. The wealthier lodges, including Grand Lodge itself, saw the purpose of the order as essentially one of sociability, with charity as a lesser and optional one. Those which had been more recently created, especially in the industrial areas, wanted it to function primarily as a friendly society, insuring members against misfortune. This was a period of dramatic growth in English manufacturing, when workers had surplus earnings to spend on insurance; but, in turn, the health risks of industrial labour made such insurance virtually essential. At the same time, membership of a lodge gave young men who had immigrated into the manufacturing regions something of the sense of close-knit community of the agricultural villages they had left. It was theoretically open to them to join both the AOD and a friendly society, but to do so would in practice stretch both their funds and their time, and many of the new members of the AOD thought that the order should adapt to their needs. In 1821 the Grand Lodge attempted a compromise by allowing individual lodges to use funds as they wished. This, however, threw into greater relief the problem of the payments to the Grand Lodge itself, which were not generally applied to charity, and created one in which poorer lodges could have their funds overwhelmed by demand, while the richer amassed a large surplus.

The crisis came in the years 1831–34, the same period as that in which a Whig government was elected with a mandate to sweep away control of British central and local government by self-perpetuating oligarchies. It can be no coincidence that the years in which sustained pressure built up for the alteration of the

Above: 38. W. O. Gellar's engraving of a Druid ceremony at Stonehenge, from 1832, not only epitomises the concern with dramatic movement and light of Romantic art, but embodies the growing sense of Druidry as a religion of demented superstition.

39. The wicker man is back, in a Victorian print. The ogre's head of the image and the emphasis on young women as favourite victims are both further signs of the increasing demonisation of the Druids.

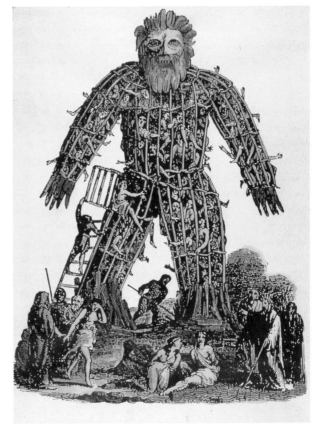

Above left: 40. The frontispiece to William Kingston's *Eldol the Druid* (1874) sums up Druidry as a furtive, nasty and bloodthirsty cult.

Above right: 41. And here comes the solution: Druids engaged in Pliny's mistletoe ritual realize that a new and better faith has arrived, removing their congregation and leaving them (literally) in the shadows. A nineteenth-century engraving from a painting by Francis Hayman in 1752.

42. Horace Knowles makes the same point in cruder and more symbolic form in an early twentieth-century illustration. The Christ Child represents youth, calm, light, power and self-confidence; the Druids the opposite qualities.

43. A scene from the 1968 B movie, *The Viking Queen*, shows that the Victorian mixture of pious horror and prurience could translate easily to the modern screen.

44. And here is the most famous recent reappearance of the wicker man, in the 1973 film of that name, which has become a cult classic. It was remade in 2006, transplanted to the United States; but the sacrificial structure, and accompanying rite of burning a man alive, was transplanted almost unchanged.

45. Sir Cyril Fox, the analyst of the finds from Llyn Cerrig Bach.

46. 'Lindow Man', the body from the Cheshire peat bog, on display at the British Museum.

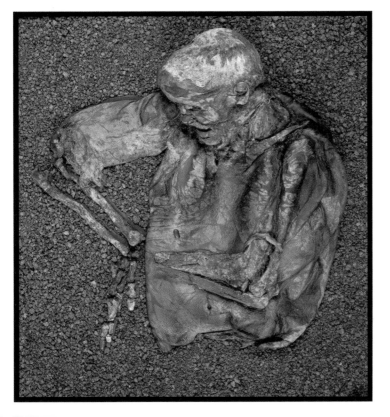

In offering our subscribers the above sketch, our aim has been to convey the minds of those Brothers, whom distance and other circumstances prevented from being present, an idea of its extent and respectability.

Particulars of this meeting will be found in page 57.

A pleasant joyous band were we, upon that blissful night
When from afar each Druid met, in pleasure to unite ;
Whilst music's brightest tone and melody's soft voice
Breathed a deep spell upon our minds, bidding each heart rejoice.

We met as happy Brethren meet, who long have parted been,
The *friendly* grip was given by each, the smile of pleasure seen,
And they we never saw before, were hailed as brethren now,
And loved, with all a brother's love, so sacred is our vow !

As speaks a crowned monarch, from his proud and regal throne
So breathed our Noble Arch his words, with soft and eloquent tone :
The earth with all its cares, were as a mantle flung away,
Each joy we felt, sprung from the scource of pleasures bright array.

But pleasure such as this, was far too bright to last for ever,
From all we prize the most on earth, we still are doom'd to sever ;
Yet would we fain once more behold a sight so fair as this,
And deem it were the proudest height of earthly happiness.

47. An engraving from *The Druids' Magazine*, 1832, showing the Treasurer of the Grand Lodge, enthroned and wearing the regalia of his office and of the Ancient Order of Druids. It amply reflects the self-confidence and prosperity of the order in general, and Grand Lodge in particular, at this moment, the eve of the first great internal crisis, and schism, in fraternal Druidry.

48. Another illustration from the same issue, showing a procession opening a ceremony in the Grand Lodge of the Ancient Order. Note the musicians.

49. Members of the local lodge of the Ancient Order of Druids, parading through the streets of Salisbury in 1832, in full costume, to support the Great Reform Bill, to liberalize and standardize the nature of parliamentary elections. The drawing demonstrates the confidence and ease with which the order was by then integrated into local society, and also its identification with the upwardly mobile middle class that stood to gain from reform.

50. The title page of the official magazine of the Ancient Order, in 1909. Its identification with traditional views of ancient Druidry, and the major influence of freemasonry upon it, are both evident.

Below: 51. The Druids arrive (at last) at Stonehenge. The opening procession of the Ancient Order's grand ceremony at the monument in 1905.

52. Sleeping savant: William Stukeley dozed off in a chair in the inn at Avebury, sketched by a friend after a hard day's fieldwork in 1722.

Middle: 53. Stukeley's sketch of the Christian 'Hermitage' he had built in his garden at Stamford by 1738. He has portrayed himself showing it off to his new wife. It is a lovely example of the charm of his drawings, but also of his taste for decorating his property with religious monuments. No image, alas, seems to survive of the pagan shrines that he constructed in his grounds at Grantham ten years before.

Bottom: 54. The rocking stone on Pontpridd Common, enclosed by the stone circle erected by Myfyr Morganwg and his friends, as it is on a winter afternoon at the present day. Some of the stones in one of the avenues leading to it were stolen in the 1950s, and the gaps are apparent.

The Hermitage Stamford 1738.

55. The head of the stone serpent represented by the avenues passing through the circle at the rocking stone with its bulging 'eyes'. This design was taken directly from Stukeley's (incorrect) reconstruction of the Avebury megalithic complex in Druidical times.

56. A firebrand held by a firebrand: William Price, in his famous (or notorious) habitual costume. In his right hand is the torch with which he lit his son's pyre; in the left, the crescent moon which was his symbol of Druidry.

57. Price on stage in 1884, demonstrating Druid costume at one of his public lectures. The garment is scarlet, embroidered with the letters – Price's own Druidical hieroglyphics – in green. It is easy to see why people sometimes mistook this ritual dress for long combinations, and wanted to know why he was in his underwear.

Ancient Order of Druids were those in which the Whigs pushed through the Great Reform Act to widen and standardise the national system of parliamentary representation. The process is chronicled in successive issues of the newly established magazine of the order, by an editor sympathetic to reform. It began in 1831 with a request from junior lodges for the establishment of a general fund to relieve members in need. The editor commented in support of this that the outside world saw the order as 'a mere convivial body without any redeeming touches of utility'. The Grand Lodge rejected it in 1832, whereupon the next year over seventy of the lodges in Lancashire and Cheshire broadened the attack, demanding that the Grand Lodge halve the fees paid to it, account for how it spent them, and allow the rules of the order to be revised by a general assembly of elected delegates. The council appointed by the Grand Lodge to run the order attempted another compromise, whereby a central pension fund was to be established, but kept under its own control even while the bulk of contributions were made by junior lodges.

This was the signal for revolt, as the lodges demanding reform established a United Provisional Committee of their own, and called for control of the order to be vested in a council consisting of every past and present lodge leader, and for a fund for charitable purposes to be created by every lodge. Four-fifths of the rebels were in the northern and midland industrial areas, but two lodges in London and Surrey were also prominent among them. It was these that the Grand Lodge selected as examples near the end of 1833, expelling them both from the order. In reponse, fifty lodges held a meeting in London in December. Amid tumultuous scenes at 2.30 a.m. on the 20th, they decided to secede and form their own order. More than fifty others joined them, representing about half of the total membership, and so the United Ancient Order of Druids was created.

The split, however traumatic, proved to be a creative one. Both halves of the original order were now free to recreate it according to their differing ideals and did so. The remnant that supported the Grand Lodge, naturally retaining the name of the Ancient Order of Druids, immediately enacted a modified form of the reforms demanded by the rebels, vetted by all members and approved by majority vote. Under these, the Grand Lodge still enforced the rules of the order and made minor amendments to them, controlled all ceremonies and insignia, levied annual payments from the whole order and retained the sole right to recognise new lodges. Leadership of the order was, however, now vested in a committee on which members of the Grand Lodge were equalled in number by those from others, and the Grand Lodge had to produce annual accounts for the use of all money sent to it. The new system worked well for it, and by 1843, ten years after the great schism, the AOD had 381 lodges, having almost doubled the membership that it had achieved before the secession. They were spread even further across the nation, and had made up the ground lost in the industrial regions by the losses of 1833. A generation after the latter, on 1 November 1858, the AOD replayed the same drama, as its Cheshire lodges seceded to form a friendly society, this time calling itself simply the Order of Druids. Those lodges ran the new order until 1872, when its headquarters moved to Manchester and it took on a board of management elected from the whole membership. Its distinguishing feature was that lodges in each district that had a surplus of money had to use this to remedy any shortfall suffered by others. The heartland of the order remained in the expanse of Britain between Birmingham and Glasgow, though it still gained a good presence in the south east. By 1871 it had 55,151 members in 955 lodges, and by 1927 the total membership had risen to 160,000.

Once again the remnant of the Ancient Order repaired its losses, with new lodges being founded in Britain and a string forming across Australia during the 1860s. In 1888 further secessions were prevented by an internal revolution that finally removed any control of the order from the existing Grand Lodge and vested it in a board of management comprised of former leaders of lodges which met at a London hotel. The lodge that had been Henry Hurle's closed down, for twenty years, thereby making the devolution of power absolute. Provincial lodges now, of necessity, became the most dynamic parts of the organisation, such as the Albion Lodge, based in Oxford. On 10 August 1908 it held a ceremony in the park of Blenheim Palace, as guests of the Duke of Marlborough, who was formally a member, in which it initiated the latter's relative, the future Prime Minister Winston Churchill.

Meanwhile the United Ancient Order shared much the same fortunes. In just over ten years from its formation, it tripled in size, having 330 lodges in England

and Wales by 1846. They were scattered across most of northern, midland and south-eastern England and south-east Wales, though the order's main strength remained in the industrial regions. This expansion was sustained, but in the process the UAOD proved no more shatterproof than its parent, and before the end of the century some of its northern lodges had seceded to form new Druidical friendly societies based on Sheffield and Manchester, while another had been created out of its membership in the South Wales coalfield. Alongside the AOD and its progeny, new fraternal bodies of Druids continued to be founded all through the reign of Victoria, such as the Independent Order of Modern Druids, at Liverpool, the Loyal Order of Modern Druids, the Druids under the Grove, the Bolton Unity of Druids, and the United Order of Modern Druids. They tended to lack the staying power of the older orders, some not lasting into the twentieth century, and those which did generally collapsing soon after that began. As well as such corporate organisations, those consisting of a single group continued to appear, such as the Druid Friendly Society established at the George Inn, Amesbury, in 1853, which existed to provide health care and funerals for people living within four miles of the town. Its name was no doubt chosen because of the fact that Stonehenge lay within its catchment area.

Women had been barred from all these, but in 1853 some at Leigh, in the Manchester cotton-manufacturing area, founded a Noble Order of Female Druids. The initiation rites of the male orders had been relatively simple, but those of the ladies – if the source is to be trusted – were far more elaborate. The candidate was required to leap from a 'symbolic mountain' towards a 'double row of sharp steel spikes'. When she landed, however, a 'soft green sward' had replaced the spikes. Lights suddenly shone to reveal a 'fairy scene of green fields, shady trees, and babbling fountains … The officers were seated on gorgeous thrones, while the sisters were all clad in white and adorned with badges and scarfs of various colours'. In 1876 a United Ancient Order of Female Druids was formed alongside the existing UAOD, and in 1910 the latter decided to prevent further secessions, and move with the times, by establishing branches for both women and children. The former were treated like the men, save for added admonitions on the importance of motherhood in promoting the order. The latter were given simplified ceremonies and lectures on the nobility of the ancient Druids.

The records of fraternal Druidry, or at least those that survive in the public domain, lack much information of value to a social historian, such as membership lists that provide solid evidence of the age, social status, religious beliefs and occupations of members. They are richer in information for students of cultural history. They show, for example, that these orders shared in the growing respectability and public acceptance of voluntary societies, including those that had secret meetings protected by signs and passwords, in nineteenth-century Britain. In the 1830s the Dartford Lodge of the AOD, the one that had already founded its own school, instituted an annual feast at the town's Bull Hotel. The hotel was decorated with huge branches of oak, numerous flags and two silk banners bearing 'Druid devices'. In the centre of the hotel was mounted a hanging showing the ceremony of mistletoe-gathering described by Pliny. The lodge room had another, covering the ceiling, of an azure sky with the harp of Apollo in the centre, while the walls were decorated with flowers and portraits of leading members. The parish church rang its bells in honour of the meeting, and local brewers contributed bowls of punch to the meal, at which speeches were made, toasts offered and (of course) songs performed. Two decades later, in July 1856, the Mona Lodge of the same order (actually based in Bristol) had an outing to view the megaliths at Stanton Drew. They arrived in a series of coaches containing a total of 150 people, being members, wives and friends, and processed through the village to the stone circles, wearing robes and inignia and carrying wands, cups, flagons, a Bible on a velvet cushion and a banner showing Noah's Flood. They were welcomed by the lord of the manor, who owned the prehistoric remains, and joined by a crowd of curious villagers. Having reached the north-eastern circle of the complex, which was (and is) the best preserved, they sang a chorus, listened to a personal view of Druidical history, provided by the lodge's First Bard, chanted an 'ode', and passed round a cup of mead. They then adjourned for dinner at the home of a (very generous) member who lived in the village, followed by dancing to a band in his orchard until sunset.

The First Bard's lecture in the stone circle took a personal and idiosyncratic view of history. Being a Welshman, he made use of Iolo's forged Druidic wisdom, but mixed in the worship of snakes, a corn goddess called 'Godo', and priests who danced wildly and lacerated themselves at festivals. These were all features of his view of Druidry as a religion that had degenerated from the pure teachings of the Old Testament patriarchs. The individual nature of his ideas was typical of the Ancient Order of Druids from the beginning. The magazine that it published in the early 1830s, and was taken over to the United Ancient Order after the schism, shows that members held a variety of views of ancient Druidry. Some took up Iolo's teachings, while others were more interested in the association of Druids with prehistoric monuments, and they had differing notions of the extent of the goodness of the former Druids and admitted to doubts over whether they had sacrificed humans. The official books of rules of the order issued in the course of the century vaunted its ancient models for their power, learning and solidarity, without inspecting their religious or moral beliefs.

Other orders had more of a party line, but this proves to be relatively weak on close inspection. The Loyal, founded in 1829, had, as said, absorbed a lot of Iolo's teachings, though its official book of ceremonies also warned initiates (without going into specifics) that in some respects the ancient Druids would have no place in modern society. The United Ancient Order had a vested interest, initially, in emphasising the manner in which ancient Druidry had become corrupt and degenerate, and drawing parallels with the behaviour of the Ancient Order's Grand Lodge. This stress on degeneration had, however, faded away by the end of the century, when the official book on ceremonies ensured that initiates were lectured only on the enlightenment and virtue of their ancient predecessors. The Order of Druids that seceded from the AOD in 1858 claimed both that the original Druids had been founded by Noah and his sons, and that they had later turned into bloodthirsty and superstitious beings with whom modern Druids had little in common. This reservation was, in turn, challenged by individual members of the order. The emphasis on Noah had probably already been present in the Ancient Order from which the Order of Druids had split, to judge by the banner at Stanton Drew. It drew attention to a view of Druidry as derived from the pure religion of the Book of Genesis, common in the early nineteenth century, but also may have been intended to reaffirm a literal belief in that Book, in the face of the doubts beginning to be cast on it by geologists and prehistorians by the middle decades.

Fraternal Druidry faced the twentieth century with a major conceptual problem. The mid Victorian period had indeed destroyed complete faith in the Book of Genesis among most educated people, removing the framework into which Druids had been fitted as practitioners and teachers of true religion. The late Victorian one had seen scholars sever the connection between Druids and megaliths, and depose the former from being the central characters in ancient Britain to being latecomers on the margins of prehistory. At the same time, appalling images of them as savage pagan priests were circulating in works of history and fiction alike. The Druid orders met this challenge in a number of different ways. One was to put themselves more obviously, and glamorously, into the public eye. This was aided by a growing investment in costume on the part of the older orders. In the early nineteenth century, the AOD had prescribed a white robe for Archdruids, with medallions, sashes and ribbons of the masonic kind for officers in general. By the end of the century, robes had proliferated to become general for members, and they had also taken to carrying wands and staves, those of officers being topped with golden sickles, and to donning bushy white false beards for ceremonies. There was a flurry of alarm in the order's magazine in 1911 over whether borrowed beards could harbour tuberculosis; but it blew over. Costume in the United Ancient Order seems to have evolved similarly; by 1906 members were expected to dress for ritual in special robes and collars and carry staves, while the person presiding was expected to wear a long, sky-blue gown with a hood, a string of glass beads and a long beard.

These developments gave members high and dramatic visibility when they performed rites in public spaces; and the greatest and most charismatic that they chose was Stonehenge, the most important monument that had become associated with Druidry. Some leading members of the AOD, at least, knew by 1907, and broadcast to the order in general, that prehistorians no longer believed that Druids had built it. Instead, they played cleverly on the residual possibilities that Druids had used the monument, and rebuilt it, in the Iron Age, and that there had been an evolutionary relationship between Neolithic priests and Druids. Until the end of the nineteenth century, the stones had remained relatively difficult to reach, standing on the edge of the bare expanses of Salisbury Plain that were left to shepherds and wildlife. Now, however, improvements in highways and in transport – especially the invention of the bicycle and the motor charabanc – were making access much easier. The owner, Sir Edmund Antrobus, had opened the century by enclosing the monument and installing a custodian who charged an admission fee; this in turn made it possible for an organisation to book the stones for an exclusive event.

In August 1905 the Ancient Order did just that, occupying the monument for a day in order to hold a mass initiation ceremony of 259 people; tactfully, it numbered Sir Edmund among the new entrants. The order fielded about seven hundred members, including the most illustrious, who now included the Duke of Leeds as well as the Duke Marlborough and the Earl of Warwick. Luncheon was served to all in a marquee beforehand, as a Druid brass band played, with tea afterwards, 'including four kinds of the best cake'. The occasion received coverage in both national and local newspapers, and four years later the Royal Gloucester Lodge of the order returned for a much smaller rite, of two initiations. The First World War then intervened, but in 1925 the order was back for a service, three hundred strong. Six years later the United Ancient Order followed its example, to celebrate the centenary of the events leading to its foundation. It brought with it members from New Zealand, Germany and Norway together with guests from several other Druid orders, and installed a new Archdruid and his deputy. This launched a tradition whereby individual lodges or provincial Grand Lodges of the AOD or the UAOD, or both, held rites at the monument every year for the rest of the 1930s. These were halted by the new world war but resumed as soon as peace returned. Since 1918 Stonehenge had been in the custody of the national Office of Works, but the orders made a relationship with this body as cordial as the one that they had formed with Antrobus. They applied formally for permission to hold their ceremonies, well in advance and avoiding dates of maximum general interest in the stones such as the summer solstice. The rites themselves were full of points of reference to which conservative members of the general public could respond, such as the singing of well-known Christian hymns (though those that extolled God rather than Christ, to make them more cross-confessional), and speeches in favour of charity, brotherhood and patriotism. Newspaper coverage of these events was always supportive and generally deeply respectful. In 1925 the AOD performed its own version of the national anthem, reproduced word for word in a local newspaper:

Hail! Mystic Light Divine,
May'st Thou ne'er cease to shine
Over this land.
Wisdom in thee we find,
Beauty and strength combined
Druids are ever joined
In heart and hand.

Come then, ye sons of light,
In joyous strain unite,
God save the King!
Long may Our Monarch reign,
King of the azure main:
Druids respond the strain,
God save the King!

Another way in which fraternal Druids strengthened themselves during this period was by greater co-operation between orders. The pressure for this came initially from abroad, as a rebound effect resulting from the expansion of both the AOD and the UAOD into the United States during the early nineteenth century. The American divisions of both orders amicably separated themselves into parallel bodies, which got on with each other so well that in 1858 the Grand Secretary of the American UAOD proposed to the orders in Britain that they combine in a federate structure similar to that of the United States themselves. The Ancient Order and United Ancient Order accordingly twice attempted to reunite in the late nineteenth century, but could not agree on a means to do this. One was provided, again, from abroad, and this time from the opposite geographical direction. In the course of the nineteenth century Germans who had lived in the USA, and been initiated into the AOD or UAOD there, returned home and founded similar Druid orders in their own country, which spread from there to Sweden, Denmark and Switzerland. At the opening of the twentieth century, and partly as a reaction against the growth of international tension that led eventually to world war, Brother Fricke, the national leader of the German fraternal Druids, approached his American counterparts with a scheme for a worldwide association of their kind. The Americans encouraged a meeting between the British and German UAOD at Hull in 1906, and all three got together in Munich in 1908. In 1913 representatives of the AOD, UAOD and the Manchester Order of Druids (one of the offspring of the UAOD) met in London with delegates from the German, American, Australian and New Zealand equivalents to their orders, and formed an International Grand Lodge of Druidism.

One year later, war ruptured the bonds that had thus been created, but they were reformed after the bloodshed and endured. Members of each order in the association were able to visit lodges of the others, and attended major events held by each other as guests. Once more the Germans featured as especially enthusiastic proponents of international fraternity. Hugo Wiese of Hamburg, Noble Grand Arch of the German Order of Druids, served as president of the International Grand Lodge in the early 1930s, and was prominently present at the UAOD's centenary celebrations at Stonehenge. He and his friends subsequently published a guide to the world's fraternal Druid orders. Now, however, the former difference between official attitudes to secret societies on the Continent and in the English-speaking world reappeared with a vengeance; on coming to power, the Nazis outlawed Druids along with all other kinds of society that represented potential foci for independent opinion, and poor Wiese died of the treatment that he received in prison. The tragedy of his fate is not lightened by the irony that he had at first led German Druidry in supporting Hitler's regime, as a bulwark against Communism. The international co-operation, and the domestic amity that he and his compatriots had encouraged among the older British orders, none the less survived.

In coping with the intellectual challenges of the new century, the fraternal orders could call on the flexibility and variety of belief that they had already displayed in the former one. The manner in which the Ancient Order managed to adapt to changing views regarding the relationship between the Druids and Stonehenge illustrates this well; likewise, claims of a connection between Druidry and Old Testament patriarchs had quietly disappeared by 1900. The private mythologies of orders, which had never had any connection with history, could continue to be repeated with an unknown degree of genuine belief. Since the early nineteenth century, if not before, the Ancient Order had claimed a wholly fictitious ancient ancestor called Togodubiline; even in a credible ancient

Brythonic form, as Togodubilinos, this is a character unknown to history. Initiates were told that he was the son of a British Bard called Tacitus Magallas, slain by the Romans on Anglesey, and a Druid priestess called Sensitoria Roxiana. He had been found as a babe abandoned under an oak tree, in a Druidic equivalent of the infancy of Moses, and brought up by refugee Druids. Togodubiline, the fable went, grew up to become a great scientist and philosopher, the founder of the order and – a nice touch of humour here – the inventor of the brewing of beer.

None the less, the orders still felt a need to keep some kind of purchase on demonstrable, or at least possible, historical truth. The formal ceremonies drew on the classical sources, with some traditional misreadings and omissions, to convey a view of ancient Druidry as a religion of one Supreme Being which preached the immortality of the soul, with reward or punishment for conduct in life, and extolled justice, benevolence and learning. During the first quarter of the century, both the AOD and the UAOD imported ideas from the writings of Iolo Morganwg to take the place of the now distintegrating associations with megaliths and Genesis. This was, of course, just in time to collide with the final discrediting of Iolo as a forger; but some members, at least, swiftly adapted to that as well. In 1932 a member of the Ancient Order called Wilhelm North, who had carried out some impressive research into its actual origins, published two articles on Druidry in a London newspaper. He acknowledged courageously that the eighteenth-century view of Druids had been 'a pure fairy tale', that Iolo's triads had been refuted by 'competent Welsh scholars', and that the ancient sources were difficult to interpret and unreliable. He clearly felt that modern fraternal Druidry could stand up in its own right.

The second half of the twentieth century, however proved to be a hostile environment for fraternal Druids. The Welfare State eliminated much of the need for their charitable functions, while the multiplication of forms of entertainment, both inside and outside the home, removed many of the attractions of lodge nights. Changing economic contexts broke up the old-fashioned manufacturing industries and the artisan communities that they had nurtured, and removed the traditional role of market towns; both developments that eroded the social basis for the fraternal orders. In a deeper and more general sense, they shared in the end of the Victorian framework of, and agenda for, British life, which in many respects lasted until the 1960s. During the early twentieth century their association with an earlier period seems to have been a reassuring and a stabilising feature; in the later part it just made them seem old-fashioned. They disappeared from the public view and public consciousness; symbolically, no more of them held ceremonies at Stonehenge after 1955. For a historian who is not an initiate, there are few materials from which their story in this period can be written.

In the 1990s, it seemed as if further social and political changes might give them a new lease of life, as the decay of the Welfare State, and the increasing need for private pension schemes and health insurance, could bring about a revival of friendly societies and benefit clubs. What happened instead was that new government rules were introduced for the regulation of such bodies that proved too difficult for the United Ancient Order to adopt. It dissolved itself a few years short of the new millennium. A splinter of the Order of Druids that had been formed in 1858, based in Sheffield, managed to make the adaptation successfully, and survives as the Independent Druids' Friendly Society.

The great survivor has, however, been the grandparent of fraternal Druidry, the Ancient Order of Druids itself, which carries on under a dynamic and imaginative leadership which reaches out both to the general public and to other kinds of contemporary Druid order. After more than two centuries, the society started by Hurle and his chums in the King's Arms, and which has directly or indirectly produced so many progeny, still holds it own.

The Rebel Druids

In the strict sense of the expression, there were probably no rebel Druids in antiquity. They feature in the ancient and medieval texts as, by definition, part of the established leadership of their societies. Those mentioned by Tacitus, as stirring up revolt against Roman rule at the far end of Gaul in 69 CE, would certainly count as rebels in Roman eyes. They themselves, however, would almost certainly have regarded their activity as intended to free their peoples from foreign invaders, whose power had been legitimised only by force; as such, they belong more to the category of patriot, as defined at the beginning of this book. The sort of rebel Druid that is the concern of this chapter is definitively a modern phenomenon. Once Druids had seized the imagination of the British, and appeared attractive to many as forebears and examples, it was only a matter of time before some people used them to criticise and oppose orthodox forms of belief and institution within their own societies. It seems, indeed, that the more fervently modern British people have identified themselves with ancient Druidry, the more likely it is that they will have to some extent been in collision with prevailing social and religious norms. The image of the Druid could thus be put to one final, and enduring, use in modern Britain: as the hallmark of a counter-culture.

It is possible that this sort of Druid appeared in Europe in the sixteenth and seventeenth centuries, but there seem to be no reports of any. People like the German authors Celtis and Trithemius, who promoted admiration for ancient Druidry among their people, referred to each other affectionately as Druids, but this seems to have been no more than banter. The first person in Britain to have taken on the self-perception of being a Druid, since the end of the ancient world, seems to have been the one who was most influential in bringing Druids into the national consciousness: William Stukeley. At first sight it seems odd to find him reappearing in a category devoted to individuals and movements that challenged social norms; after all, he became an orthodox Anglican clergyman, and was prominent in the respectable intellectual circles of the capital with friends among the gentry and aristocracy. Nor have previous studies of his life and work brought out such an aspect to them. They have either portrayed him as a rationalist who underwent a sudden (and regrettable) conversion to religion in early middle age, or as somebody who was always a devout Anglican and merely chose at one point to make a profession out of it.

Three bodies of evidence suggest a different story. The first consists of his position as one of the founder members of a Society of Roman Knights, formed in 1722 among genteel antiquarians who wanted to foster interest in ancient Britain. Each member assumed a nickname taken from a British and Gallic notable of the Roman period. All but one chose that of a tribal chief. The exception was Stukeley, who donned that of a Druid, or rather a presumed one: Chyndonax, a name found with a cremation burial of the Roman period in France in 1598 which the discoverer had identified (almost certainly falsely) as Druidic. He retained it for the rest of his life, among friends and in his public writings, as a symbol of his intense personal identification with the ancient priesthood. The friends concerned affectionately referred to him thereafter as 'the Druid'.

Stukeley's interest in Druids had itself been part of a conversion experience, resulting from reading a copy of John Aubrey's unpublished book on megalithic monuments. It inspired him to undertake his own famous fieldwork among such remains, and on the basis of this he prepared a book of his own during the mid 1720s. The surviving manuscripts of portions of this provide the second body of evidence for his beliefs. Their significance in this context has not been appreciated hitherto because, failing to get them published, he subsequently turned them into notebooks, adding extensions and interpolations. In this embellished and altered form they became major sources for the famous volumes on Stonehenge and Avebury that he actually did publish in the early 1740s. To recover the original text, of the 1720s, it is necessary to ignore all the later additions, which in most cases is easy because the latter are in a heavier and larger handwriting. When this is done, a consistent and dramatic argument appears: for Stukeley's personal belief in a primeval religion which had been shared by all the peoples of the remote past, because he saw it as the natural one for primitive humanity to embrace. It venerated a single all-powerful god who had created the universe on a framework of numbers, geometric figures and musical notes. Stukeley had got this concept from the ancient pagan philosophers known as Neoplatonists and Neopythagoreans, and applied it to Britain's prehistoric monuments. In his belief, these not only reflected the religion concerned, but acted as receivers, by which the divine power emanating from the creator was drawn down more effectively to earth. Druidry, in his opinion, had been the finest expression of this universal religion. To him it was not a dead faith, of only intellectual interest, but the reality on which the cosmos was based. By contrast, his references to Christianity are few and slighting, and he denied the fundamental doctrine – in Christian orthodoxy – of the Trinity. There seems little doubt that, during this period, he was what his contemporaries called a 'deist', an umbrella term for a freethinker who believed in a single omnipotent deity who had created the natural world and concerning whom Christianity, at best, did not teach the whole truth. Even among deists, however, Stukeley was unusual in his indifference to Christianity and his passionate personal engagement with pagan ideas.

The third collection of evidence consists of letters written to and from his friends during the late 1720s, when he had left London in a fit of anger and disappointment, and set himself up with a medical practice in the quiet country town of Grantham, Lincolnshire. Part of the reason for this move may have been his failure to obtain the support that he had expected from his aristocratic friends, to get his book published, and this lack of support, in turn, may have been at least partly due to the heretical nature of the ideas in it. The letters disclose that he had adorned his new home with objects from various different ancient civilisations, according to their symbolic properties: thus, the Egyptian antiquities in his bedroom were designed to drive off evil. In his garden he constructed 'a temple of the Druids' modelled on Stonehenge, with concentric circles of hazels and evergreens and an apple tree grown with mistletoe at the centre. He also built a 'chapel' beside the temple, which contained a Roman altar with a camomile bed in front on which to kneel. When his wife suffered a miscarriage, he buried the foetus in this fragrant little lawn, 'with ceremonies proper to the occasion'.

It is hard to tell how much of this was play-acting and how much genuine religious behaviour, but, given Stukeley's strongly mystical temperament it is difficult to believe that it was less than half serious. What this re-evaluation of his earlier career does make easy to understand is the amazement of his friends when he suddenly reinvented himself as an Anglican parson in 1729, and why he himself wrote of this at the time as a conversion. It may be argued that he had become weary of the isolation, idiosyncracy and loneliness of the spiritual system that he had adopted, and longed for one that he could practise in public, as a priest, and with the full support of a national and local community. In early Georgian England there was only one such religion on offer; and he entered it. For the rest of his life, he strove, with unflagging energy, to integrate his imagined Druidry with Anglican Christianity. His love of Druids never faltered, but he now made megalithic monuments reflections of the doctrine of the Trinity and Druidic teaching a prediction of the coming of Christ. The poacher had turned gamekeeper.

If Stukeley's heretical propensities have long remained concealed, there has never been any doubt concerning the radical credentials of another major figure in the development of modern perceptions of Druidry: Iolo Morganwg. At the *gorsedd* on Primrose Hill in September 1792, the first of which a description survives, he recited an ode that called for the end of despotism and the return of liberty to England. In his book of poems, which appeared two years later and contained the longest explanation of ancient Druidic teachings that he ever published himself, he began by declaring that 'there is too much priestcraft in every sect; too much kingcraft in all, even republican, governments'. He went on to boast of his independence as a self-employed stonemason, and that his pen was used against 'scoundrelism, though captained by *ever so great a name*' (his emphasis). Some of the poems that followed celebrated freedom and pacifism, which was an especially politicised stance as the war that Britain had just commenced was against a French revolutionary republic that had just established itself by executing a king and disestablishing a church. Others celebrated working men, as lacking the corruptions and diseases of the wealthy, and accused monarchs of being responsible for all of history's wars. Another poem was in praise of the United States, which had thrown off British and monarchical rule only in the previous decade. Iolo was also opposed to cruelty to animals, practising vegetarianism as one aspect of this, and supported the campaign to abolish slavery. While the fraternal Druid orders appearing in his lifetime automatically banned women, Iolo permitted them in principle, and after a time in practice, to be admitted to his *gorseddau* on equal terms with men as Bards and Ovates.

Many of Iolo's friends shared his political views. The Gwyneddigion, the London society in which he was most active, was dedicated to promoting both a Welsh cultural revival and the reform of British institutions. Owen Jones, 'Owain Myfyr', the financial patron of the edition of medieval literature to which Iolo eventually contributed so many forgeries, wrote to a friend in 1789 that 'freedom in Church and state is the aim of the Society … It is for these rights that the French are struggling at this moment, just as our ancestors have been doing for hundreds of years.' Among his non-Welsh allies he counted Thomas Paine, author of *The Rights of Man* and a major figure in the American Revolution and a participant in the French one. It is hardly surprising that the authorities observed his activities with some alarm. Two of the principles that he laid down as having been essential to the ancient Bards and Druids – that they abhorred violence and that they always met in the open air and in daylight – were intended to reassure the government that he and his friends rejected physical force as a means to revolution and were not conspirators. This was not invariably effective. In 1796 Iolo attempted to hold a *gorsedd* in Glamorgan, only to have it banned by local magistrates because of his 'democratic principles'. The following year he addressed one in the same county at Forest Mountain, north of Cowbridge, at which he compared Napoleon to a legendary Welsh hero who slew tyrants. He and his companions were watched by twelve justices and a mounted troop of vigilantes. In 1798 he started to hold another, on Mynydd y Garth (Garth Mountain) in the north-east corner of the Vale of Glamorgan, but it was broken up by the armed horsemen of the county yeomanry who feared that Iolo and his audience were in league with the French.

Iolo always emphasised his devotion to what, in the introduction to his poems, he called 'the transcendently lovely Christian religion'. He went on to declare, however, that this religion, in its true form, was 'entirely subversive of all the present establishments in *Church and State*, and opposed by the *priesthoods*, etc., of every country'. He predicted the return of a society genuinely based on peace and love, in which Christianity could be practised without any clergy. At the meeting on Garth Mountain, he spoke of the achievement of a good religion without denominational squabbles. In most respects, the Christianised Druidry that he attributed to the medieval bards was his blueprint for such a faith. After 1800, as – like many 1790s radicals – he lost faith in the possibility of rapid political reform, he concentrated more on religious renewal and was one of the founders of the South Wales Unitarian Society in 1802. Unitarianism, by this date, had become another linguistic umbrella, covering a range of individuals and groups who rejected both established churches and the the older dissenting traditions, wanting to construct a more open and democratic form of Christianity on a local basis. In his later life he composed between two and three thousand hymns for it, in Welsh. Though pushed into the background of his activities, his commitment to the principle of political liberty never faltered until his death. In 1802 his friend Robert Southey, the English poet, historian and essayist, could describe him as 'brim full of genius and Jacobinism' (the Jacobins being the extreme wing of the French revolutionaries). In old age he still liked to talk avidly about his championship of reforming ideals.

Iolo's subsequent influence ran down two different channels. The broader was that which became the National Eisteddfod, initially the result of his cooperation with the established Church in Wales, an organisation which, in theory, he wanted to see destroyed. It may be suggested that ultimately he gained much more from the alliance, because the church failed to halt the weakening of its hold on the Welsh people or to retain any primacy in the eisteddfod movement, while Iolo's Gorsedd remained embedded in the latter. The other route taken by his intellectual inheritance was into a religious and political radicalism more extreme than his own; and it did so in one particular district of his county of Glamorgan. It lay on a natural frontier where the rolling farmlands of the southern Vale met the 'other' Glamorgan, the sharply-etched south-flowing river valleys of the northern uplands, divided by high hog-backed ridges of moorland and forest, rising to the massif of the Black Mountains. Fit in a pre-industrial society only for forestry and rough grazing, the mineral wealth of this area turned it between 1780 and 1850 into one of the great industrial areas of the world, with towns sprouting all along the valleys. One of these was placed where the Rhondda Valley ran into that of the Taff, a score of miles above the latter river's outlet into the sea at Cardiff, which became the main port for the whole region. Its focus was one of the triumphs of eighteenth-century engineering, a single-span bridge that arched across the Taff and gave the settlement its name, of Newbridge. During the nineteenth century, as the place became a centre of coal-mining and steel-working, and of Welsh cultural nationalism, it was changed to a Welsh form, as Pontypridd. Seven miles south west was a very different community, the small medieval town of Llantrisant, occupying the saddle between the two peaks of a steep isolated hill; an outrunner of those that rose just to the north and would swell into the mountains beyond. It had twisting cobbled streets, splinters of ruined castle, and a proud collective tradition which included memories of sending archers to the Hundred Years' War, and which helped compensate for its relative economic decline during the nineteenth century. These two towns, representing between them the two classic faces of Glamorgan, became for a hundred years the focus of a vibrant and colourful tradition of Druidry.

In the broader sense, this was one expression of the cultural and social ferment of Wales in general, and the southern mining and iron-working districts in particular, during the early nineteenth century. It was an aspect of the extreme religious nonconformity which ensured that, by the time of the first national religious census in 1851, three-quarters of the people of Wales worshipped in dissenting chapels rather than parish churches. They were chapels, moreover, divided between a rapidly multiplying number of sects; Pontypridd today preserves twenty-one different houses of worship. The first half of the nineteenth century, in particular, was the heyday of *crach-pregethwyr*, which may be translated as quack-preachers, or more generously as a free market in religious enterpreneurs, offering their own concepts of faith to whomever would listen. The Druids of Pontypridd and Llantrisant may be regarded as a manifestation of these. The political ferment of their region, during the same period, was almost as great. It produced secret societies of working men such as the Scotch Cattle, intended to terrorise unpopular employers or landlords, and the most determined supporters of the national movement known as Chartism, intended to produce an immediate and fundamental democratisation of British politics.

For anybody who wished to shape their religious and cultural identity around Druidry, Pontypridd possessed a great symbolic asset: in a region apparently devoid of megalithic monuments, it included an impressive equivalent. On Pontypridd Common, a long and narrow area of public land taking up a terrace of twitch grass, gorse and bracken in the steep eastern slope of the Taff Valley, there stood a large boulder of grey sandstone that nature had left balanced on top of another rock. The balance was so fine that the massive upper stone could be rocked with a child's hand, making it one of those wonders that the Cornish called logans and which had been regarded, since Toland invented the idea and Borlase supported it, as constructions of the ancient Druids. It thus represented the area's only apparently convincing Druidical monument, and its position and nature made it a natural focus for meetings. Locals called it by two different Welsh terms denoting a rocking stone: Carreg Siglo and Yr Maen Chwyf (which to English ears sounds like Ur Mine Hweev).

It was Iolo Morganwg himself who inaugurated its active association with Druidry, leading local *gorseddau* there from midwinter 1814. After his death, this activity was carried on by some of his followers, including his own son, inevitably called Taliesin, who strove to maintain his father's heritage, both by editing and publishing his papers, and by conducting *gorseddau*. In 1834 he initiated as a Bard a young man from the Vale who had made a name for himself as a poet at provincial eisteddfodau, a maker (or at least repairer) of clocks and watches, and a preacher in Congregational chapels, called Evan Davies. By 1846 Davies had settled in Pontypridd. When Taliesin Williams died the next year, he decided that he was the spiritual heir of Taliesin and Iolo, and so of the whole line of Glamorgan bards whom Iolo had claimed to be the true transmitters of Druidic knowledge. He and his friends in the local society dedicated to Welsh culture (the Cymreigyddion of Yr Maen Chwyf) turned the Pontypridd rocking stone into part of a sacred landscape, enclosing it in a double stone circle with an avenue of stones running to it on either side in the form of the two halves of a snake. This design, of a serpent gliding through an egg, had been William Stukeley's reconstruction of Avebury as a Druidical temple. In 1849, when the work was complete, Davies declared that the *gorsedd* that met at the stone was the oldest in Wales, with supreme authority over all the others. In 1852, at a midsummer ceremony at the site, he became the first known person in history to take the title of Archdruid of the Isle of Britain, with the name of Myfyr Morganwg, which – perhaps coincidentally – blended those of Owain Myfyr and Iolo Morganwg.

Myfyr seems to have been an impressive figure, with a bushy black beard which turned white with age, and the ceremonial dress of a white robe and an oval crystal, representing Pliny's 'Druid egg', hung around his neck. He also had the showman's gifts of the popular preachers of his time: at midsummer 1853 he scattered handbills around Pontypridd announcing that a prophecy of Isaiah would be fulfilled at the rocking stone on the longest day. Thousands turned up there, to see Myfyr and his friends unveil 'several irons' hung from poles, representing swords beaten into ploughshares and spears into pruning hooks; the audience cheered him and returned to the town very amused. He developed a personal theology, based ultimately on just three texts. One was Stukeley and another the Bible, with its references to the erection of megaliths in ancient Palestine. The third was the least expected and the most important: the tenth volume of the journal *Asiatic Researches*, founded to promote British knowledge of eastern culture. From that he drew the conclusions that Christianity was based on the legend of the ninth incarnation of the god Vishnu, and that 'the Indian system of religion is Druidism in confusion'. His own religion, acted out in ceremonies at the rocking stone on the solstices and equinoxes between 1849 and 1881, therefore became a blend of Hindu elements with those of ancient Druidry; at the rite of midsummer 1878 the prayer offered by him was to the goddess Kali, as creatrix 'of the sun, moon, stars and universe'. Large crowds watched these rituals, and he regularly intiated newcomers at them, including some American visitors. Another point of contact between him and representations of the ancient Druids was his love of astronomy, part of that instinctual feeling for order and mechanism that had turned him into a maker or servicer of timepieces. He built a small observatory above Pontypridd where he could spend nights observing the stars.

Local opinion regarding his views and activities was, unsurprisingly, mixed, and he attracted much open hostility from chapel preachers, which he returned with interest; one reason why the books that he wrote to expound his theological system (always in Welsh) are so scarce is that his enemies encouraged their flocks to buy them up and burn them. To balance this he had many friends and initiates, including several major poets. One of these was Evan James, composer of the lyrics of what became the Welsh national anthem, 'Hen Wlad Fy Nhadau' ('Land of My Fathers'). Another was John Williams 'ab Ithel', the editor of *Barddas*. Myfyr's own son acted as 'Under Archdruid' to him, taking his place to lead rites at the rocking stone on the increasing number of occasions in his old age when illness enforced his absence. It was not his son, however, who emerged as his heir among the Pontypridd Druids when he died in 1888, but another of his followers, a journalist working for a prominent regional newspaper. He was Owen Morgan, who as a Bard chose to be known as 'Morien', which was the Welsh name that had become attributed to the great late Roman Christian heretic Pelagius, who had come from Britain. Several of the nineteenth-century books that had argued (following Iolo) that ancient Druidry had been converted into a native British Christianity, superior to that of Rome and looking forward to the Protestant Reformation, had hailed Pelagius as a hero. The choice signalled Morgan's determination to make his own mark as a theologian.

There seems to be no hard evidence that Morien continued to lead Myfyr's group or to stage ceremonies at the rocking stone; in his writings after Myfyr's death, he treated the man himself with affection but disparaged his beliefs, his followers and his rituals. What is certain is that Morien was prominent in the gatherings of poets and musicians held in Pontypridd and that he developed his own elaborate theory of ancient Druidry, expressed in several books. It was based on a concept developed by a succession of British writers in the late eighteenth and early nineteenth centuries: that all primitive religion depended ultimately on a polarity, and creative union, of female and male principles. He proceeded to craft this idea together with Iolo's teachings and the famous medieval Welsh story known as *Hanes Taliesin*. To Morien the two divine principles were represented by the earth goddess Cêd or Cariadwen, alias Isis, and a heavenly god, Cêli, Celu or Coelus, whose sperm descended into the vessel of Cariadwen (variously described by him as a ship, egg or cauldron) to produce the sun god, Hu Gadarn, alias Arthur, alias Pan, alias St George. Hu in turn sent forth his semen in the form of divine words, which became personified as Christ, alias Apollo, alias Taliesin, the representative of the sun's life-giving warmth on earth. Cariadwen had, however, independently produced a son of her own, Avagddu, alias Pluto, Satan or Set, who as spirit of darkness and destruction was automatically opposed to Hu. She also, however, produced a beautiful daughter, Crairwy, alias Diana, spirit of the moon and of the virgin earth. To Morien the greatest seasonal rite of the Druids had been at midwinter, when they acted out the annual destruction of the sun's old body by darkness, and his rebirth from Cariadwen in a new one. The spring equinox commemorated the fertilisation of Crairwy by Taliesin (alias Jesus), whose power of fecundity had been conferred by his consumption of three drops of semen (or seminal words) emanating from his solar father. From these divine couplings, the living things of the world were created. To this cosmology, Morien tacked a system of salvation based on Iolo's circles of existence, with their inbuilt message that the order of creation enables humanity to rise to grace, rather than that humanity suffered a primal fall from it. He kept a place for the biblical Jesus, as a British Druid born of the seminal words of the sun which (in Morien's view) had fertilised the Virgin Mary. In this legendary history, Jesus turned the ancient world from worshipping the old sun of autumn to worshipping the new one of spring, and on his death was identified with that sun himself.

One of the most delightful aspects of Morien's writings was the manner in which he populated the district around Pontypridd with imagined ancient Druidical rituals. The latter included a re-enactment of the pursuit of Taliesin by Cariadwen, starting at the rocking stone and crossing the Taff and Rhondda valleys. The people representing them had to be ferried over the Rhondda, as Druids stood on both sides of the river, costumed as hobgoblins and satyrs, carrying flaming torches and chanting dirges to represent the cries of ghosts. The chase continued up to a mountain lake, a journey symbolising that through (Iolo's) circles of existence, where the priest taking the part of Taliesin took refuge in a cave. From this he re-emerged, 'with a loud melodious shout – cry of the birth … in white and his brow dazzling with a gold crown with radiating gold beams'. Hilariously, Morien's imagined ancient Welsh Druidry fragmented into warring sects, with their holy places situated at different points in the valleys, exactly as Welsh Christianity had done. It is not clear whether anybody but he took this recreated religion as a personal faith, or whether he and friends ever acted out any of these hypothetical rites, even in miniature. What is clear is that, unlike Iolo, Taliesin Williams or Myfyr, he left no successors, and the Druidry of Pontypridd seems to have died with him in 1921. The megalithic complex that Myfyr had built around the rocking stone still survives, although some of the avenue stones were pilfered in the 1950s, and it remains open to all on common land; but the famous stone itself, alas, no longer rocks.

If Myfyr and Morien alone had represented the Druids whose religion was focused on Pontypridd Common, then they would still be remarkable illustrations of how far the religious imagination could extend at the local level of Victorian and Edwardian Wales. Beside them, however, must be set a third figure, far more famous than either, who succeeded in changing national life for ever: William Price of Llantrisant. It is a measure of this man, and of his reputation, that the most detailed and valuable scholarly appraisal of his life is a postgraduate thesis produced in 1960 by a medical student who wanted to determine from which kind of mental illness he had suffered (the conclusion was a variety of schizophrenia called paraphrenia). A common alternative label for him found in publications is as an 'eccentric'. Neither category seems entirely satisfactory for him. Leaving aside the fact that the author of the thesis came close at times to suggesting that for a modern man to grow his hair long and don colourful clothes is itself a sign of mental disturbance (he must have had a tough time later in the decade), Price was certainly no straightforward lunatic. He held down a demanding medical practice until his death in advanced old age, winning great respect from his patients, and won a string of court cases by impressing judges or juries. As for eccentricity, the term's usual connotations of harmless and ineffectual oddity hardly come up to the measure of somebody whom the central government of his day regarded for a period (with justice) as a dangerous political revolutionary. He is perhaps best described more temperately as a determined nonconformist, with a combative and extrovert nature, who occasionally said and did wild things when under extreme emotional pressure.

Having said that, it remains true that lunacy – of an unmistakable clinical kind – did cast a long shadow over Price's life. This is because his father, a clergyman from the extreme east of Glamorgan, went completely and permanently mad when Price himself was still a child. One of his earlier and more benevolent signs of instability was to marry an uneducated serving girl, who was left to bring up their offspring in poverty, from which young William fought his way into a medical career with the aid of charitable friends and relatives, hard work and sheer determination. These formative experiences left lasting marks. They probably had much to do with his prickly, competitive and rebellious personality. They also gave him a passion for genealogy, and for emphasising the genteel background of his father's family and adding further heroic ancestors. Whereas the other modern Welsh Druids claimed to inherit their status by initiation, Price claimed to be a Druid simply by blood. He wanted even greater things for his own children than he did for himself, and built these expectations (along with his unfailing impulse to offer provocation) into their names. His first child, a daughter, was called Gwenhiolan Iarlles Morganwg, literally Gwenhiolan, Countess of Glamorgan, while his second and third, both boys, were successively named Iesu Grist: Jesus Christ. It must be significant that his published testament of Druidical belief bore a title which translates as *The Will of My Father*.

Like Myfyr Morganwg, Price first made an impact on public awareness through cultural nationalism, being prominent at eisteddfodau in the 1830s. By the end of the decade he had become part of the society based at Pontypridd, dedicated to Welsh culture, that was to give Myfyr his following. What was different about Price was his commitment to politics. He became the leader of the district's Chartists. As the national movement grew more frustrated, and its Welsh division more extreme, he became involved in local plans for an armed uprising; government agents reported that he had collected not merely hand weapons but seven pieces of field artillery. When the rebellion came, in 1839, Price was too shrewd to launch his men into it, and so escaped involvement in its destruction at Newport. He was then cunning enough to flee abroad in disguise, so evading the subsequent wave of arrests. He was soon back and once more under official surveillance, and it is important in the present context that a local aristocrat, reporting to the government in 1840, accused him not merely of 'republicanism' but of 'infidel opinions'. Two of these were clearly already a rejection of marriage and a rejection of established religion, represented by the fact that he was living with a woman (Ann Morgan) out of wedlock, and that their child, Gwenhiolan was 'baptised' by him personally at the rocking stone in 1841.

By 1848 Price had adopted the habitual costume for which he became famous, and which set him off at a glance from all other people: beard and hair worn very long, scalloped jacket and trousers of emerald green, lined with scarlet and adorned with many gilt buttons, and a fur cap, first of sable and later of fox, with the tails or tail hanging behind. This seems simply to have been the outfit that he wanted, and designed, for himself: at various times he told those who asked that it was Druidic, or from the ancient royal court of Glamorgan, or the dress of the Welsh soldiers at Bosworth, or inspired by Egyptian hieroglyphs. Such trappings must have added considerably to the physical presence of a man who unadorned stood only five and a half feet tall. It is significant that he is remembered much more for what he wore than for anything he said or wrote, and that he is always called by his given name rather than his Bardic one (which, as written, included hieroglyphs not used by anybody else); whereas Myvyr and Morien were primarily people of words, Price was one of action. None the less, his conduct was regulated by certain major principles, which he articulated in speech and print. Although, like Iolo's generation of radicals, he turned from political to cultural reform, he remained committed to social justice. He treated poor patients for free and made fiery speeches in support of striking miners. He was another animal-lover and vegetarian, supported various aspects of natural medicine, and condemned smoking as a health hazard. His love of and pride in the Welsh, as the most important nation on the globe, never faltered.

Price had a theology in which the cosmos originated in an egg, an idea taken from the ancient Orphic poems and much discussed by authors interested in religion during the decades around 1800. It also included a creator god whose will had put the universe in place, but Price did not believe that people should regard themselves as servants or followers of this being, and insisted instead that they should take responsibility for their own affairs and destinies. Nor did he hold out any hopes of a future life, stating (again hearking back to his sense of pedigree) that true immortality lay in one's children. He did think that prayers should be offered in honour of heavenly bodies, such as the moon. He held his own rituals at the rocking stone, and certainly had some collaborators or followers for them – his procession to the stone at the spring equinox of 1881 included 'three respectable women representing the three Graces' – while they were watched by large crowds. It should be noted that his dress for ceremonies was a white robe, of the now expected Druidical kind, and not his usual, and celebrated, green and red outfit. He had an affection for Myvyr Morganwg, and recognised him as Archdruid; with Morien he had a profound mutual rivalry and disgust, inflamed further when both claimed Myvyr's title of Archdruid on his death.

Price's status as a national hero, in both Welsh and British terms, is the result of a pure accident, or, if readers prefer, a remarkable intervention by destiny. In 1881, when he was eighty years old, he married a young woman called Gwenllian Llewellyn in a Druidical ceremony at the rocking stone; Anne Morgan had died in 1866. They settled down together in the home that he had made for himself at Llantrisant. His views on health were triumphantly vindicated in his own case, at least, because they rapidly produced a son. The importance of this event to him may be surmised from his views on the life-perpetuating qualities of children, and from the name of Iesu Grist that he and Llewellyn bestowed on the boy as a sign of their expectations of him; it may have reinforced his feelings that Gwenhiolan had not achieved anything of note on her own account. In reality, the poor little lad was to give his father immortality, but not in the manner expected; he precipitated it by dying in infancy, at the opening of 1884. One of Price's tenets was that burial of corpses was 'barbarous', and burning of them the only wholesome and decent method of disposing of them. Many people agreed with him by this date, but pressure to have cremation recognised by the law had thus far failed, despite agitation. Price chose both to ignore this and to kindle his son's pyre on the summit of one of the two peaks that dominate Llantrisant, on a dark Sunday evening when people were coming out of chapel. He could not have chosen a time and place more perfectly guaranteed to attract attention; either he was engaging in his customary determination to provoke or was so crazed with grief that practical considerations did not occur to him.

When a crowd reached the spot, it saw a child's body burning in a cask, while Price stood in front of the blaze, in his white ceremonial robe, his arms extended, chanting a version of a medieval poem attributed to Taliesin; the stereotypical image of a demonic Druid. Fortunately, policemen arrived at the same moment, and arrested him; it was also very lucky that the cremation had been interrupted while the corpse was still unconsumed and an autopsy could establish that death had resulted from natural causes. None the less, Price still had to stand trial, for attempting to cremate a body; and the event showed him at his coolly courageous best. He was no stranger to courtrooms, having long before been acquitted, in separate cases, of charges of perjury and manslaughter. He had the equally brave and constant support of Gwenllian Llewellyn, and a sympathetic judge. He did not base his defence on Druidry, but on practical arguments and the point that cremation was not in fact positively forbidden by law. The verdict in his favour established its de facto legality, and the first public crematorium in the United Kingdom was under construction (in Essex) within three months.

William was now a national figure, and he and Gwenllian returned home safely and proceeded to produce two more children in four years, Iesu Grist (II) and Penelopen (sic). Iesu got a minature version of his father's costume, with the prophecy that he would grow up to reign over the earth. When William himself died in 1893 – his last words were 'give me champagne' – his own cremation became a huge public event, with hundreds of spectators admitted by ticket only. He left no spiritual heirs; Iesu changed his name to Nicholas, and he, Gwenhiolan and Penelopen lived the remainder of their lives in respectable obscurity. In every sense, Price's was an impossible act to follow. At the present day there are no memorials to Myvyr Morganwg or Morien at Pontypridd, and they (so far) get only a glancing notice in the town's museum; but a statue of William Price dominates the main square of Llantrisant, as the memory of him does the town.

It was more than a hundred years before England produced Druids of the counter-cultural hue of Iolo Morganwg, let alone of his successors around Pontypridd; but it had begun to do so as they died out in Wales, and has continued ever since. Admittedly it needed a Scot to kick off the process, a tall, massively-built man with a luxuriant moustache, calling himself (eventually) George Watson MacGregor Reid. Like Iolo and Price, he moved from radical politics to radical spirituality, by a process that was a change of emphasis rather than of kind. He appeared in the years around 1890, as an agitator working to get dockers into trade unions, in ports in Britain and America, and a would-be politician in the United States. In 1893 he published a testament in which he set forth his three enduring beliefs: in socialism (with sympathy for anarchism), in natural lifestyles and medicine, and in a universal religion of pacifism, equality and mutual love that blended elements of all the world's greatest faiths. All were aimed against exploitation, privilege, established and inherited authority, and the ability of the rich and powerful to abuse or use the poor and vulnerable. Between 1893 and 1906 he vanished from any known records, to reappear with a wife and a private fortune (the latter perhaps provided by the former), intent primarily on pursuing his interest in natural healing. He had founded a British Nature Cure Association, led by himself, and a journal to give it voice, edited by himself, both designed to promote vegetarianism, outdoor living, wholesome food and natural medicines, and condemn all the opposites of those, along with vaccination and vivisection. Within three years, however, his interests had shifted again in their balance, from physical healing to spirituality, and his association was likewise starting to shift shape, from a medical to a religious movement.

The form that it took was that of the religion in which Reid had believed, in principle, during the early 1890s; except that now he set out to construct it in practice. By 1913 it had acquired the name of 'The Universal Bond of the Sons of Men' – though some of its most active members were women – and had a base at Clapham, London, and a smaller but elder group at Leamington Spa. It was fashioned from six components: esoteric Christianity, Druidry, Cabbala, Buddhism, Zoroastrianism and mystical strains of Islam. Each of these seems to have been dominant in the mixture at different points of the 1900s and 1910s, and the last three, at the least, were associated with particular personalities who impressed and influenced Reid at different times. Behind three of them stood the greatest society of ceremonial magicians in nineteenth-century Britain, the Hermetic Order of the Golden Dawn. One was launched by Samuel Liddell MacGregor Mathers, who composed the main ceremonies for the order and came to lead it. Reid regarded him as his master in cabbalistic teachings, and seems to have added 'MacGregor' to his own string of names in honour of his influence. Another of Mathers's pupils, Alan Bennett, opened his eyes to the riches of Buddhist tradition. Around 1913, Islam claimed more of his attention, associated with one of its main British defenders, Charles Rosher, who was another product of the Golden Dawn. Reid and his associates made contact with a group of Muslim mystics called the Senussi. These had made themselves unpopular with both French and British colonial administrators in north Africa by preaching resistance to foreign imperialism, focused on Islamic cultural resurgence. By this time their last stronghold, in the Libyan Sahara, was being threatened by Italian colonial expansion, and Reid and his friends championed their cause and sent them encouragement. Indeed, it was claimed that regular visits were made to them, and that nineteen members of the Universal Bond, including one of Reid's own relatives, had died there alongside them and were buried at their base in the desert. This focus of interest was, however, distracted in turn by the outbreak of general war in Europe, and by a different conflict at home, minuscule and bloodless but destined to bring Reid and his companions to national attention as nothing else had done: at Stonehenge.

That monument had been transformed in the years around 1900 from an isolated site on the edge of a wilderness, lying open to all and visited by occasional travellers, to one fenced about, subject to an admission charge levied by a custodian and sought out by growing numbers of tourists. As Andy Worthington has shown, between 1870 and 1900 it had become the custom for crowds, largely of local people, to assemble there to watch the midsummer sunrise. By the 1890s these could be thousands strong and cheerfully rowdy. As the national profile of the stones rose, there were strong reasons why Reid should regard it as the main British shrine of his religion. It was still, to him as to most people outside the intellectual elite, associated with the Druids. Behind his concept of a universal religion lay the biblical one of an original true faith revealed to all humanity, and the modern development of that into a vision in which all the great and venerable religions of the world were a fragment of that revelation. Reid followed many nineteenth-century writers in believing that Druidry had been the ancient British representation of it, and that the biblical tradition had been given a recent post-Christian restatement by Sir Norman Lockyer's assertion that astronomy proved the existence of a uniform archaic faith focused on the sun. Reid's own universalist religion was based partly on an adoration of figurative and literal light, of which the sun was the obvious physical representation, and Lockyer's work had highlighted the emphasis made since Stukeley's time on Stonehenge as a solar temple. The Ancient Order of Druids had, in the course of the 1900s, set a well-publicised precedent for the holding of successful group ceremonies at the monument with the support of the owner, Sir Edmund Antrobus. The problem was that Reid followed the precedent while ignoring every point of the example.

The AOD was a large, long-established international society, with no religious or political connotations and a titled upper crust which made Sir Edmund's baronetcy look humdrum. It had carefully applied in advance for permission to use Stonehenge, avoided the turbulent and crowded period of the summer solstice, incorporated and flattered Antrobus in the course of its rites and (to judge from its later recorded practice) made the occasion handsomely worth his while in financial terms. Reid and four friends turned up at the monument for the midsummer sunrise of 1912, and held services then and in late morning, reciting liturgy, singing hymns and making a declaration of faith that did not mention Christ but used Muslim, Judaic and Zoroastrian names for their supreme being. In keeping with the currently eastern tendency of their movement, they wore robes and turbans, and bore Persian, Turkish and Sanskrit titles. They had not apparently bothered to warn Antrobus but cultivated the journalists present, handing out copies of their declaration. Sir Edmund was clearly livid, for when Reid returned with nine followers the following year, he found that a ban had been imposed on religious ceremonies, with police present to enforce it. He protested both against the ban and the right of Antrobus to charge an admission fee, was ejected physically after refusing to promise not to hold a service, and pronounced a loud and solemn curse on Sir Edmund. Similar scenes were repeated in 1914 and 1915, with the addition of protest meetings and ceremonies held outside the precinct, and harangues by Reid to the crowds upon the iniquities of Antrobus and the police. All these episodes received widespread coverage in newspapers.

The reports were generally unsympathetic to Reid, but he had one great source of strength to add to his own determination, pugnacity and love of publicity: the sympathy of Lord and Lady Glenconner, a pair of local Liberal notables who happened to own the land immediately south of Stonehenge. They gave him and his friends a safe base on her husband's estate, where they could camp and hold rites, and from which they could sally forth to the stones. In particular, they came to use for meetings there a rare kind of prehistoric monument that provided a natural amphitheatre: a pair of Bronze Age disc barrows surrounded by a common ditch to which they gave the name 'the Double Circle'. The benevolence of the Glenconners, and Reid's stamina (and perhaps his curses), were rewarded when Sir Edmund died and his heir sold Stonehenge to a genial and upwardly mobile local businessman, Cecil Chubb, who allowed the Universal Bond to hold their ceremonies at the monument undisturbed, providing they paid the price of admission. The result was a trio of peaceful summers, between 1916 and 1918, in which they enacted their rites without trouble. By 1918 they were staging six separate rituals in or near Stonehenge at the solstice, spread over four days. Reid's party had swollen to about thirty, and they now dominated the popular assemblies to watch the midsummer sunrise, occupying the centre of the stones for their rite while Reid treated the local people, who had been gathering there unregulated for decades, as if they had become a congregation. The manner in which these assemblies had come to represent the public image of his religion seems to have brought about another shift in its focus, as Druidry displaced eastern faiths as the main focus of its identity. The society that he led retained the name 'Church of the Universal Bond', but had also adopted for its usual working title the Gaelic (and so more 'Druidic') equivalent of 'An Druidh Uileach Braithreachas', with headed notepaper bearing a trilithon.

In late 1918, when Chubb presented Stonehenge to the nation, it came into the care of the government's Office of Works. Immediately Reid's ceremonies became contentious again, as a pattern was established that was to obtain for the next one and a half decades. The civil servants and politicians who were now in charge of the site viewed the Druids as individuals on a level with all other members of the general public. They had no sympathy with or respect for their beliefs and rites, but were prepared to tolerate the latter if they happened just once a year, caused no trouble or expense, and were preceded by payment of the normal admission fee. To Reid and his most vociferous followers, they themselves had become the true heirs of the ancient Druids and therefore the true moral custodians of Stonehenge, with appropriate privileges owed to them. The potential for a clash was worsened by Reid's automatic response to opposition – already displayed in the case of Antrobus – which was to resort to confrontation rather than diplomacy. When the Office of Works showed any disinclination to grant his requests in full, he always blustered, hectored, threatened and denounced, wildly exaggerating the size of his organisation, the illustrious nature of its past and present membership, the length of its existence and of its connection with Stonehenge, and the privileges granted to it by previous owners.

Between 1919 and 1922, the Office and the Universal Bond argued constantly over the number of services that the latter could hold, the fee that members should pay to get in for each, and how the cost of policing the solstice assemblies could be met. The Office shut the Druids out in 1920, but allowed them back thereafter and gave way on most of points in dispute, only to face a fresh explosion of anger from the Bond in 1922, when a group of officers from a nearby army base staged a burlesque of its rituals at midsummer, at a time when Reid's Druids themselves were absent. To the custodian and Office, the soldiers were just another part of the public, on a level with Druids. The Universal Bond, however, expected any signs of disrespect to itself to be crushed by official force, as a sign of its privileged position. When neither this nor apologies were forthcoming, it informed the Office and the public visiting Stonehenge of its outrage, and withdrew to the Double Circle. Lord Glenconner was now dead, but his widow continued her patronage and kept the vital piece of land available. In 1923 the Bond returned to Stonehenge, and attempted to gain a much closer relationship with the site in 1924 because of the election of Britain's first Labour government. During the war years Reid had returned to active socialist politics, becoming leader of the Labour Party's local division in his part of Clapham. With a new First Commissioner of Works installed to lead the Office, chosen from the ranks of the new government and therefore in a sense a comrade of his, Reid expected better treatment. He therefore requested services at midsummer and the equinoxes, those at the former to be spread over eleven days, and the formal right to bury a small portion of the cremated ashes of deceased members of his order at the monument. The Commissioner, a bluff former mill-hand called Frederick Jowett, agreed to these proposals, providing that the ashes were only put into the topsoil and kept outside the circle of stones itself. In doing so both he and Reid had reckoned without a new power that had arrived on the scene: archaeologists.

As part of its remit on taking over the monument, the Office of Works had committed itself to sustained scholarly investigation of it. Accordingly, its bureaucrats invited the main national body that represented British prehistorians, the

Society of Antiquaries, to recommend a fit person to conduct excavations. It had proposed Colonel William Hawley, who proceeded to work at the stones between 1919 and 1926. His activities gave the community of scholars interested in national prehistory a sustained interest in Stonehenge, which produced in turn a sense of corporate responsibility for all matters relating to its archaeological character and potential. When news of the agreement made with Reid's Druids leaked out (through the site custodian, who had come to detest the Universal Bond), the Wiltshire Archaeological and Natural History Society orchestrated a national campaign among experts in prehistory to induce the First Commissioner to revoke permission to deposit any ashes. It took the form of letter-writing to politicians and the press, and was remarkably comprehensive, uniting surviving giants of Victorian scholarship such as Sir William Boyd Dawkins, old-fashioned antiquaries, and pioneers of the new-style professional archaeology such as O. G. S. Crawford. Much of it was based on apparently innocent misunderstandings. What Reid was actually intending was that only a sixth of the contents of an urn should be deposited, in areas already excavated by Hawley. His opponents seemed to think that entire cremations would be dug into the earth, that the deposits would be at any depth and anywhere around the stones, and even that whole bodies would be interred. Their expressions of outrage were, however, all the more effective for such mistakes.

The Office of Works kept what seems to have been a complete record of all press coverage of the issue, in a large number of national and local newspapers. Journalistic comment was overwhelmingly hostile to the Druids, and to the First Commissioner for humouring them. There was a minority opinion that disparaged the antiquaries and archaeologists as self-important and self-appointed spoilsports, but with no positive feelings for the Universal Bond. Most of this pattern was doubtless due to automatic prejudice against the Druids as odd people doing unfamiliar things, but – once again – Reid and his followers did not improve their own case. To judge from the single letter that they succeeded in getting published in a newspaper – out of many apparently written – they chose as usual to take the course of trumpeting their own historic and present importance and claim to be the natural custodians of Stonehenge, instead of bidding for the middle ground by presenting themselves as gentle and reasonable individuals victimised by pompous and intolerant intellectuals. After a month Jowett, buckling under what seemed to be a tremendous pressure of public indignation, revoked his permission to inter ashes at the monument. There was a curious sequel to the whole affair. In 1956, when excavating inside the henge, Richard Atkinson found fragments of a 'Victorian' glass bottle containing the ashes of a 'Chief Druid', with a note saying that it had been interred 'by ceremony of BEMA'. What these initials mean, and how, if at all, this find relates to the Universal Bond, remains open to debate. A different and much less enigmatic memorial to the whole episode was left by Sir Thomas Kendrick of the British Museum. It seems to have provoked him to write the first full-length study of the ancient Druids to be published by a respected scholar in the wake of the Victorian revolution in views of the ancient past. It reinforced the conclusion that they had not built megalithic monuments, and had been late and marginal figures in prehistory, and added a verdict that they had possessed no remarkable learning, no admirable religious or philosophical beliefs, and nutured 'only the elementary superstitions of simple folk'. As for their modern imitators, he denounced the 'extravagances and impostures' of 'Neo-druidism', which produced 'a wearisome and ungrateful task for a student in earnest search of druidic survival'.

All that was left of the deal struck between the government and the Universal Bond was the right to hold up to four services at the summer solstice, at an entry fee of half price per member; and that came to grief the next year, 1925. A misunderstanding with the custodian over the reduced entrance price produced fisticuffs at the gate. Following those, Reid allegedly incited the crowd to charge the entrance, which some of it did, destroying part of the enclosure surrounding the stones, at which the police had to intervene. Once more the Druids withdrew to the Double Circle, making verbal and written denunciations of the Office, and held their ceremonies there for the next two summers. In 1928, there was a change of custodian, which produced an immediate improvement in relations. The Universal Bond applied to hold three services in the stones on the longest day, and were allowed back. For four years they returned annually for these rites, co-operating perfectly with the Office and its representative on the spot and receiving sympathetic reports in the local paper; an illustration, as in the years of Cecil Chubb's ownership, that Reid's Druids caused no problems at all if they were treated kindly.

Over the period between the mid 1910s and the mid 1920s, the Druids had changed significantly in their appearance, organisation and ideology. Gone were the eastern costumes and turbans, to be replaced by white robes similar to those of the fraternal orders, sometimes with headdresses like those of ancient Egyptians (or of modern ritual magicians such as Mathers, who imitated the latter). Instead of Buddhist monks and Islamic sages, the predecessors held up for admiration were overwhelmingly British (with a few French and Americans), being a mixture of religious, political and social radicals from the eighteenth and nineteenth centuries. Although the liturgy at the Stonehenge services honoured a 'God' who could be acceptable to a range of different faiths, that deity was saluted in terms that were familiar enough to most orthodox Christians. The rites, like those of the fraternal orders, now included familiar Christian hymns. The true story of the development of the Universal Bond between 1906 and 1912 was obliterated – at least to outsiders – to be replaced by a claim that it was the heir to a continuously existing Druid tradition that had come down from ancient times. The question of whether it was a spiritual and symbolic, or a literal, descendant was left obscured; but the claimed existence of the Bond itself was explicitly pushed back to the seventeenth century. It was now organised into lodges, on the fraternal Druid (and masonic) model, with those at London and Leamington still being pre-eminent. Its numbers had also grown, to an average of fifty at the midsummer celebrations. The latter had settled into a repeated pattern, whereby three services at Stonehenge were followed by one at the Double Circle on the evening of 21 June, at which Reid delivered a set-piece oration. Thousands of people, many local, attended this, and it easy to see why working folk, many reared in a tradition of dissenting religion, would have warmed to these in the era of the General Strike and the Great Depression. Reid's speeches were couched in an idiom that most evangelical Christians would appreciate. He denounced the crimes of the rich and powerful, and predicted the coming of a new era in which the true message of Christ would prevail, and equality and mutual love prevail across the earth.

This happy annual tradition came to an abrupt end in 1932, when Reid found a new reason for a breach with the Office of Works. He asked the latter for official permission for members of his organisation to distribute copies of its own journal to members of the public at Stonehenge. This was denied, as the Office's regulations forbade the sale or distribution of any literature other than its own at the site. The significance of this was that the Office's literature consisted principally of the official guidebook to the monument, written by a local museum-keeper who bitterly disliked the Universal Bond and laid great emphasis on the lack of any proven connection between Stonehenge and the Druids. Reid, who took this as the effective declaration of an official propaganda war against his organisation, declared to all who would listen that he was withdrawing from the stones in response to the insult. His first plan was to have a complete replica of Stonehenge built at the Double Circle, but, when the normally compliant owner refused permission, he withdrew from it in turn. He never returned to the district, leaving the fraternal orders, who had been holding ceremonies at the monument regularly since 1925, without a single moment of controversy, as the only Druids to appear there. Behind this gesture of pique lay another shift in his interests. Reid had begun to give increasing attention to his old enthusiasm of natural healing, and had established a centre for it in Sussex. At the same time the increasing equation of his religious attitudes with Christianity became more pronounced, and he had ceased to speak of Druidry by the mid 1930s. Instead his organisation became simply 'The Universalist Church', and he and his closest followers worked on fostering links with American churches that preached universal salvation. They were still doing so when he died in 1946.

At his worst, George Watson MacGregor Reid was a bully, a braggart and a charlatan. At his best, he was a visionary of heroic and generous ideals, capable of inspiring great devotion in others. The latter aspect of the man ensured that he left a rich, dynamic and varied inheritance to his followers. The most Christian of them attempted to continue as a universalist church in London, eventually blending with the Unitarians in the 1950s. Others formed a group in the Bayswater district of the capital, dedicated to working a system of personal spiritual progress based on Caballa but substituting Arthurian names for the Hebrew spheres on the Cabbalist Tree of Life that symbolises the cosmos. Most of those who wished to continue Reid's legacy within a Druidic framework, however, gathered round another Londoner, G. W. Smith. Here it is necessary to retreat for a while from the 1940s, to understand the context within which Smith and his people were working. We need, in fact to go back to the West Riding of Yorkshire in the 1820s and a very unusual country gentleman called Godfrey Higgins. Higgins fulfilled the usual demands on somebody of his rank, managing his estates and acting as a magistrate, but he had an unusual streak of radicalism, campaigning for the reform of lunatic asylums, the system of electing Parliaments, the laws that kept high the price of bread, and the use of child labour in factories. His private life was devoted to the history of comparative religion. His overall view of this was absolutely typical of his place and time, for he believed in the former existence of a pure primeval religion, revealed to humanity at the creation of the world, which had fragmented and decayed, and of which Druidry had been one of the most admirable vestiges. Three aspects of his views were far less typical. One was his extreme hatred of clerics, summed up in his declaration that 'priests have been the curse of the world', and his desire for a 'rational Christianity', purified of them; in this respect he was even more extreme than Toland or Iolo. The second was his faith in reincarnation. The third was his belief that this doctrine, along with other cosmic truths, had been taught secretly through history by a group of sages who were incarnated for the purpose in each generation.

The notion of great secrets about the nature of the universe, handed down from antiquity by closed groups of initiates, made a profound appeal to some Victorians, blending as it did three of the age's strongest desires: that for increased knowledge and mastery of the world; that for sustained faith in an original divine plan for the universe and revelation to humanity; and that for a social and intellectual life arranged in clubs with controlled membership. It became a frequent assumption of books about the Druids that they had possessed both a public doctrine and also esoteric teachings, of greater importance and imparted only to their own initiates. The same system, of hidden histories kept by closed groups and revealed on initiation into them, was of course part of the mystique of the Freemasons and of orders modelled on them such as the fraternal Druids. In those cases, however, the traditions involved were incidental to the main purposes of those organisations, of providing conviviality and charity. Towards the end of the nineteenth century, societies began to appear that depended for their appeal upon the teaching of esoteric wisdom, in some cases joined with the enactment of ceremonies designed to change the participants and – at their most ambitious – produce an impact on the world at large.

The Hermetic Order of the Golden Dawn was one of the greatest of these, being specifically devoted to the study of ritual magic. Another was the Theosophical Society, which repackaged the traditional belief in one original true religion by teaching that this religion was maintained by semidivine beings seated in the Himalayas, who were in psychic communication with chosen and gifted individuals in the present world. Druidry was easily absorbed into this system, as an ancient version of the doctrines taught by modern Theosophists. Occasionally, a Victorian esoteric society was poured into a Druidic mould, such as the Ancient and Archaeological Order of Druids, founded in 1874 by Robert Wentworth Little. It was open only to Freemasons who wanted to work rituals based on images and ideas taken from Celtic literatures. In a classic illustration of the way in which ancient information influences modern activity, and the latter then rebounds on the interpretation of the ancient information, these activities began to mould representations of the original Druids. By the early twentieth century writers interested in the occult were attempting to reconstruct the secret ceremonies and doctrines that were presumed to have been at the core of Iron Age Druidry.

The first was Dudley Wright, in 1924, whose portrait was a curious mixture of information from classical texts, Iolo's writings and pure fantasy, as free as any employed by a Victorian imagining the iniquities of demonic Druids. One such flight involved the initiation ceremony of a novice, which Wright imagined as being in a cave. Three officers presided: 'Cadeiriaith', the chief, standing in the east, 'Goronwy', representing the moon goddess Ceridwen, in the west, and Fleidwr Flam, representing the sun god Hu, in the south. In masonic fashion, the north was left empty. The candidate took an oath of secrecy and was invested with an ivy crown and a robe of white, blue and green sections, symbolising light, truth and hope respectively, over which a pure white tunic was donned. His hair was then shaved back in a crescent above his forehead from ear to ear (actually the tonsure of early medieval Welsh and Irish monks) and he was made to crawl through a holed stone. After that he was shut into a coffin for three days, to signify his death and rebirth. On being released, he was led blindfold into a reassembled company as this chanted a hymn to the sun, and then nine times round the space, as it shouted and screamed. He then took a second and more solemn oath, was immersed in water, hauled out into a blaze of light, and presented to the archdruid on his throne. The novice was expected to achieve a succession of five further grades over the period of twenty years that Caesar had said comprised the training of a Druid.

The second reconstruction of the esoteric rites was made four years later by a Scottish journalist and nationalist politician called Lewis Spence. He boasted that it was the first work to approach ancient British tradition in a 'scientific manner' and 'the light of modern research'. Indeed, it was better based on evidence than Wright's, though, as the evidence concerned consisted of Iolo's writings plus unprovable interpretations of enigmatic Welsh medieval poems, the result was no less imaginative. He restated a belief in a single ancient religion covering the whole of the very ancient world, but this was no longer that of the biblical patriarchs and it no longer came from the Middle East. Instead it was a cult of the dead and originated in north-west Africa, an idea he had got from late Victorian archaeologists who had suggested that the megalithic tombs of the Neolithic had been built by a small dark race akin to the Spanish and Berbers. It had found its highest subsequent expression in Britain, turning the island into 'the Tibet of the ancient world'. His reconstruction of an initiation into the Druidic mysteries made it an exploration of the divine Otherworld of Celtic literatures, which he equated with the 'astral plane' of modern occultists. It involved the acting out of a journey into Iolo's Annwn, the source of all life and container of the secrets of death, by being enclosed in a cell. Initiates who passed through it, and desired to progress to the status of a true adept, were cast adrift in vessels on the sea, as Taliesin was by Ceridwen in the medieval tale. Those who survived had achieved full membership of the Druidic order. By this means, Spence claimed to have provided the British with 'the Secret Tradition' of their land, capable of rivalling any of the teachings of India and China, to which (as he noted with irritation), too many of his compatriots now seemed to treat as superior wisdom to anything in the West.

This, then, is the background to a society that appeared in London in the late 1930s and took the name of the Ancient Order of Druid Hermetists; thus neatly combining echoes of fraternal Druidry with those of occultism. It was a study group, concerned with what could be known of the teachings of the ancient Druids, inspired by a commitment to pacifism, faith-healing and benevolence between human beings. In this it converged with the ideals that Reid had always preached and so easily took him as a hero. It rapidly became a focus for members of the Universal Bond who wished to continue with an emphasis on Druidry. From 1938 it began to celebrate the summer solstice at Stonehenge, at first just five strong and in ordinary dress but then gaining numbers and ceremonial trappings. It became the only Druid group to continue to do so during the Second World War, dedicating its liturgy to peace, and gained Reid's invaluable right to hold longer ceremonies at the Double Circle. When Reid died in 1946 it was in a perfect position to assume the name of the Circle of the Universal Bond and become the heir to the whole Druidic tradition that had gathered around that in the 1920s. Its leading figure was G. W. Smith, who made a point of emphasising the equality of all members rather than chiefly power; and so the final division of the dead chief's inheritance was made. Smith's Druids behaved in a way that won the respect of the Office of Works, the press, the British Broadcasting Corporation and the general public alike, and their three services held at Stonehenge at each solstice of the post-war years were as free from controversy as those of the fraternal orders had always been.

Controversy, however, came to them from quite a different quarter. George Watson MacGregor Reid had left a son, Robert, who had been an active member of the Universal Bond in the 1920s. In the 1930s, having quarrelled with his father, badly enough to be spiritually and legally disinherited, he joined the Druid Hermetists instead. On his father's death, Smith clearly expected him to keep to this allegiance and become a key figure in the revived Universal Bond. Members of the old order in Leamington and Bristol, however, supported Robert in a coup in December 1946, by which he proclaimed himself to be his father's true heir and established a rival Circle of the Universal Bond, using the same names and adding the further, provocative one of 'The Druid Order'. Over the following couple of years. Robert's group produced a set of new rituals, and in 1949 they

were ready to start holding meetings at Stonehenge. As Smith's order had occupied
the prime position of the solstice, Robert's was forced to celebrate a week or two
later; attempts by the younger Reid to compose relations between them foundered
upon Smith's implacable hostility and feeling of betrayal. This feud continued
until Smith collapsed and died in 1954, and his order with him. Robert's one now
moved smoothly into the solstice position at Stonehenge, and as the fraternal
orders ceased to celebrate there after 1956, it was left as the only group of Druids
working at the monument, with the eyes of the nation upon it.

Robert was not the same man as his father, and his Universal Bond was
proportionately different. The elder Reid may have believed strongly in peace
between nations, but he was by nature a battler while the younger was a diplomat.
He dealt smoothly with the Office of Works over Stonehenge; after all, he was
himself a civil servant by profession. He had good relations with the mass
media and cultivated MPs, writers and academics. He proved equally expert at
building bridges between different parts of the world of alternative spirituality
and religion. Among those whom attracted as supporters or patrons of his
order were Lewis Spence, Gerald Gardner, the founder or publicist of modern
pagan witchcraft, or Wicca, and Charles Cammel, the friend and biographer
of the most celebrated of all modern ritual magicians, Aleister Crowley. When
a group of Rosicrucians began to hold rites at Stonehenge, Robert befriended
them so well that they became a loyal lodge of the Universal Bond. He had no
apparent feeling for Christianity, and does not seem to have been deeply religious,
but was profoundly attracted to the personally transformative effects of ritual
magic, and in particular that of the Golden Dawn. He personally knew and
respected Crowley, and signalled his own position in the Golden Dawn tradition
by retaining the name 'MacGregor' that his father had assumed in honour of
Mathers. Indeed, it was now commonly hyphenated with Reid, to give a greater
impression of gentility.

The rites of his order accordingly shed most references to 'God', and became
based far more clearly on the four elements and on human potential, placing
the participants in an interplay between the individual and generalised cosmic
forces. There was still an emphasis on the essential unity of all beings, and in
particular of all humanity, but the apocalyptic themes so important to Reid

were now missing; and that itself fitted the transformation of the Britain of the General Strike into that of the Welfare State. There was still an emphasis (though slight and kept for private rituals) on an original holy land from which the original true wisdom had spread, but this now took the more abstract, notional, dechristianised and remote form of Atlantis. Ideas and motifs were imported into the ceremonies from Golden Dawn magic, the writings of Spence and Iolo, the Welsh Gorsedd, and translations of medieval Welsh verse. The main figure held up in them for admiration was not a deity, philosopher or holy man but King Arthur. Rather than a universal religion, old or new, Robert's order represented a philosophy – or, rather, in the telling word of the time – a 'science', designed to promote self-knowledge. It had constructed a new legendary history for itself, with a list of chiefs that stretched back to John Toland. A few of the religious freethinkers honoured by George Reid were retained at the end, but further back it was a chain of famous writers on Druids; significantly, all were still – at least at points of their careers – political or religious radicals, or both. Enough current scholarship had been absorbed to leave out Iolo, although the order actually owed more directly to him than any of the others. There was also a lot of creativity, as well as borrowing and synthesising, in the making of the order's rites. In 1956 it added to the midsummer rites at Stonehenge regular celebrations of the equinoxes at Tower Hill, London, a site associated with medieval Welsh legend (and so 'Druidical') and convenient for the core of the order's membership, which was based in and around the metropolis. A new verse appeared at the first of these Tower Hill rituals, that sums up the ideals of Robert's order:

> We swear, by peace and love to stand
> Heart to heart, and hand in hand;
> Mark! O Spirit, and hear us now,
> Confirming this, our sacred vow.

Peace and love did indeed prevail in MacGregor-Reid's order under his leadership, but, despite all his efforts, it evaporated once more at Stonehenge. The problem here lay in the origins of the celebration of the summer solstice at the monument, as a spontaneous gathering of mainly local people. Even before the end of the nineteenth century, the large size and disorderly nature of these crowds had sometimes caused alarm among commentators. The arrival of the Universal Bond at Stonehenge in the 1910s, as described, represented in one sense an irruption into this tradition of a foreign body, that had come by 1918 to take it over. Some among the general public attending regarded the Druids with hostility or derision, and this tendency was reinforced during the early 1920s by the open antipathy of the custodian towards them, the coolness of the government department, and the appearance of another alien element in the gatherings. This consisted of young officers from the army bases now constructed on the nearbly plain, who could be even less reverent than the general populace and even less restrained in expressing this.

When the Universal Bond returned in 1928, however, the benevolent attitude of the new custodian, and perhaps the numbers of the Druids and the colour of their rites, induced a greater respect. The Bond's ceremonies dominated the solstice gatherings without difficulty until it departed in 1932, and subsequent development seemed to prove that they had become a major attraction of these events. Certainly, the number of people attending the midsummer sunrise dwindled away, once they were gone, to a few hundreds. This meagre attendance made it easier for Druids to re-establish themselves at the stones each solstice from the late 1930s, and by the mid 1950s their actions there had become a traditional and accepted feature of a British midsummer. The problem was that the crowds had now returned in force to watch them, thousands strong, and were growing increasingly drink-fuelled and badly behaved. The trouble-makers among them were drawn mainly from three groups of young men – army officers, students and working-class youngsters (in the language of the time, 'teddy boys') – who attended largely to heckle the Druids, and, in 1956, to throw thunderflashes at their procession.

The courage and dignity shown by MacGregor-Reid and his companions won them much sympathy in the press but did little to allay the disorder of the crowds. The unruly elements in the latter, unsurprisingly, showed as little respect for the monument as for the Druids, particularly by climbing on the stones, which posed a particular danger at a time when Stonehenge was being excavated and restored. By 1960 the authorities had become convinced that better policing and lighting of the circle was achieving little, and that more drastic action was needed. That advocated by the Wiltshire police was to ban the Druids, whom they admitted to be blameless but whom they regarded as the focal point that attracted the crowds. In this they had the support of some archaeologists, who had returned to attempting to make policy for the conservation of the stones for the first time since the 1920s. This was partly because their kind had got back into the monument; just as Hawley's excavations had emboldened the community of prehistorians in the earlier decade to change the government's actions, so Atkinson's programme in the 1950s engendered a renewed sense of moral custodianship. One of the most eminent archaeologists of the time, Glyn Daniel, used his post as editor of the profession's foremost journal, *Antiquity*, to campaign for the prohibition of all religious ceremonies at Stonehenge, equating 'hooliganism' with 'neo-Druidism', and calling the Druids 'foolish', 'unreasonable', 'bogus', 'ridiculous', 'ludicrous', 'horrid' and 'dotty', and their rites 'antics', 'junketings', 'nonsense' and 'lunacies'. To his fury, the Ministry of Works, as the controlling body had now become, eventually took the opposite decision in 1964: to exclude everybody except the Druids (and journalists and a few locals to watch them) from the monument at sunrise on the longest day, penning the general public behind a barrier of barbed wire. In this manner, the Universal Bond had – however unintentionally – completed the takeover of the stones on this numinous date that it had begun in 1912. I confess that, on ordering up the ministry's file on the affair from its storage place in the National Archives, I expected that this policy had been decided because of a gallant sympathy for the MacGregor-Reid's order, as well-behaved and courageous people who had by now established a long connection with the site. I was wrong. When I read the critical memorandum, it proved that the civil servants responsible had reacted to what they had found in the Office of Works's earlier papers on the involvement of Druids with Stonehenge, kept since 1919. There they found the diatribes and threats sent by the elder Reid and some of his closest associates in the 1920s, and records of the persistence and defiance with which they had kept up pressure on their predecessors. They became convinced that to exclude the Universal Bond would provoke it to a renewed campaign of vilification and disobedience, and decided that to keep out the general public would be much less trouble. In this fashion, the most unreasonable aspects of George Watson Reid's character served, long after his death, to hold a shield over his order. As a result, instead of keeping the Druids out of the stones, the police found themselves, at times, fighting to get them in, such as in 1969 when several hundred 'drunks and hippies' forced their way through the barbed-wire fence and climbed the stones. A civil servant commenting on the incident was careful to establish the limits of the responsibility that his ministry felt towards Druids: it was 'not concerned in any way with facilitating their solstice exercises, [or] affording them opportunities for publicity', but it still felt them to be entitled to access.

Archaeologists reacted with fury to the decision, and left equally enduring memorials. Daniel called for both the Universal Bond and the Ministry of Works to be punished in courts of law. His friend Stuart Piggott followed the example of Kendrick, after the previous clash between Druids and archaeologists, and set to work on the full-length history of Druidry that has been considered in a previous chapter. It was emphasised there that it was hostile to ancient Druids; but it was no kinder to modern people who had taken their name. It opened with the image of the Universal Bond worshipping at Stonehenge and asked if it should be there. Its conclusion was, predictably, a resounding negative. On the way, Piggott described the various kinds of Druidry constructed since 1800 as 'almost unbelievably fatuous speculations and fantasies', 'moonbeams from the larger lunacy', 'a compelling magnet for many a psychological misfit and lonely crank', 'a non-rational universe where every form of belief and unreason may meet', 'almost unrelieved lunatic darkness', and 'a world at once misleading and rather pathetic', representing 'a sad pilgrimage through error'. To that latter category he consigned the whole of fraternal Druidry and the Universal Bond, adding that investigation of their true history was 'virtually impossible'. A decade later, another leading archaeologist of the same (now ageing but still dominant) generation, Leslie Grinsell, published a pamphlet that focused directly on the issue of Stonehenge's relationship with Druids. Its subtitle, 'The Story of a Myth' signalled its message at once, as did its expressions of gratitude to Stuart Piggott and Richard Atkinson for commenting on the text before publication. It did not deal in abuse, but concluded with no less firmness that 'the ancient Druids had little or no more to do with Stonehenge than did the Romans, the Saxons, the Normans, or any later peoples who inhabited the region'.

The Universal Bond of Robert MacGregor-Reid did not survive to enjoy this triumph, for Robert died suddenly of a heart attack at the beginning of 1964. As his death was unexpected, no provision had been made for a successor, but two strong candidates presented themselves, both Londoners as Robert had been. One was a practitioner of natural medicine called Thomas Maughan, the other the manager of a well-known teaching agency that provided extra lessons for pupils to get them through examinations, Philip Ross Nichols. Maughan was elected by a very narrow margin, in circumstances that Nichols felt to be unjust, so he seceded with some of his supporters to found his own Order of Bards, Ovates and Druids. The two societies enjoyed opposite fortunes. The Universal Bond (or Druid Order) now led by Maughan had less creativity but more staying power, while Ross Nichols and his Bards, Ovates and Druids were more original but (in the short term) more perishable.

The two did not compete for space and attention at Stonehenge, as MacGregor-Reid and Smith had done, for Nichols retired completely from the monument, and his people celebrated festivals in and around London and at Glastonbury. Maughan kept the Universal Bond more or less as MacGregor-Reid had left it, and soon made up the numbers lost with Nichols's secession. Indeed, the full strength of the Universal Bond at Stonehenge seemed to peak at the same point, of around fifty, in each generation: in the 1920s, the 1950s and the 1970s. Its public rites (at least) during the 1960s and 1970s were unchanged, and so was its legendary history, while its basic ideology remained one of fostering peace and enhancing human potential: in Maughan's own striking phrase, 'Man is God in the making'. Once more, however, its peace was to be disrupted, and at the point at which it had always encountered most trouble, and won most attention, Stonehenge.

This was because of a new development in the midsummer celebrations at the monument: the growth between 1974 and 1980 of an annual free festival in an adjoining field. Although its formal focus consisted of rock or folk-rock bands, it became the nation's most flamboyant and accessible showcase of the counter-culture that had appeared in the late 1960s: a hippy city. In the modern history of Stonehenge, the festival could be put into one of three quite different contexts. One was that of a resurgence of the ebullient popular presence at the stones that had commenced with the spontaneous and unregulated solstice gatherings in the late Victorian period. From almost the beginning, these had included some music and provoked anxiety on the part of authorities, and they represented, after all, the oldest and most continuous tradition of celebration at the monument. A second context was that of the intrusion of another alien element into that tradition, following fraternal and rebel Druids, soldiers, students and 'teddy boys'. A third would be to view many of the festival-goers, and probably most, as a fresh wave of radical spirituality to burst upon the stones. They were a repetition, on a huge scale, of the appearance of the Universal Bond at the site in 1912, as strange figures in exotic costumes, challenging established authority in church and state in the names of worldwide peace and love. There is no doubt that the symbolic significance of the monument, as an ancient holy place, enigmatic enough to provide a setting for many different visions and beliefs, was the principal impetus for the development of the festival.

It is also clear that while the Druids of the Universal Bond were privileged – in an important sense 'established' – figures there in comparison to the festival-goers, the latter often regarded them with affection and interest as people opposed in their own way to social norms and condemned by leading academics. Their rites were watched with interest and affection by some of those attending the festival, and though the attitudes of others among the latter were more ambivalent, none tried to disrupt the ceremonies, something the more significant in view of the sheer scale of the latter. Whereas not many more than fifty Druids had ever been present at the solstice, and the general public had never outgrown a few thousand, at its peak in 1984 perhaps a hundred thousand people passed through the Stonehenge festival at some point in its duration. In apparent official recognition of both the general good behaviour of the participants and their genuine spiritual attachment to the site, from 1979 they were allowed into the stones together with the Druids, and able to return later on the longest day to enact their own rites. This all ended traumatically in 1985, when English Heritage, the semi-independent official body to which guardianship of ancient monuments had been devolved by the civil service, decided to close the monument to anybody at the solstice. This was, explicitly, to kill off the festival, which was now pronounced to be a danger to the monument and its surrounding ancient sites, but the Druids were banned as well. In contrast to their historic behaviour, they went quietly, and within a relatively short time struck a deal with English Heritage whereby they could continue to hold ceremonies at Stonehenge outside public opening hours on dates away from the solstice. In doing so, they have effectively slipped out of the public eye: the Universal Bond continues to flourish, but, having been the best-known, most dynamic and most influential of modern Druid orders, it has now become – at least to an outsider – one of the most isolated and reclusive.

Ross Nichols's Order of Bards, Ovate and Druids pursued a different course. He was himself a man of three different periods. Born an Edwardian, to some extent he pursued a continuing nineteenth-century agenda. He could not accept the apparent full implications of the doctrine of evolution, preferring to believe in some divinely-granted quality or revelation that was peculiar to humans. He also retained faith in the previous existence of a universal true religion, which could be equated in Britain with Druidry but of which Christianity, Greek philosophy, mystical strains of Islam and Chinese and Indian teachings all represented parts. In another of his guises, he was a classic freethinker of a kind not uncommon in Britain in the period between the world wars: a socialist and pacifist, and a naturist, who belonged for many years to the Utopian community at Spielplatz near St Albans. He remained, however, interested in new ideas and information that harmonised with his ingrained convictions. This was associated with his interest in young people, reflected in his patronage of woodcraft societies that provided liberal alternatives to the Boy Scouts and Girl Guides, and in his career as head of the teaching agency. In the 1960s it led him to take up eagerly novel concepts such as Alexander Thom's argument that prehistoric stone circles and rows had been the instruments of sophisticated prehistoric scientists, and John Michell's, that ancient people had laid out a system of straight lines across the planet that reflected magnetic flows of earth energy. He wrote for magazines that acted as voices of the late '60s counter-culture, and some of his order's rituals in the period look like gatherings of Flower Children. He was a close friend of Gerald Gardner, and absorbed into OBOD, from Gardner's pagan movement of Wicca, the system of eight festivals – the solstices, the equinoxes and the quarter days that opened seasons – that made up the wheel of its year. He remained himself a person of structure and correspondence, fascinated by the way in which things relate, connect and form patterns. His order did well enough as long as he led it, but it died with him in 1975, lacking either a successor to him or the will to find one.

His greatest achievement was, in fact, to be posthumous. In 1970, at the festival of Beltane that opens summer, he had initiated on Glastonbury Tor a young Londoner with a luxuriant Afro hairdo called Philip Carr-Gomm. Fourteen years later, and nine after his own death, Nichols appeared in a vision to Carr-Gomm and urged him to consider the value of Druid teachings in the contemporary world and to hunt down and regather his own writings. Philip devoted four years to the task, and in 1988 was invited by surviving friends of the old chief to revive his Order of Bards, Ovates and Druids. The time was well chosen, in both the particular and the general respects. The former gave Carr-Gomm a wife, Stephanie, who added her enthusiastic hard work and creative power to the project. The latter ensured that British society was repeating a pattern in its relationship with alternative spirituality that it had manifested a hundred years before. This had begun with a surge of enthusiasm, all over the Western world, for ideas taken from eastern traditions; essentially from Hinduism, Taoism, Islam and (above all) Buddhism. This in turn set up a reaction among some Western writers, who protested that the European past contained, or ought to contain, esoteric wisdom as profound and valuable, and that Westerners should at least be aware of the value of their own spiritual heritage. This was played out in the 1880s and 1890s, with the Theosophical Society representing the most celebrated conduit for oriental mysticism and the Golden Dawn being set up in part as a Western reaction. Lewis Spence reinvented a Druidic system of philosophy and initiation as an explicit balance to the continuing enthusiasm for eastern teachings. The late 1960s brought a new wave of that enthusiasm, with esoteric Hinduism being valued above the other faiths but all playing their part. One aspect of the reaction that occurred to this in turn during the 1980s was represented by the work of two more Londoners, Caitlín and John Matthews.

The dominant cultural influence obvious upon them both was a love of medieval Irish and Welsh literature, and of the Arthurian legend that had spun off from the latter. The dominant structural influence was that of the closed initiatory groups of ritual magicians that had descended, directly or spiritually, from the Golden Dawn. These taught techniques of guided visualisation intended to enable practitioners to open themselves to contact with otherworldly beings and to project their own spirit-selves to travel on other planes of existence. These interests led both, in turn, to study shamanic traditions associated with traditional societies in Eurasia and North America, and to find apparent parallels for these in the British and Irish past. In so doing, they deftly incorporated a new movement within Western alternative spirituality: to venerate and imitiate selected aspects of the cultures of tribal peoples who had survived into the modern era, especially the American Indians. From 1985 onwards, they published jointly or individually a very large number of books (twenty-five in the first ten years) that extracted esoteric teachings from Welsh and Irish literature, mixed with elements of shamanism and often accompanied by practical meditative exercises. The theological basis of these was a belief in a single, united, formless deity on whom human beings imposed image and gender, by visualisation. This put the traditional concept of the one true God into a postmodern mould. They added a strong feminist hue to it by arguing that in the present world there was great value in visualising the one deity as female. In doing all this, they both gained benefit from and greatly reinforced another new development in European and American spirituality: a tendency to regard Celtic cultures, especially the Welsh and Irish, as the western European equivalent to traditional peoples, providing a built-in antidote to the perceived materialism and secularism of contemporary Western culture.

All this has an obvious relevance to Druidry, and it was made the closer when Philip Carr-Gomm enlisted the help of the Matthewses in composing a correspondence course to disseminate the teachings of his revived Order of Bards, Ovates and Druids, while John Matthews undertook with him the work of editing and publishing the main teachings of Ross Nichols. The device of the correspondence course was another one taken from the societies of magicians, and that for OBOD, despite the help from others, was essentially Carr-Gomm's own. He is a man of great social grace, conventional good manners, and an extensive education both in traditional learning (his school was Westminster) and forms of alternative spirituality. He manages to combine successive enthusiasms for new interests and a loyalty to accustomed responsibilities, the latter anchored by the fiery determination of his wife Stephanie. His professional training was as a psychologist, which lent an instinctual sureness of touch to his enterprise of turning the OBOD correspondence course into a means by which people could explore their own natures and needs and strengthen and stabilise themselves while realising their talents. It was the dream of the later Universal Bond to foster human potential in a manner that led to a great harmony between individuals and peoples. It drew on two different aspects of the wise Druid of antiquity: as sage and teacher, and as bringer of peace, capable of halting contending armies. In sum, the OBOD correspondence course arguably represents one of the major documents of British spirituality from the late twentieth century.

The system that Philip Carr-Gomm set up was so successful that, within ten years of its refoundation, the Order of Bards, Ovates and Druids was the largest Druid order in the world devoted primarily to spiritual matters, with members in every English-speaking land and more in continental Europe. Those taking, or who had taken, the correspondence course, were able to meet at regular camps and assemblies, and to form local groups, or 'groves' roughly on the model of the 'lodges' of fraternal Druids (and Masons). It also, in the manner of rapidly expanding organisations with high ideals, generated new orders as people broke away from it. Two of these in particular deserve comment, because they were the first Druid organisations to be led by women. Ever since Iolo got his *gorseddau* up and running, women had been present, and sometimes prominent, in all of the organisations in which the image of the Druid was pitted against dominant beliefs and attitudes in British society; as the public life of that society had remained dominated by, and often restricted to, men, this was one aspect of the counter-cultural nature of these groups. The first lodge of the Universal Bond had been established by a woman, and both the surviving part of that order, and the Order of Bards, Ovates and Druids that had split off from it, had a strong female presence among its leading officers in the 1960s. The same was true of OBOD as refounded by Philip Carr-Gomm; his wife Stephanie was its secretary, and the most important of its local groves in Britain were either jointly or wholly led by women. It remains true, however, that in every case, the groups concerned, from Iolo's onward, had men as their ultimate leaders and guiding sprits.

It was significant, therefore, when during the mid-1990s Veronica Hammond left OBOD to found the Cotswold Order of Druids, and Emma Restall Orr did so to become joint chief of the British Druid Order. The nature of the groups concerned was very different. The Cotswold Order remained small and compact, with a family atmosphere, while the British Druid Order grew rapidly into an international organisation on the model of OBOD. Its success lay in the creative partnership between Emma Restall Orr and the original founder of the BDO – also for a time a member of OBOD – Philip Shallcrass. The latter had already made a name for himself by speaking on modern Druidry at academic conferences. Now he and Emma both became considerable authors, jointly and (more often) individually, and developed a more freestyle form of ritual practice, based on an intimate interaction with the natural and spirit worlds; which to them, of course, were the same. In the process, they applied consistently to the specific case of Druidry that introduction (or, as they would say, revival) of shamanic practices which Caitlín and John Mathews had already brought about in their intepretation of Celtic literatures. Shortly before writing this paragraph, I asked an undergraduate pupil in the course of a tutorial how he found the books of Philip Carr-Gomm to differ from those of Emma Restall Orr. He replied that the latter seemed to do more things in the woods. While I felt that this answer lacked something of the forensic precision encouraged in scholarly analysis, it had truth to it. By the end of the 1990s, Restall Orr was the most famous Druidess in the world; certainly the first since antiquity to occupy such an influential position and perhaps the first of all time. In the first years of the new century, she left the BDO to establish an organisation unequivocally under, or responsive to, her own guidance, the Druid Network.

Readers who are hard-nosed political animals may question whether it is appropriate to apply the term 'rebel Druids' to the organisations from the late twentieth century. After all, compared with Iolo confronting armed vigilantes because of his opinions, Myfyr getting his books burned because of his, Price facing a judge and jury because of his, and George W. M. Reid's comrades going to die beside the Senussi because of theirs, the later Druid leaders discussed here have had an easy ride. From another perspective, those who propound personal growth and human potential as a means to a better world, and who are attached to groups and teachings to which the word 'esoteric' can be applied, have often incurred scorn from those to whom the improvement of the human condition is best achieved by direct political action. Against this view, it can be stated simply that this chapter is dedicated to people who have used the name and identity of Druid to oppose and alter prevailing social, political or religious norms; and, according to that test, all who have appeared in it thus far deserve their place. There can be hardly any doubt, however, of the fitness of the label 'rebel' for the last, and most recent, group of Druids to be treated in it.

These furnished the strongest possible proof that the Stonehenge Festival had contained a core of highly-charged spirituality, focused on the monument. When English Heritage banned it, some of those who represented this most avidly realised that it had to have formal expression, in order to be taken seriously as a force in its own right. There was a chance that the Universal Bond, had it wished to do so, might have come forward as a priesthood for the festival by championing its cause. This was never a practical option, as the Bond had a completely separate identity and point of origin, and had never possessed either a practical or an emotional investment in the event. Left thus alone, those festival-goers who regarded Stonehenge as a national temple, bequeathed to the modern British by a past innocent of Christianity and the exploitative features of modernity and susceptible to a range of different visions, had to make Druids of themselves. In an important sense they were more purely religious than the Universal Bond itself, for they were united by a post-Wiccan pagan cosmology centred largely on a goddess who was either regarded as a personification of the forces of nature or as being represented by the entire planet, which was literally her body.

Propelled by these emotional and practical needs, three new orders, in particular, came into being between 1986 and 1992: the Secular Order of Druids, the Glastonbury Order of Druids and the Loyal Arthurian Warband. Each strove to avoid the temptation to function as any kind of counterpart to established clergy: the Secular Order by its very name; the Glastonbury Order by declaring equality between its component parts; and the Warband by making practical politics, rather than the enactment of ceremony, its main purpose for existence. All, in turn, inevitably found the conducting of rituals to become a major part of their activities: especially to mark seasonal festivals and human rites of passage. Each was led by a charismatic male figure, though – once again – women were prominent in the second-rank membership of all. The Secular Order was founded by Tim Sebastion, a former Catholic schoolboy from Essex who had acquired the air, and habits, of a jovial and generous rough diamond (or, as he would prefer it, 'a slightly soiled sapphire'); a persona in some respects belied by his love of music (in particular) and poetry, and of the fostering of events that encouraged both. The Glastonbury Order was the child of Rollo Maughfling, the son of a member of the Cornish Gorseth of Bards and a man who strongly resembled Myfyr Morganwg in his passionate speechmaking, bushy dark beard, very personal approach to scholarship, association with cultural events dedicated to a particular town (in his case Glastonbury), and assumption of the title of Archdruid of the Isle of Britain.

The chief of the Loyal Arthurian Warband was to acquire the highest profile in the mass media, and indeed to become something of a national figure, under the name that he took, legally and absolutely, in 1986: Arthur Uther Pendragon. He was the only one of the three to come unequivocally from the working class, but his family inheritance is more strongly marked in a different way; that both he and his father successively went into the British Army, enjoyed it, and in a sense never quite left it. Half of Arthur remains a soldier, expressed first in a notable career as leader of a tough (motor)biker club and then in his enduring role as a Druid chief dedicated to political campaigning. The other half is a mystic, with a strong sense of having been called by destiny to his present role as the contemporary representative (and perhaps literal reincarnation) of the legendary King Arthur. In enacting it he strikes a constant balance between treating the part as a sacred duty and as a joke, as a self-conscious compromise between shirking the responsibilities of the position and succumbing to follies of grandeur. Around him gathered what became the largest recent Druid order in Britain after OBOD, and the only one dedicated to direct political action: especially against controversial road, quarry and building schemes, especially those that do unusual harm to the natural environment, and government measures perceived to diminish civil liberties. In all cases its professed aim is to agitate and demonstrate boldly while avoiding physical violence: in that sense, its guiding historical example seems for much of the time to be not Arthur but Gandhi.

What the Warband's colourful costumes and titles ensured was attention from the mass media, which gave the causes for which it strove – and does still – the publicity on which demonstrations and non-violent direct action depend for success. In some cases, and at any rate in its earlier career, they served to deflect or qualify hostility on the part of security personnel, police and members of the general public who would otherwise automatically have been hostile. They also, however, lay within two different historical traditions. One was that of King Arthur, as a sleeping hero lying with his warriors within an enchanted cavern, or Otherworld, waiting for the call to return and save his nation. This had been deployed before during the twentieth century, especially in the Second World War, as a patriotic motif to encourage resistance to foreign enemies. What the Druid Arthur had done was to activate it as a symbol of resistance to domestic threats to what he and his companions deemed to be the land and liberties of Britain. To put the same point in a different context, the Universal Bond of MacGregor-Reid had made King Arthur the leading figure of its mythology, with full emphasis on his attribute as a hero who might yet return. Now a different sort of Druid had realised the potential of the association. The other tradition was of English rebels, emerging from parts of society underneath the usual political nation of nobility, gentry and wealthy merchants, who took ritualised names to nerve themselves up to challenging the established order, and to put a space between their normal social roles and that now adopted by them. This first appeared in the Peasants' Revolt of 1381, and was a feature of rebellions and riots during the next half a millennium: Jack Straw, Robin Hood, Reynold Greenleaf, Captain Pouch, Lady Skimmington and Captain Swing have been some of the names and titles adopted. The donning of costume by rioters, further distancing those who did from their everyday selves and places in the social order, has also been found intermittently across the later half of that period. The last examples before the Warband were in the Captain Swing disturbances (aimed at farmers whose methods were putting labourers out of work), and the Hosts of Rebecca (who destroyed toll gates) in the early nineteenth century. The Warband represents a non-violent continuation of the same tradition.

Although all three orders drew on members from a broad expanse of Britain, especially the Loyal Arthurian Warband, their heartland lay – and lies – in the counties of Somerset, Wiltshire and Hampshire, which is why they have collectively taken the name of the West Country Druid Orders. The chiefs have (usually) been firm friends, and co-operated, and never longer nor more firmly than in the campaign to reopen Stonehenge at midsummer. If English Heritage keeps its records as well as the central civil service did, it will be fascinating for a later generation of historians to peruse those that deal with both ends of the process. It is still not absolutely certain why the decision to close the monument was taken in 1985, though the obvious broader context seems to be the determination of the reigning Conservative government, of Margaret Thatcher, to suppress what seemed to it to be the more disruptive dissident elements in British society. Similarly, it is not at present clear whether the decision to revoke the ban completely in 2000 was more the result of the relentless pressure of the West Country Druid Orders, the more temperate and conciliatory negotiations of the British Druid Order and similar groups, or the shift of majority opinion among archaeologists from supporting to condemning the closure. Each has confident and apparently well-informed advocates.

What happened in 2000, and has happened since, is that the solstice gatherings at the stones have come full circle. They began well over a hundred years ago as formless assemblies of ordinary people, sometimes rowdy and often including spontaneous musical performances. Now that situation has returned, as a huge, chaotic and ebullient crowd, including drummers and pipers, mills in and around Stonehenge all night before the midsummer sunrise, and cheers it on without structured rites. This is exactly what the West Country orders, at least, wanted – a free right of assembly of the common folk to enjoy the sight of the midsummer dawn – but it has involved the marginalisation of Druids in general at the event. After dominating it for much of the twentieth century, it could be that their particular association with it is done; but then, in Druidry (and especially at Stonehenge), no situation remains the same for long.

During the years between 1940 and 1985 a few smaller Druid orders, devoted to ritual and/or the pursuit of occult wisdom, appeared (and generally disappeared) in Britain, mostly in London. Since 1990, new formal groups of people who embrace the identity of Druid in the context of modern alternative spirituality – roughly according to the OBOD or West Country model – have

appeared at the rate of five or six every year, most short-lived but others with
apparent staying power. Some have been ceremonially and ritually impressive,
some colourful and led by memorable characters, and some have been both.
All have been ignored here, as the constraints of space have limited attention to
those who have made the most impact on national and international attention.
Likewise, the concentration on leading figures has obscured many second-rank
people who contributed significantly to the groups concerned. In particular this
policy has left women almost completely in the shade. It is at one with it that the
fraternal Druids considered in this book have been virtually all collective and
anonymous, as have been scores of people who wrote extensively about Druidry,
and hundreds who mentioned it in passing, simply because they were typical.
The writing of history is a remorselessly selective process.

Each chapter hitherto has had a neat and logical ending; this one cannot be
given it. The sort of Druidry with which it deals is still developing too fast. At the
time at which these words are being written, the government has just declared
that it is prepared to countenance a whole range of construction projects to
remove the present problem of the major roads that pass Stonehenge; and Arthur
Pendragon has announced that he will declare war on any that seriously disturb
the natural and archaeological landscape. Tim Sebastion is sponsoring a project
to link schools directly to the annual competition that his order has founded,
to choose a Bard of Bath. Rollo Maughfling has retired to Wales, leaving a new
pair of joint leaders for his Glastonbury Order who have set about campaigning
on political and environmental issues around the town. Philip Carr-Gomm is
halfway through a complete rewriting of the OBOD correspondence course.
Emma Restall Orr has instigated an organisation called Honouring the Ancient
Dead, to persuade archaeologists and museum keepers to treat ancient human
remains with the same respect as those accorded to those of Christians and Jews,
and to work with an enhanced sense of the sacredness of ancient ceremonial
sites. Meanwhile, controversy has at last broken out at Avebury, the second most
famous of those sites in England, over the number of people, many of them
Druids, who are celebrating there at midsummer. Any of these developments
may usher in events of enduring historical importance.

In a sense, that was signalled at the end of each, the themes of the first three chapters of this book all converge upon this final one. That of the patriotic Druids, which has pretty well totally faded out of British culture as a whole, has found a new strength in a counter-cultural setting. The Loyal Arthurian Warband, in particular, strongly identifies with the image of the Druid as resistance leader on behalf of the land and of the liberty of its people. The Romans, however, are no longer identified with foreign aggressors, but with the forces of intrusive government and exploitative and damaging construction schemes. This requires less of a leap of imagination than may at first appear, because the ancient Druids were, after all, the spiritual leaders of a simpler and more traditional society than the Romans. The latter were the people who invented reinforced concrete, drove straight highways across conquered lands to connect new towns built according to standardised patterns, and used all to support a system of high taxation and despotic government, with an increasing eradication of local liberties and political identities. It is significant that the greatest cleavage among contemporary British people who use the name of Druid is between the Welsh Gorsedd and the counter-cultural organisations, who have rival senses of the relationship between Druidry and nationhood. The wise Druids are now most clearly personified in the OBOD correspondence course and the other orders that make teaching, and personal self-development, the core of their objectives. They have broken free, on the whole, of any attempt to retrieve ancient Druidic knowledge or to relate Druidry to biblical history and cosmology; instead, for most, it is sufficient that the ancient Druids were credited by several classical and medieval texts with being scientists and sages worthy of respect. This puts them at the head of a British tradition of thinking and learning which is the more open-ended for the twin facts that their actual doctrines are lost and that at present no seats or traditions of established learning make anything of them as ancestors or examples. The green Druids flourish now more than they have for almost two hundred years, as fear for the natural environment grows on both a national and a global scale. A connecting characteristic between kinds of contemporary Druidry that are essentially concerned with personal growth and those that are essentially concerned with cultural and political campaigning is an intense sense of affection for the natural world, and especially for trees. Thus movements that in many respects exist upon the cultural and social fringe of Britain (though some would call it a cutting edge), are the stronger and more confident for the fact that they embody ideas and images that were once central.

Future Druids

Historians make notoriously bad prophets, and there is no reason to believe that this record is likely to be better in the case of future attitudes to Druids. Any informed observer in 1980, when there was very little interest in Druidry apparent in society in general, or among alternative kinds of spirituality, or political and social counter-cultures, would have been very imaginative to expect the tremendous growth of new orders that began in the later half of the decade. In that year, also, anybody looking for a book in print that dealt with the subject would have virtually no choice other than Stuart Piggott's brilliantly composed but hostile polemic from the 1960s. Now the problem is where a newcomer should start, as there is a wide and ever increasing range of texts, from the wholly scholarly to the completely experiential, and from brand-new works to reprinted classics, that deal with Druids from almost every possible viewpoint. None the less, it is tempting to make certain suggestions regarding the likely fate of Druidry in twenty-first-century Britain, if only to allow posterity the fun of comparing them with what happens instead.

They can be most easily made by following the successive characterisations of Druids that made up the chapters of this book. It does not seem at present as though there is any obvious future for 'patriotic' Druids in the national imagination. They formed part of a British identity developed to fit a United Kingdom, but both the identity and the kingdom proved perfectly capable of doing without them when nationalist enthusiasm for them wore off. If they are expendable to a sense of Britishness, then at present a British identity itself is on the wane, in an era of Scottish and Welsh devolution and an increasing incorporation of the United Kingdom into a European Union in which small, strongly-defined states thrive as well as larger and more complex nations do. In this context, it seems likely that the Welsh will hang on to their particular nationalist association with

Druids, achieved during the nineteenth century and expressed most obviously in the Gorsedd at the National Eisteddfod. The very success of this association makes it a conservative one, as the Gorsedd itself has tended to function as a conservative force in Welsh culture during the twentieth century. In this respect, Druids in Gorsedd circles occupy something of the same emotional space in Welsh identity as cricket on village greens does in the English; but the more strongly settled for that.

Even less chance seems to exist for a revival of 'wise' Druids as important figures in the national scholarly imagination. As the Victorians removed the connection with megalithic monuments and with the Old Testament that the Georgians had successfully installed, the ancient Druids have gone back to being the silent, enigmatic, intangible people with whom Tudor and Stuart authors struggled to come to grips. Indeed, they are even more remote, because the imaginative lifelines thrown to those authors – forged or mistranslated texts, extrapolations from literal belief in Scripture, and a simple and trusting reading of Greek and Roman texts – are denied to the present. It always remains possible that archaeology will give voices and faces to them, but it is also unlikely, in the nature of that discipline, that any new evidence dug up will win a unanimous and uncontested interpretation.

From the perspective of the present, 'green' Druids seem to have been even more of a passing literary fashion than part of a sustained cultural movement. Even among the writers of sentimental nature poetry, they were always less familiar and useful characters than the deities, nymphs and satyrs of Greek and Roman mythology, and really represented an imaginative experiment confined to the late eighteenth century. Occasional echoes of them, which continued for a hundred years longer, faded away from mainstream British literature after the First World War as such poetry finally fell out of favour. It is interesting that, at the present time, most of the circumstances that attended the flourishing of images of Druids as priests of the natural world have returned: above all, an acute love of, and identification, of people with an endangered natural environment, and an admiration for traditional societies as examples of human beings living in harmony with the latter. To fit the Druids back into this, in British culture in general, would however, require the revival of a sense of them as central personalities in the ancient British past; and our present knowledge of prehistory makes this unlikely. Furthermore, television has replaced poetry as the principal medium through which the natural world is celebrated, and biology has replaced mythology as the vehicle for celebration. Advances in our knowledge of how ecosystems work, and in a technology that can film their workings for home consumption, have made Pan and the nymphs largely superfluous; it is real animals and plants who personify the woods and streams, and whose adventures are celebrated in works of education and entertainment.

It is difficult to predict the fate of 'fraternal' Druid orders. At first sight they seem to belong as much to a disappearing British world as the empire, heavy industry, closed village communities, working men's clubs, and parents who expect their children to follow them in their trades. On the other hand, it may be that, in a mutated and refreshed form, they could earn the dividend of respect given to institutions that have survived centuries, and retain clear links to the past, while serving the social needs of the future. Two developments in particular might ensure their survival and prosperity, if they could only adapt to meet them, or be allowed to do so. One has been mentioned: the decline of the Welfare State, and the corresponding growth of private insurance and pension schemes to compensate for the shortfall of public provisions. The other is the increasing mobility of the population, and the need for safe, stable social spaces with which people can identify. Neither at present looks as if it is necessarily going to benefit fraternal Druidry, but a further change in social conditions, and some creative reinvention on the part of the orders concerned, might bring all into a productive relationship.

In contrast to all this, the future of 'demonic' Druids seems to be assured. Societies as fundamentally peaceful, prosperous, secure and well ordered as Britain has been for many decades, seem to have more of a taste than most for erotic and violent images in works of entertainment. Greek and Roman writings about Druids contain vivid examples of both, which may be accepted (with some blindness to the problems of the sources) as historic, and therefore as having the additional power of 'reality'. There are three different forces that are likely to propel use of those images into an indefinite future. One is simple sensationalism: the fact that, when presenting Iron Age Britain to an audience, to bring in some evil Druids is a sure way of spicing up the material and one which is, arguably, justified by the evidence. This is a bait which film-makers, novelists, dramatists and (perhaps) archaeologists and museum curators are unlikely to resist. The second force is pessimism regarding human nature and the human condition. Such pessimists have always found a handy retort to those who admire societies with a lifestyle that predates the development of cities and state systems (and which may therefore be termed more 'natural'), in pointing to alleged or proven atrocities habitually committed by their members. The Druids fulfil that function with regard to the British past. The third force is that demonic Druids have always been used, since they were observed or invented in the ancient world, as symbols of the wrong sort of religion. As such, they have proved to have a seemingly effortless and endless potential for being used to castigate religious opponents, and sometimes organised religion in general. A proponent of this tactic might say that it highlights the dangers to which human religiosity can always lead. An opponent could reply that demonic Druids are a standard conceptual weapon in the armoury of human intolerance.

The 'rebel' Druids are the hardest of all to place in any predictive pattern. It would be easy to argue that the current explosion in Druidry, as an expression of alternative British spirituality, is likely to become an enduring aspect of national culture. After all, as the West seems in general to be turning into an increasingly similar set of societies, characterised by individual self-expression and consumer choice, what critics call a 'pick and mix' approach to religion and other spiritual systems is surely going to be sustained and increased. Amid the large number of traditions now on offer, Druidry has proved itself to have a flexibility, and a relevance to human potential and environmental concerns, that would seem to make it an attractive choice. On the other hand, it must also be recognised that consumer choice is notoriously fickle, and that spiritual systems which are based on the free choice of members, and not supported by an established framework of financial support and training, are particularly vulnerable in a fast-changing world. What must be pointed out is that Druidry as an expression of a counter-culture now has a continuous history in Britain of more than two hundred years. It therefore has been afforded plenty of time to show how well it can adapt to change. The very evaporation of the Druids as major figures in national culture

58. Owen Morgan ('Morien') in old age, enthroned in a bardic chair at Pontypridd.

59. The illustration to accompany one of Morien's oracular utterances: 'The Infant Son as the Infant Body of Jupiter or Jove: and the Infant Body of Pan. Lamb and He Goat to imply their respective Zodiacal signs. Goddess with the Horn of Plenty, Nest of Birds to imply Springtime.' The actual images are taken from Roman period reliefs found in France.

60. George Watson MacGregor Reid in his pre-Druid days as an advocate of natural healing, 1907.

61. Reid's Edwardian journal, which was to transform slowly into a vehicle for spiritual, rather than physical, regeneration.

62. A new Druid in the process of initiation, drawn by Wendy Wood as the frontispiece to Lewis Spence's *The Mysteries of Britain* (1929).

63. Wendy Wood's depiction of 'A Druidic Orgy' for Spence's book: even by Victorian literary standards the proceedings seem rather innocent, but perhaps things are only getting started.

64. Robert MacGregor-Reid (note the added hyphen) prepares to resheath the ceremonial sword at an autumn equinox ceremony of his Circle of the Universal Bond on Primose Hill, London, in 1957. The gesture, like the place, marks the spiritual descent of much of his order's identity from Iolo Morganwg.

65. Robert MacGregor-Reid and his order at Stonehenge at dawn on the summer solstice of 1956. The press of public around them is an indication of the problems of crowd control which were to become critical by the end of the decade.

66. One of MacGregor-Reid's two successors, Thomas Maughan, leads the Universal Bond in a spring equinox ceremony on Tower Hill, London, in 1966.

67. MacGregor-Reid's other successor, Ross Nichols, leads his breakaway order of Bards, Ovates and Druids in another rite at London on the same festival of 1966.

68. Another part of the same ceremony, which usefully serves to emphasize the prominence of women in this sort of Druidry by the 1960s.

69. Philip Carr-Gomm, Chief of the revived Order of Bards, Ovates and Druids, about to join a ritual at his order's summer camp in 2001.

70. A gathering of Druids on Dragon Hill, below the Uffington White Horse, in July 1994. Philip Shallcrass is the one striding robed and staffed across the right of the picture.

71. Druid gathering at Avebury at Beltane (May Day) 1996. Emma Restall Orr is in the centre of the picture, Philip Shallcrass, appropriately, just to her right, head turned away, in wolfskin.

72. Caricature of Tim Sebastian, made by a friend, as he appeared on a television programme in 1986, around the time of the launching of his Secular Order of Druids.

73. Rollo Maughfling, Chief of the Glastonbury Order of Druids, at a Beltane gathering at Avebury in 1998.

Below: 74. Arthur Pendragon manages to look regal even when seated in a suburban garden, August 2000.

Above: 75. A cartoon against the closure of Stonehenge against all summer solstice celebrations, from 1985. It neatly links the traditional association of the monument with Druids through the French Iron Age cartoon figure of Asterix. It also represents a good example of the way in which resistance to the Romans could be turned from a general patriotic motif into one of internal politics.

76. A column from the Order of Bards, Ovates and Druids newsletter, in 2005, showing how Druidry can be assimilated to modern campaigns to protect ancient sites and the natural environment.

United Kingdom

Thornborough Henges quarry threat-
Stop the quarrying at Britain's largest ritual site:
http://www.thepetitionsite.com/takeaction/790535280
Stop Silbury Hill collapsing -
This petition asks for Silbury Hill in the UK to be fixed - it started subsiding five years ago due to archaeological interventions of the past. Five years later little has been done.
http://www.petitiononline.com/Silbury1/petition.htm
Save Priory Park and its ancient burial ground
Trees will be cut and the ancient burial ground of a Saxon King will be tarmacked over. Stop the insane roadbuilding mania! Don't let cars rule the world! Save precious natural and historical sites in Britain and elsewhere!
Sign this petition and pass it on. Please!
http://www.thepetitionsite.com/takeaction/730475056

United States

Save Native American burial grounds -
http://www.petitiononline.com/JW5004/petition.html

Ireland

Hill of Tara motorway threat -
Petition to re-route the M3 away from Tara.
http://www.petitiononline.com/Temair/petition.html

Please pass these on - saving 5,000 years old heritage sites also saves 5,000 year old landscapes and habitat, it stops development and thus helps with global warming.

77. Druidry looking into the future. A member of the Universal Bond, and also of the Bards, Ovates and Druids, gazes at the midsummer sunrise at Stonehenge in 2002. His position among the great crowd, at once striking and isolated, indicates the way in which modern Druids have become firmly associated with the monument and yet marginalized in the recent public celebrations of the summer solstice there.

has released their full potential as models, emblems and metaphors for people opposed to elements of that culture. Whether or not Britain later in this century contains a rebel Druidry that resembles the kinds which it has now, it is likely to have some.

The imaginative use of Druids, therefore, will most probably be sustained at polarised extremes. On the one hand, there are good reasons why images of them as bloodstained and barbarian priests should continue to flourish, and to be presented as an objective truth about the past. On the other, there are equally good grounds for expecting that more positive, though vaguer, concepts of them, as philosophers, mystics, defenders of their people and priests of a nature-centred religion, will continue to inspire people seeking spiritual growth and regeneration for themselves and change in their society. The two attitudes represent a perfect example of the opposed uses to which the past can be put; because they depend upon radically different views of humanity. It would be melodramatic, and indeed unrealistic, to declare that they will struggle between them for the soul of the British. The British soul is large enough to comprehend both.

What would I myself most like to see happen? I would like to see expectation confounded again – even though in this case it is my own – and Britain show the world the continuing richness and vitality of its culture and heritage, by finding a role for the image of the Druid that differs from any of the above.

Source Materials

Full publication details will be given for all books that have appeared after 1950; for those earlier, only the place and date at which they were published. To make it easier for readers to trace works in these endnotes, date and place, at the least, will be given anew for a book that is cited in more than one chapter.

Introduction

The books mentioned in the first paragraph were, in order of citation, Stuart Piggott, *The Druids* (London: Thames and Hudson, 1968); Anne Ross, *Druids* (Stroud: Tempus, 1999); Miranda J. Green (now Aldhouse-Green), *Exploring the World of the Druids* (London: Thames and Hudson, 1997); Nora Chadwick, *The Druids* (Cardiff: University of Wales Press, 1966), Ward Rutherford, *The Druids and their Heritage* (London: Gordon and Cremonesi, 1978); Peter Berresford Ellis, *The Druids* (London: Constable, 1994); and John Matthews, *Secrets of the Druids* (New York: Black Dog, 2002). A. L. Owens's book was *The Famous Druids: A Survey of Three Centuries of English Literature* (Oxford: Oxford University Press, 1962).

Chapter One: The Patriotic Druids

The passages of Tacitus that mention Druids are in his *Annals*, xiv. 28–30, and his *Histories*, iv. 54. The former contains the famous passage on Anglesey. The recent analyses of his treatment of British events are E. W. Black, 'The First-Century Historians of Roman Britain', *Oxford Archaeological Journal*, 20 (2001), 415–28, and David Braund, *Ruling Roman Britain* (London: Routledge, 1996), pp. 118–76. For a representative recent overview of his techniques, see Holly Haynes, *The History of Make-Believe* (Berkeley: University of California Press, 2003). The gulf that now seems to exist on this matter between classicists and archaeologists is well illustrated by Guy de la Bédoyère, *Gods with Thunderbolts* (Stroud: Tempus, 2002), p. 61. It shows how great the lag of communication between disciplines has become that even a well-informed, sensitive and justly popular expert in Romano-British archaeology, such as de la Bédoyère, should be completely unaware of the problems associated with treating Tacitus like a modern historian.

The Renaissance German and French love affair with Druids is examined in Noel L. Brann, 'Conrad Celtis and the "Druid" Abbot Trithemius', *Renaissance and Reformation*, new series, 3 (1979), pp. 16–28; Frank L. Borchardt, *German Antiquity in Renaissance Myth* (Baltimore: Johns Hopkins University Press, 1971); R. E. Asher, *Nationalist Myths in Renaissance France* (Edinburgh: Edinburgh University Press, 1993); and D. P. Walker, 'The "Prisca Theologia" in France', *Journal of the Warburg and Courtauld Institutes*, 17 (1954), pp. 204–59. Classic French texts include Jean Picard, *Le Prisca Celtopedia* (Paris, 1556); Noël Taillepied, *Histoire de l'Estat et République des Druides* (Paris, 1585); and Sebastian Rouillard, *Parthenie* (Paris, 1609).

The edition of Hector Boece's *Chronicles* that I have used is the Scots one, edited by R. W. Chambers and Edith Batho for the Scottish Text Society in 1936. Spottiswoode's book is his *History of the Church of Scotland* (London, 1656). The Welsh historiography cited is Humphrey Llwyd, *The Historie of Cambria* (London, 1584) (quotation about Druids on p. 7) and *Cronica Walliae* (edited by Ieuan M. Williams, Cardiff University Press, 2002); Sir John Price, *Historiae Brytannicae defensio* (in British Library, Add. MS 14925); and Maurice Kiffin, *Deffyniad Ffydd Eglwys Loegr a Gyfieithwyd I'f Gymraeg* (edited by W. P. Williams, Bangor, 1908) p. xi. The letter from Henry Vaughan is in Bodleian Library, Aubrey MS 12, folio 240.

The classic work of Irish Counter-Reformation historiography is Geoffrey Keating, *The History of Ireland*, and his treatment of Druids is in the 1908 Irish Texts Society edition by Patrick Dineen. The full text of it is missing from earlier editions of the same work, which is why I am all the more grateful to Caitlín and John Matthews for drawing my attention to this one.

Polydore Vergil's *English History* was edited by Sir Henry Ellis for the Camden Society in 1846. Leland's *Commentarii de scriptoribus Britannicis* was eventually published in 1709. The relevant work by Bale is *The Actes of Englysh Votaryes* (2nd edition, London, 1550). I have used the 1807 London reprint of the 2nd, 1586, edition of Ralph Holinshed's *Chronicles*. For Camden I faced a tougher problem as there are many editions and they are very different from each other, so I drew on a sample of six, from the original Latin one of 1586 to the English translation of 1610. Coke's comments are in the preface of *Le Tierce Part des Reports* (London, 1602), a reference which I owe to Benjamin Carter. Selden's are scattered between his annotations to the poem 'Poly-Olbion', in *The Works of Michael Drayton*, iv edited by J. William Hebel (Oxford, 1933); *Jani Anglorum Facies Altera* (London, 1610); and Nathaniel Bacon, *An Historical and Political Discourse of the Laws and Government of England* (London, 1689).

Henry Fletcher's *Bonduca* (sic) is in volume 4 of *The Dramatic Works in the Beaumont and Fletcher Canon*, edited by Fredson Bowers for Cambridge University Press in 1970. Carew's masque is in the edition of his poems by Rhodes Dunlap, published by Oxford University Press in 1949. Elias Ashmole's cryptic line is in his *Theatrum Chemicum Britannicum* (London, 1652), on sig. A3, while Diaper's poem is *Dryades* (London, 1713).

Lhuyd's preliminary work is in the Henry Gibson edition of Camden's *Britannia*, published in 1695; the nearest thing to a biography of him is Frank Emery, *Edward Lhuyd* (Cardiff: University of Wales Press, 1971), though Glyn Daniel published a neat appreciation of his contribution to our understanding of antiquity in the *Welsh History Review*, 3 (1967), pp. 346–8. Rowlands published *Mona Antiqua Restaurata* in Dublin in 1723, and Martin *A Description of the Western Isles of Scotland* in London in 1703. John Toland's characteristically inconsistent and opportunistic views of Druids were published in his *Pantheisticon* (London, 1720) and (much more extensively) in the posthumous edition of his works by P. Desmaiseaux, *A Collection of Several Pieces of Mr John Toland* (London, 1726).

Thomson's 'Liberty' may be found in any anthology of his work: the Druids are in book IV, lines 626–33. Stukeley's two great books were *Stonehenge* (London, 1740), and *Abury* (London, 1743). The only biography of him is still Stuart Piggott's *William Stukeley* (London: Thames and Hudson, 1950; 2nd edition, 1985), but its conclusions concerning Stukeley's ideas have been overturned by David Boyd Haycock, *William Stukeley* (Woodbridge: Boydell, 2002). *The Modern Druids* was written by James Wheeler and published at London. Pope's notes for *Brutus* are in British Library, Egerton MS 1950, folios 4–5v, and the Druidical verse of Collins's 'Ode to Liberty' is in lines 109–12.

Linda Colley's book is *Britons: Forging the Nation, 1707–1837* (New Haven: Yale University Press, 1992). Macpherson's were *Fragments of Ancient Poetry* (London, 1760); *Fingal* (London, 1760); and *Temora* (London, 1763). The controversy over them was resolved largely by D. S. Thomson, *The Gaelic Sources of Macpherson's 'Ossian'* (Edinburgh: Oliver and Boyd, 1952). A good recent survey of Macpherson's life and work is Fiona J., Stafford, *The Sublime Savage: A Study of James Macpherson and the Poems of Ossian* (Edinburgh: Edinburgh University Press, 1988). Gray's contribution is analysed in Edward D. Snyder, 'Thomas Gray's Interest in Celtic', *Modern Philology*, 11 (1913), pp. 559–61; and *The Celtic Revival in English Literature* (Cambridge, Massachusetts: Harvard University Press, 1923); and in Sam Smiles, *The Image of Antiquity: Ancient Britain and the Antiquarian Imagination* (New Haven: Yale University Press, 1994), pp. 48–61. Snyder also chronicles the success and influence of Mason's 'Caractacus'; other material on Mason is added here from his entry in the *New Dictionary of National Biography*. Cowper's 'Boadicea' is in H. S. Mitford's edition of his poetical works, published by Oxford University Press in many reprintings, of which I used that of 1967; where the poem can be found on pp. 310–11. William Sotheby's poem is *The Cambrian Hero* (London, n.d. but *c*.1800).

The Scottish cultural revival, including the element of myth-making and forgery, is summed up by Hugh Trevor-Roper, 'The Invention of Tradition: The Highland Tradition of Scotland', in Eric Hobsbawm and Terence Ranger (ed.), *The Invention*

of Tradition (Cambridge: Cambridge University Press, 1983), pp. 21–40, and again in
Ronald Hutton, *Witches, Druids and King Arthur* (London: Hambledon and London,
2003), pp. 2–5. That of modern Wales has been charted by Prys Morgan, *A New History
of Wales: The Eighteenth-Century Renaissance* (Llandybie: Christopher Davies, 1981),
and Geraint Jenkins, *The Foundations of Modern Wales 1642–1780* (Oxford: Oxford
University Press, 1987). Iolo still awaits a full and detailed scholarly biography in
English. For the time being we have Prys Morgan, *Iolo Morganwg* (Cardiff: University of
Wales Press, 1975) (verdict on Iolo on p. 91); Ceri W. Lewis, 'The Literary Tradition of
Morganwg down to the Middle of the Sixteenth Century', in T. B. Pugh (ed.), *Glamorgan
County History*, iii (Cardiff: University of Wales Press, 1971), pp. 449–54 (verdict on
Iolo on pp. 450–1), and 'The Literary History of Glamorgan from 1530 to 1770', in
Glanmor Williams (ed.), *Glamorgan County History*, iv (Cardiff: University of Wales
Press, 1974), pp. 535–641; Elijah Waring, *Recollections and Anecdotes of Edward Williams*
(London, 1850); Gwyneth Lewis, 'Eighteenth-Century Forgeries with Special Reference
to the Work of Iolo Morganwg' (Oxford University D.Phil. thesis, 1991); Mary-Ann
Constantine, 'Pious Frauds and Perjurers: Iolo Morganwg's Truth Against the World',
in Peter Knight and Jonathan Long (eds), *Fakes and Forgeries* (Cambridge: Scholars
Press, 2004), pp. 119–34 (verdict on Iolo on p.133; I am very grateful to the author for
an offprint); and Geraint H. Jenkins, *Facts, Fantasy and Fiction: The Historical Vision
of Iolo Morganwg* (Aberystwyth: University of Wales Centre for Advanced Welsh and
Celtic Studies, 1997) (verdict on Iolo on p. 16). Geraint Jenkins is currently leading a
team at the centre that published this last book, which includes Mary-Ann Constantine,
to study Iolo and his work. Its findings should make a quantum leap in knowledge
of the subject. The Madoc episode is recounted in Morgan, *The Eighteenth-Century
Renaissance*, with the verdicts on Iolo on pp. 114 and 134. His position as a Glamorgan
bard is examined in the two essays by Ceri Lewis, while Rachel Bromwich's study of his
triads is *'Trioedd Ynys Prydain' in Welsh Literature and Scholarship* (Cardiff: University
of Wales Press, 1969).

Iolo's early 'Drudic' material can be found in William Owen, *The Heroic Elegies and
Other Pieces of Llywarch Hen* (London, 1792), and Edward Williams, *Poems, Lyric and
Pastoral, in Two Volumes* (London, 1794). His later published forgeries appear in Owen
Jones, Edward Williams and William Owen Pughe (eds), *The Myrvyrian Archaiology of
Wales* (London, 1801–7, 3 volumes). His papers survive in the National Library of Wales,
MSS 13061–80, the letter to Owen being in MS 13221E, folios 99–106. The subsequent
publications of them are Taliesin Williams (ed.), *Cyfrenach Y Beirdd* (1829), *Coelbren Y
Beirdd* (1840), and *Iolo Manuscripts* (1848), and J. Williams ab Ithel, *Barddas* (1862–65,
2 volumes). Geraint Jenkins's point about opium is on p. 9 of Jenkins, *Facts, Fantasy and
Fiction*. The metaphor of pollution is found in Morgan, *Iolo Morganwg*, p. 66; Stuart
Piggott, *The Druids* (London: Thames and Hudson, 1968), p. 169; and Geraint Jenkins,

'*Perish Kings and Emperors, but let the Bard of Liberty live*' (Aberystwyth: Centre for Advanced Welsh and Celtic Studies, 2006), p. 4. I am grateful to Mary-Ann Constantine for giving me the last work.

Studies of the critical reception of Iolo can be found in Morgan, *The Eighteenth-Century Renaissance*, pp. 115–16, and various sections of his *Iolo Morganwg*; Iorwerth C. Peate, 'The Gorsedd of the Bards of Britain', *Antiquity*, 35 (1951), pp. 13–15; Bromwich, '*Trioedd Ynys Prydain*', pp. 34–41; Jenkins, '*Perish Kings and Emperors*'; and Constantine, 'Pious Frauds and Forgeries', p. 131. The three classic works of Griffith John Williams were *Iolo Morganwg a Chywyddau'r Ychwanegiad* (London, 1926), *Traddadiad Llenyddol Morganwg* (Cardiff, 1948) and *Iolo Morganwg: Y Gyfol Gyntaf* (Cardiff, 1956). For a published example of modern Druid rumours, see Ross Nichols, *The Book of Druidry*, edited by John Matthews and Philip Carr-Gomm (London: Aquarian, 1990), pp. 272–73. I have myself worked through the catalogue of Iolo's papers in the National Library, which identifies the nature of each, and read those parts – the great majority – which are in English, actually his first language. My knowledge of the Welsh portions is based on conversations with Geraint Jenkins and his team in the Centre for Advanced Welsh and Celtic Studies next door, who have entertained and advised me splendidly.

The key articles on Druids by John Williams ab Ithel are in his *Cambrian Journal* for the years 1855–61, while the same periodical has a biography of him by James Kenward published in instalments under the years 1862–64.

Iolo's famous description of the 1792 *gorsedd* is in the *Gentleman's Magazine* 62 (1792), pp. 956–57. The two great classic studies of the National Eisteddfod and the *gorsedd* ceremony, respectively, are both by Dillwyn Miles: *The Royal National Eisteddfod of Wales* (Swansea: Christopher Davies, 1978), and *The Secret of the Bards of the Isle of Britain* (Llandybie: Gwasg Dinefwr Press, 1992). I have added material from Prys Morgan, 'Archbishops and Archdruids', *The Historian*, 76 (2002), pp. 28–32 (I am grateful to my colleague William Doyle for lending me a copy of this), and Beriah Gwynfe Evans, *The Bardic Gorsedd: Its History and Symbolism* (Pontypool, 1923). The relevant works by Southey and Peacock are, respectively, *Madoc* (Edinburgh, 1805), part 1, pp. 108–16, and *The Misfortunes of Elphin* (London, 1829). The campaigner for home rule was 'Griffith', *The Welsh Question and Druidism* (London, 1887).

Recent general works on the problems of nineteenth-century British national identities, of special relevance to this question, include Hugh A. MacDougall, *Racial Myth in English History* (Montreal: Harvest House, 1982); Norman Vance, *The Victorians and Ancient Rome* (Oxford Blackwell, 1997); Richard Hingley, *Roman Officers and English Gentlemen* (London: Routledge, 2000); and Krishan Kumar, *The Making of English National Identity* (Cambridge: Cambridge University Press, 2003), pp. 175–225.

Hemans's 'Druid Chorus' is in her *Poetical* Works (Oxford, 1914), p. 165. Peacock's

'The Genius of the Thames' is in the sixth volume of the 1927 London edition of his collected works, with the Druid on pp. 123–29. Tennyson's 'The Druid's Prophecies' is on pp. 116–20 of the first volume of Christopher Ricks's edition of his poems (London: Longman, 1987). Hankinson's poem was published as *The Druids* at Cambridge in 1827, and again as 'The Druid's Lament' in his collected *Poems* (London, 1844); quotation on p. 327. The English version of Romani's libretto for *Norma* was published in London in 1841, and its British performance history discussed by Sam Smiles in *The Image of Antiquity*, pp. 108–9. Sarah Hamilton's poem was published (anonymously) as *The Druid and Holy King* (Leamington Spa, 1838) – quotation from p. 12 – and Esther Le Hardy's as *Agabus* (London, 1851); quotation from p. 124. Gilbert's opera was published in London in 1869; the quotation is from p. 28. The quotation from H. T. Mackenzie Bell is in 'Meadow Musings', published in *Old Year Leaves* (London, 1883), and that from Hughes in *The Scouring of the White Horse* (Cambridge, 1859) on p. 44 of the 1889 edition.

The quotations from *Under Milk Wood* are in the edition by Daniel Jones (London, 1954), on pp. 20–22. The Terry Pratchett novel richest in references to Llamedos is *Soul Music* (London: Victor Gollancz, 1994).

Chapter Two: The Wise Druids

The classical texts concerning Druids are translated into English in J. T. Koch (ed.), *The Celtic Heroic Age* (Andover, Massachesetts: Celtic Studies Publications, 1997), between pp. 13 and 31. Most were also translated, with a commentary, in T. D. Kendrick, *The Druids* (London, 1927), pp. 75–97, with the original Greek and Latin at pp. 212–21. Other comments on them are found in Hugo Last, 'Rome and the Druids', *Journal of Roman Studies*, 39 (1949), pp. 1–5; J. J. Tierney, 'The Celtic Ethnography of Poseidonios', *Proceedings of the Royal Irish Academy*, 60 (1959–60), pp. 189–275; A L. Owen, *The Famous Druids* (Oxford: Oxford University Press, 1962), p. 16; Nora Chadwick, *The Druids* (Cardiff: University of Wales Press, 1966), p. 35; Stuart Piggott, *The Druids* (London: Thames and Hudson, 1968), pp. 92–111; Daphne Nash, 'Reconstructing Posidonius's Celtic Ethnography', *Britannia*, 7 (1976), pp. 112–36; J. F. Drinkwater, *Roman Gaul* (London: Croom Helm, 1983), pp. 38–9; Miranda Green, *The Gods of the Celts* (Gloucester: Sutton, 1986), p. 14; Graham Webster, *The British Celts and their Gods under Rome* (London: Batsford, 1986), p. 26; J. F. Drinkwater, 'For Better or Worse? Towards an Assessment of the Economic and Social Consequences of the Roman Conquest of Gaul', in Thomas Blagg and Martin Millett, *The Early Roman Empire in the West* (Oxford: Oxbow, 1990), pp. 210–19; Peter Berresford Ellis, *The Druids* (London: Constable, 1994), pp. 50–69; Jane Webster, 'The Just War: Graeco-Roman Texts as Colonial Discourse', in *TRAC 94: Proceedings of the Fourth Annual Theoretical Roman Archaeology Conference* (Oxford: Oxbow, 1994), pp. 6–7; David Rankine, 'The Celts through Classical Eyes', in Miranda J. Green (ed.), *The Celtic World* (London: Routledge, 1995), p. 29; Sean B. Dunham, 'Caesar's Perception of Gallic Social Structure', in Bettina Arnold and D. Blair Gibson (eds.), *Celtic Chiefdom, Celtic State* (Cambridge: Cambridge University Press, 1995), pp. 114–15; Jane Webster, 'At the End of the World', *Britannia*, 30 (1999), p. 8–11; and Bernhard Maier, *The Celts* (Edinburgh: Edinburgh University Press, 2003), pp. 65–66.

The number of relevant Irish texts, scattered among many different editions, is far too large to list here, though I would like to record my gratitude to Christina Harrington for having, long ago, given me a list of the most important. An analysis of them will be work for my succeeding book. The revisionist scholarship is well summarised in Kim McCone, *Pagan Past and Christian Present* (Maynooth: An Sagart, 1990); and J. P. Mallory (ed.), *Aspects of the Tain* (Belfast: Universities Press, 1992). Recent examples of a more conservative attitude are John Minahane, *The Christian Druids* (Dublin: Sanas, 1993); Dáithi Ó hÓgáin, *The Sacred Isle: Belief and Religion in Pre-Christian Ireland* (Woodbridge: Boydell, 1999), p. 72; and Christian-J. Guyonvarc'h, *The Making of a Druid* (Rochester, Vermont: Inner Traditions, 2002). The trouble with the latter group of works is that none of them actually engage with the points made by the revisionists; they prefer instead to ignore the latter and proceed as if they had never written.

I have used the translation of Conrad Celtis's account of the statues in John Selden, *The Reverse or Back Face of the English Janus*, in Redman Westcot (ed.), *Tracts Written by John Selden* (London, 1683), pp. 13–18. Camden's thoughts on Druids are at their most devleoped in the Philemon Holland translation of his *Britannia* (London, 1610), pp. 4–14, 68, 149. The original passage from Origen is in Marcel Borrett's edition of his *Homiliae in Ezechielem* (Paris: Editions du Cerf, 1989), no. 4, ch. 1, lines 154–56. The initial Scottish linkage of stone circles to Druids is chronicled in Owen, *The Famous Druids*, pp. 30–31. Caius's reference is in *De antiquitate Cantabrigiensis academiae* (London, 1568), p. 18, and Milton's in *The Doctrine and Discipline of Divorce* (2nd edition, London, 1644), sig A4, and *Areopagitica*, edited by Ernest Sirluck in *Complete Prose Works of John Milton*, ii (New Haven: Yales University Press, 1959), pp. 551–52.

Edmund Dickinson's book was *Delphi Phoenicizantes* (Oxford, 1655), and the classic follow-up texts are Thomas Smith, *Syntagma de Druidism Moribus* (Oxford, 1664) and Theophilus Gale, *The Court of the Gentiles: Part Two* (Oxford, 1671). Gale was also an admirer of Bochart's *Geographica Sacra* (Paris, 1646). Aylett Sammes's book was *Britainnia Antiqua Illustrata* (London, 1676).

John Aubrey's letters and papers survive in the several volumes of the Bodleian Library's Aubrey Manuscripts at Oxford. His unpublished work on ancient monuments is, however, in the same library's MSS Gen.Top.c.24–5, and important letters written by him are in its Wood MS F39. The best biography of his is probably still Anthony Powell, *John Aubrey and His Friends* (London, 1948), but his intellectual life is better analysed by Michael Hunter, *John Aubrey and the Realm of Learning* (London: Duckworth, 1975). The tale of Gibson's revision of Camden's *Britannia* was told by Stuart Piggott in the *Proceedings of the British Academy*, 37 (1951), pp. 199–217, and again by Graham Parry, in *The Trophies of Time: English Antiquarians of the Seventeenth Century* (Oxford: Oxford University Press, 1995), and is chronicled in the Aubrey and Tanner Manuscripts of the Bodleian Library. Toland's letters on Druids are in the posthumous edition of his works by P. Desmaiseaux, *A Collection of Several Pieces of Mr John Toland* (London, 1726).

William Stukeley's main published work was cited in the notes to the previous chapter. His papers are scattered between the Oxford's Bodleian Library, and the libraries of Freemasons' Hall, the Society of Antiquaries, and the Wellcome Trust in London, and of the Wiltshire Archaeological and Natural History Society at Devizes. The first of those is most important for his fieldwork, and the second for his religious ideas, while the last contains the notebook into which he entered sections of Aubrey's manuscript. The development of John Wood's thought can be traced in his first book, *The Origin of Building* (Bath, 1741) and the two earlier manuscript versions of it held in Sir John Soane's Museum, London, and Bath Central Library, taken together with his letters in British Library, Harleian MSS 7354–55. His later books were *An Essay Towards a Description of Bath* (two parts, 1743 and 1744) and *Choir Gaure* (London, 1747). His career and the symbolism of the Circus are studied in Timothy Mowl and Brian Earnshaw, *John Wood: Architect of Obsession* (Huddersfield: Amadeus, 1988). The development of Borlase's career as an antiquarian is documented in P. A. S. Pool, *William Borlase* (Truro: Royal Institution of Cornwall, 1986), and his classic work is *Antiquities, Historical and Monumental, of the County of Cornwall* (Oxford, 1754).

The three successive verdicts on the Welsh bardic text were by Edward Davies, D. W. Nash and Sir John Morris Jones, and the debate was carried on in Nash's *Taliesin* (London, 1858), p. 257, and Jones's *Taliesin* (London, 1918; reprinted from *Y Cymmrodor*, 28, 1918). The published works of Iolo Morganwg were listed in the sources for the last chapter; I have added material here from National Library of Wales, MS 13144A. References to supportive scholarship may be found in the edition of his writings by John Williams, 'Ab Ithel', published as *Barddas*, while the Biblical references to megaliths are in the Books of Genesis, Exodus, Joshua, II Samuel and II Kings.

The initial attacks on the use of Welsh literature for the study of Druidry were made by Thomas Stephens, *The Literature of the Kymry* (Llandovery, 1849) and Nash's *Taliesin*. Williams's definitive edition was *Canu Taliesin* (Cardiff: University of Wales Press, 1960); his ideas are presaged in his *Lectures on Early Welsh Poetry* (Dublin, 1944). Recent revisionism is represented by G. R. Isaac, 'Gweith Gwen Ystrat and the Northern Heroic Age of the Sixth Century', *Cambrian Medieval Celtic Studies*, 36 (1998), pp. 61–70. It should be noted, however, that Marged Haycock's 'Taliesin's Questions', in

Cambrian Medieval Celtic Studies, 33 (1997), pp. 19–80, still suggests that traditional native learning makes up a portion of that displayed in the later poems, and might be Druidic in origin.

Key texts in the school that ascribed megalithic monuments to the post-Roman period were John Richman, 'On the Antiquity of Abury and Stonehenge', *Archaeologia*, 28 (1839), pp. 399–419; Algernon Herbert, *Cyclops Christianus* (London, 1849); Thomas Wright, 'Discussion on Stonehenge, Avebury', *Athenaeum*, 1 (1866), pp. 136, 172; James Fergusson, *Rude Stone Monuments in All Countries* (London, 1872); and W. M. Flinders Petrie, *Stonehenge* (London, 1880).

The key scholarly works in the Scottish section are John Stuart, *Sculptured Stones of Scotland* (2 volumes, Aberdeen, 1856 and 1867); Daniel Wilson, *Prehistoric Annals of Scotland* (London, 1863); James Rust, *Druidism Exhumed* (Edinburgh, 1871), especially p. vi; Sir James Y. Simpson, *Archaeological Essays* (Edinburgh, 1872), especially volume 1, p. 37; and Joseph Anderson, *Scotland in Pagan Times: The Bronze and Stone Ages* (Edinburgh, 1886), especially pp. 134–38, 267. William Sharp's work was collected in his *Poems and Dramas* (London, 1910); for Druids, see 'St Christopher of the Gael', 'A Record (A Fragment)', 'Euphrenia', and 'Two Old Yews'.

The general background to the changes in the European view of ancient humanity can be found in Glyn Daniel, *A Short History of Archaeology* (London: Thames and Hudson, 1981), supplemented in the British case by Peter J. Bowler, *The Invention of Progress* (Oxford: Blackwell, 1989). Nilsson's lecture was published as 'Stonehenge', *Transactions of the Ethonological Society*, new series 4 (1866), pp. 244–63, and his book as *Primitive Scandinavia* (3rd edition, London, 1868). Lubbock's comment is found in a review he wrote of Fergusson's *Rude Stone Monuments* in *Nature*, 5 (1872), p. 386. Boyd Dawkins's survey was *Early Man in Britain* (London, 1880), and Clodd's views on the Bronze Age were displayed in an article on Stonehenge in the *Daily Chronicle* on 28 August 1899. The report of the British Association was published as Sir C. Hercules Read et al., *The Age of Stone Circles* (London, 1915). The remark about the antipathy of archaeologists towards Druids by A. L. Lewis was published in 'Stone Circles of Britain', *Archaeological Journal*, 49 (1892), p. 136, as part of an article spanning pp. 136–54. The diatribe that follows it is from H. N. Hutchinson, *Prehistoric Man and Beast* (London, 1896), pp. 243 and 266.

Arthur Evans's suggestion is in 'Stonehenge', *Archaeological Review*, 2.5 (1889), pp. 312–30. Also see John Rhys, *Celtic Britain* (London, 1904), pp. 67–75, and George Lawrence Gomme, *The Village Community* (London, 1890), pp. 103–4. Lubbock's comment is taken from *Pre-Historic Times*, p. 583, and Lysons's book was published at Oxford in 1865. An outline of the background to the cultural changes discussed is provided by Bowler, *The Invention of Progress*, and George Stocking, *Victorian Anthropology* (New York: Free Press, 1987).

The book by the vicar of Glastonbury was Lionel Smithett Lewis, *St Joseph of Arimathea at Glastonbury*, published in London by James Clarke. Sir Norman Lockyer's publications were, successively, 'An Attempt to Ascertain the Date of the Original Construction of Stonehenge from its Orientation', *Nature*, 65 (November, 1901), pp. 55–57; *Stonehenge and Other British Stone Monuments Astronomically Considered* (London, 1906); and *The Antiquity of the Gorsedd* (Swansea, 1907).

The quotations from Atkinson's *Stonehenge* (London: Hamish Hamilton, 1956), are on pp. 77–78, 91 and 179–80. The information that follows is in Kendrick, *The Druids*, pp. 146–56; George Engleheart, *Iron or Bronze* (Devizes, 1933); R. H. Cunnington, *Stonehenge and its Date* (London, 1935); Stuart Piggott, 'The Sources of Geoffrey of Monmouth', *Antiquity*, 15 (1941), pp. 305–19; C. F. C. Hawkes, 'Prehistory and the Gaulish Peoples', in J. M. Wallace-Hadrill and John McManners (eds.), *France: Government and Society* (London: Methuen, 1957), pp. 7–16 (quotation on p. 15); and Glyn Daniel, *Megaliths in History* (London: Thames and Hudson, 1977), pp. 37–38 and 59.

The 'definitive' study of Stonehenge's construction is Rosamund M. J. Cleal, K. E. Walker and R. Montague, *Stonehenge in its Landscape*, published by English Heritage in London. Richard Bradley published his work as 'From Ritual to Romance: Ceremonial Centres and Hill Forts', in Graeme Guilbert (ed.), *Hill-Fort Studies* (Leicester: Leicester University Press, 1981), pp. 20–27. For a general survey of the apparent fracture of belief in late prehistory, see Ronald Hutton, *The Pagan Religions of the Ancient British Isles* (Oxford: Blackwell, 1991), pp. 135–38. This book is now fifteen years out of date, in a field in which important developments occur every year, but no other has yet appeared to replace it.

John Michell's *The View of Atlantis* was published in London by Sago Press in 1969; his views on Druids are on pp. 25, 31–34, 161–84. Paul Screeton's comments are in *Quicksilver Heritage* (Wellingborough: Thorsons, 1974), pp. 195–97. Classic statements of the Goddess-centred view of the Neolithic can be found in the last books of the movement's favourite archaeologist: Marija Gimbutas, *The Language of the Goddess* (London: Thames and Hudson, 1989), and *The Civilisation of the Goddess* (San Francisco: Harper Row, 1991). For a critical view of it, see Cynthia Eller, *The Myth of Matriarchal Prehistory* (Boston: Beacon, 2000); for a contextual one, Ronald Hutton, *The Triumph of the Moon: A History of Modern Pagan Witchcraft* (Oxford: Oxford University Press, 1999), pp. 32–42 and 340–68.

Works of 'alternative archaeology' with a starring part for Druids have mostly been on the scale of the article by Meiwana, 'Jesus and the Druids', in the famous hippy magazine *Gandalf's Garden*, 4 (1969), pp. 14–15. It describes how the authoress had a vision of Christ at Glastonbury's Chalice Well, in which he revealed that he had been initiated into the highest order of Druids, which had come from Atlantis. There was, however, one wonderfully idiosyncratic book by a minister of the Church of Scotland,

Gordon Strachan's *Jesus the Master Builder* (Edinburgh: Floris, 1998). He began with the claim that the same mystical system of numbers underlies the Lady Chapel at Glastonbury, Stonehenge, the Great Pyramid, the Book of Genesis, the constellation of the Great Bear and the name of Jesus Christ. This he linked to megalithic monuments and the Druids as part of a system of ancient wisdom found from Ireland to India, of which Jesus was the incarnate god.

The comments on the Coligny calendar are from Garrett Olmstead, *The Gaulish Calendar* (Bonn: Habelt, 1992)(quotations from p. xi); Stephen C. McCluskey, *Astronomies and Cultures in Early Medieval Europe* (Cambridge: Cambridge University Press, 1998), pp. 54–60 (quotation on pp. 58–59); and Jean Louis Brunaux, *The Celtic Gauls* (London: Seaby, 1988), p. 46. Professor Olmstead has now published *A Definitive Restored Text of the Coligny Calendar* (Washington, DC: Institute for the Study of Man, 2001); but it may be feared that the term 'definitive' will prove difficult to substantiate.

Chapter Three: The Green Druids

The Greek and Roman sources, and commentaries on them, are dealt with at the opening of the references for the previous chapter. Likewise the citations of the works by Thomson, Pope, Collins and Mason all come later in those references, save for Collins's elegy on Thomson, which was studied for this context by J. M. S. Tompkins, 'In Yonder Grave a Druid Lies', *Review of English Studies*, 22 (1946), pp. 1–16. The lines from 'Caractacus' are on p. 14 of the 1777 York edition. The tributes to Mason are William Gilbert, *The Hurricane* (London, 1796), pp. 43–44; and Thomas Gisborne, *Elegy to the Memory of the Rev. William Mason* (London, 1797).

The Warton quotations are from *The Poetical Works of Thomas Warton* (London, 1805), p. 39; Joseph Warton, *Odes on Various Subjects*, edited by Richard Wendorf (Los Angeles: University of California Press, 1979), p. 39; and Joseph Warton, *An Essay on the Writings and Genius of Pope* (London, 1756), p. 7.

The admirers of Goldsmith were William Waity and John Tait, in 'The Druids' Monument', quoted in A. L. Owen, *The Famous Druids* (Oxford: Oxford University Press, 1962), p. 178. The following references are to *Stone Henge: A Poem Inscribed to Edward Jerningham, Esq* (London, 1792); Thomas Maurice, *Netherby: A Poem* (Oxford, 1796), pp. 5–10. Hawkstone's Druid is advertised in Richard Warner, *A Tour Through the Northern Counties of England and the Borders of Scotland* (Bath, 1802), ii, p. 178. Richard Polwhele's poem is in his collection *The Fate of Llewellyn* (Bath, 1777), pp. 53–54.

Hoxie Neale Fairchild's classic book is *The Noble Savage* (New York, 1928); quotation on p. 119. For further background on some of the general themes considered as context to this chapter, see Marilyn Butler, 'Romanticism in England', in Roy Porter and Mikuláš Teich (eds), *Romanticism in National Context* (Cambridge: Cambridge University Press,

1988), chapter 2. Byron's lines are from 'Don Juan', canto XI, stanza xxv, and Keats's from 'Hyperion', book II, part 1.31.

Quillinan's 'Hymn to Nature' was published in his *Woodcuts and Verses* (London, 1820), p. 24. Christopher Wordsworth's 'The Druids' was printed as a pamphlet in London in 1827. Roscoe's 'Lines Written in the Woods of Rydal Hall, Westmorland', appeared in his *Poems* (London, 1834), p. 74. The succeeding run of quotations is taken from Esther Le Hardy, *Agabus* (London, 1851), pp. 24–28; John Eliot Howard, *The Druids and Their Religion* (London, 1880), pp. 31, 40–42; C. Blencowe Dunn, *The Modern Druid* (London, 1857), pp. 8, 22; Hardwicke Drummond Rawnsley, 'The Druid Stone near Millbeck', in his *Sonnets around the Coast* (London, 1887), p. 88; Robert Leighton, 'Records XIX', in his *Poems* (London, 1869), p. 89 (and see also pp. 11 and 87); and Henry Septimus Sutton, 'On a Boulder', in his *Poems* (London, 1886), p. 52.

The concept of the Druids as the origins of fairy beliefs began with James Cririe, *Scottish Scenery* (London, 1803), pp. 347–48, and was continued in Patrick Graham, *Sketches Descriptive of Picturesque Scenery in the Southern Confines of Perthshire* (London, 1806), pp. 260–62; Alfred Maury, *Les Fées du Moyen-Age* (Paris, 1843); W. Y. Evans-Wentz, *The Fairy Faith in Celtic Countries* (Rennes, 1909); and David MacRitchie, 'Druids and Mound-Dwellers', *Celtic Review* (January 1910), pp. 1–16.

The works cited after that are Walter Chalmers Smith, 'Hilda among the Broken Gods', in his *Poetical Works* (London, 1902), p. 201; Susan L. Mitchell, 'Love's Druids', in her *Frankincense and Myrrh* (Cuala Press, 1912), n.p.; Rutland Boughton, *The Immortal Hour* (London, 1920), pp. 112–14; and Alvin Langdon Coburn, *Fairy Gold* (London, 1939); quotation on p. 7.

Chapter Four: The Demonic Druids

The sources for the classical authors quoted here, and for discussions of them, are basically the same as those cited at the opening of the notes to Chaper two. I have added material from Lucan's *Pharsalia*, 3.5.399; and Pliny, *Historia naturalis*, xxii. 2. Charles Plummer's comment is on p. clviii of his edition of *Vitae Sanctorum Hiberniae* (Oxford, 1910); see also his *Lives of the Irish Saints* (Oxford, 1922). Other Irish material is from A. B. E. Hood (ed.), *St Patrick: His Writings and Muirchú's Life* (London: Phillimore, 1978). For a consideration of the biblical background to much early Irish literature, see Kim McCone, *Pagan Past and Christian Present in Early Irish Literature* (Maynooth: An Sagart, 1990), especially pp. 33–34.

The passage about the sacrifices at Maigh Slecht is, perhaps significantly, missing from recent scholarly studies of pagan Irish religion, but was given great prominence in earlier, less rigorous, works, such as Charles Squire, *Mythology of the British Islands* (London, 1905), pp. 37–39; P. W. Joyce, *A Social History of Ancient Ireland* (Dublin, 1910), volume 1, pp. 275–76; and Lewis Spence, *The Magic Arts in Celtic Britain* (London,

1945), p. 52. The original references to the idols can be found in Whitley Stokes (ed.), *The Tripartite Life of Patrick* (London: Rolls Series, 1887), pp. 90–93; and Edward Gwynn (ed.), *The Metrical Dindshenchas. Part Four* (Dublin, 1924), pp. 19–23.

John Bale's text was *The Actes of Englysh Votaryes*, of which I have used the second edition, published in London in 1550; the Druids are on folios 12–14. I have used the 1807 reprint of the second, London 1586, edition of Holinshed's *Chronicles*: the Druids feature on pp. 33–41, 63–65, 430 and 494 of volume 1, and p. 52 of volume 5. Further quotations are from Thomas Nashe, *The Terrors of the Night* (London, 1594), sig. B4; and *The Witches of Northamptonshire* (London, 1612), sig. A3. I owe the latter reference to my pupil Madeleine Harwood.

Toland's views on rocking stones are in *A Collection of Several Pieces of Mr John Toland*, edited by P. Desmaiseaux (London, 1726), i, pp. 105–7. Those of Borlase are in *Antiquities, Historical and Monumental, of the County of Cornwall* (Oxford, 1754), pp. 19–167. The following references are to David Hume, *The History of England*, i (Oxford reprint, 1826), p. 4; Joseph Strutt, *The Chronicle of England* (London, 1779), i, pp. 189–200 (quotation on p. 190); Thomas Chatterton, 'Elegy Written at Stanton Drew', in Donald S. Taylor, *The Complete Works of Thomas Chatterton* (Oxford: Oxford University Press, 1971), volume 1, pp. 379–80; Michael Wodhull, 'Ode to the Dryads', in his *Poems* (London, 1772), n.p.; and William Wordsworth, 'The Vale of Esthwaite', lines 25–34.

What follows is from Edward King, *Munimenta Antiqua* (London, 1799), pp. 208–9 – it was Leslie Grinsell, in *The Druids and Stonehenge* (Guernsey: Toucan, 1978), p. 11, who first noticed his naming of the Slaughter Stone; Mary Russell Mitford, *Christina, the Maid of the South Seas* (London, 1811), p. 86; Stephen Prentis, *Tintern and Stonehenge* (London, 1843), pp. 33–34; George Newby, *Henllywarc: or, The Druid's Temple* (London, 1854), p. 13. The murals at the Houses of Parliament are described in T. R. S. Boase, 'The Decoration of the New Palace of Westminster, 1841–1863', *Journal of the Warburg and Courtauld Institutes*, 17 (1954), p. 341. John Harris's reference to *sati* is in *Luda: A Lay of the Druids* (London, 1868), pp. 31–32. Thomas Dudley Fosbrooke published his *Encyclopedia of Antiquities* at London in 1825; the Druids are on pp. 768–89. Charles Squire's *Mythology of the British Islands* came out in London in 1905, with the Druids on pp. 34–41, and the quotation on p. 36.

The references following those are to Robert Southey, *The Book of the Church* (London, 1824), i, pp. 3–9; Henry Lingard, *A History of England* (London: 3rd edition, 1835), i, pp. 19–26; Charles Dickens, *A Child's History of England* (London, 1852), pp. 1–10; Thomas Kitson Cromwell, *The Druid, A Tragedy* (London, 1832); and *The Dramatic and Poetical Works of Joanna Bailey* (London, 1851), pp. 152–53.

The next section is from John Walker Ord, *Rural Sketches and Poems* (London, 1845), p. 181; John Stuart Blackie, 'Columba' in *A Song of Heroes* (London, 1890),

p. 81; Frederick Paas, *The Arch Druid: An Historical Poem* (Sidmouth, 1830), sig. C;
N. T. Carrington, 'The Druids', *The Amulet*, (1828), pp. 74–77; Agnes Strickland, *The
Druid's Retreat*, bound up with *Guthred: or The Widow's Slave* (London, 1876), p. 54;
T. F. Wilkinson, *Iduna, Queen of Kent* (London, 1846), p. 5; T. B. Lomax, *A Complete
History of the Druids* (Lichfield, 1810), p. 47; William Hurd, *A New and Universal
History of the Religious Rites, Ceremonies and Customs of the Whole World* (Newcastle-
upon-Tyne, 1811), pp. 35–37; Sandford Earle, *Eanthe: A Tale of the Druids, and Other
Poems* (Edinburgh, 1830), pp. 27–28 and 74; Thomas Miller, *History of the Anglo-Saxons*
(London, 1852), pp. 12–17; William Winwood Reade, *The Veil of Isis: or The Mysteries
of the Druids* (London, 1861) (quotations on pp. 101–4, 111–12 and 172); *The Ancient
Britons: A Tale of Primeval Life* (London, 1851), pp. 321–32; J. W. Willis Bund, *The
Celtic Church of Wales* (London, 1897), pp. 103–7; John Forbes Leslie, *The Early Races
of Scotland and their Monuments* (Edinburgh, 1866), pp. 62–68, 72, 93; and George
Lawrence Gomme, *Ethnology in Folklore* (London, 1892), pp. 58–62.

The interwar texts cited are A. Hadrian Allcroft, *The Circle and the Cross* (London,
1927), i, pp. 308–15; Beth Coombe Harris, *In The Grip of the Druids* (Stirling, 1937) (the
information about Sunday schools is in the 1999 Mayflower Christian Books reprint);
and T. B. Morris, *Druid's Ring* (London, 1938).

Henry Treece's trilogy of novels containing Druids were *The Dark Island* (London:
Gollancz, 1952), quotation on p. 65; *The Great Captains* (London: Bodley Head, 1956);
and *Red Queen, White Queen* (London: Bodley Head, 1958). Rosemary Sutcliff's relevant
1970s novels were *The Capricorn Bracelet* (Oxford: Oxford University Press, 1973); *Sun
Horse, Moon Horse* (London: Bodley Head, 1977); and *Song for a Dark Queen* (London:
Pelham, 1978). Edward Rutherford's *Sarum* was published by Century Hutchinson at
London in 1987. Guy N. Smith's story is *The Druid Connection* (Sevenoaks, Kent: NEL
Books, 1983) (quotations on dust jacket); I am grateful to Nick Freeman and Joanne
Pearson for presenting this book to me. Terry Pratchett's is *The Light Fantastic* (London:
Colin Smythe, 1986) (quotation on pp. 56–57).

The recent titles are as follows: Barbara Erskine, *On the Edge of Darkness* (London:
BCA, 1998); and Bernard Cornwell, *The Winter King* (1995), *Enemy of God* (1996),
and *Excalibur* (1997), all first published in London by Michael Joseph. Robert Hunt's
collection of Cornish folklore is *Popular Romances of the West of England* (1865, but my
copy is the 1990 Llanerch Press reprint of the 1916 edition), pp. 49–51. The collection of
Glamorgan stories is Viv Small, *Glamorgan Ghosts* (Small Book Co, n.d.), with Druids
on pp. 27–28. Simon Scarrow's novel is *When the Eagle Hunts* (London: Headline,
2002) (quotation from endnote). Guy de la Bédoyère's study is *Gods with Thunderbolts*
(Stroud: Tempus, 2002), pp. 45, 61.

The sources associated with Llyn Cerrig Bach are Sir Cyril Fox, *A Find of the Early
Iron Age from Llyn Cerrig Bach, Anglesey* (Cardiff, 1945) (quotations from pp. 52–53);

Charles Scott-Fox, *Cyril Fox: Archaeologist Extraordinary* (Oxford: Oxbow, 2002), pp. 11–12, 168–72; C. F. C. Hawkes, review of Fox's *A Find of the Iron Age, Antiquaries Journal*, 26 (1946), pp. 79–80; Jacquetta Hawkes, *Early Britain* (London, 1945), p. 36; and Francis Pryor, *English Heritage Book of Flag Fen* (London: Batsford, 1991); and *The Flag Fen Basin* (London: English Heritage, 2001).

The sources for Stuart Piggott are his works *The Druids* (London: Thames and Hudson, 1968), especially p. 93; *British Prehistory* (Oxford, 1949), p. 5, 52, 101, 195; *The Dawn of Civilization* (London: Sunday Times Books, 1962), p. 15; and *Ancient Europe* (Edinburgh: Edinburgh University Press, 1965), pp. 4–20, 257; Grahame Clark and Stuart Piggott, *Prehistoric Societies* (London: Hutchinson, 1965), p. 332; and Arthur O. Loveday and George Boas, *Primitivism and Related Ideas in Antiquity* (Baltimore, 1935), pp. 7–17. Stuart Piggott's archive, now kept by the Institute of Archaeology at Oxford University, includes two files of material relating to Druids which contain further important evidence of his attitude to the subject.

The sources used here for Lindow Man are I. M. Stead et al., *Lindow Man* (London: British Museum, 1986); Don Brothwell, *The Bog Man and the Archaeology of People* (London: British Museum, 1986); J. A. J. Gowlett et al., 'Radiocarbon Accelerator Dating of Lindow Man', *Antiquity*, 63 (1989), pp. 71–79; R. C. Turner and R. G. Scaife (eds), *Bog Bodies* (London: British Museum, 1995); Bryony Coles et al. (eds), *Bog Bodies, Sacred Sites and Wetland Archaeology* (Exeter: Wetland Archaeology Research Project, 1999); R. C. Connolly, 'Lindow Man', *Anthropology Today*, 1, no. 5 (1985), pp. 15–17; and Alison Taylor, 'Burial with the Romans', *British Archaeology*, 69 (March 2003), pp. 14–19. My debate with J. D. Hill was carried on in the *Times Literary Supplement*, 30 January, 5 March and 12 March 2004, and in the *Times* on 22 March.

On Gournay and Ribemont, see Jean-Louis Brunaux, 'Gallic Blood Rites', *Archaeology*, 54 (2001), pp. 54–58, and 'Headless Warriors', Channel Five television programme, 17 October 2003. While academic archaeologists and historians may rightly deplore the number of badly researched and wildly inaccurate theories about the past that get publicity through television programmes, it is also true that the latter provide an opportunity for legitimate challenges to academic orthodoxies to reach a large audience: the first comprehensive doubts about that concerning Lindow Man were aired in the Horizon programme 'Overkill', screened on BBC2 on 2 April 1998.

Miranda Aldhouse-Green's works are 'Humans as Ritual Victims in the Later Prehistory of Western Europe', *Oxford Journal of Archaeology*, 17 (1998), pp. 169–90, and *Dying for the Gods* (Stroud: Tempus, 2001) (quotation from p. 15). J. D. Hill's famous monograph is *Ritual and Rubbish in the Iron Age of Wessex* (British Archaeological Reports, British Series 242, 1995).

Victorian works expressing a view of early British prehistory as a time of rampant savagery include William Greenwell's comments in the *Archaeological Journal*, 22

(1865), p. 107; John Lubbock, *Pre-Historic Times* (London, 1865), pp. 83–492; John Thurnam, 'On Ancient British Barrows', *Archaeologia*, 42 (1869), pp. 185–87; W. Boyd Dawkins, *Early Man in Britain* (London, 1880), pp. 282–87; and Charles Grant B. Allen, *Falling in Love: With Other Essays* (London, 1889), pp. 296–97.

For a miscellany of recent publications on relevant aspects of Neolithic and Bronze Age Britain, see Richard Bradley, *The Social Foundations of Prehistoric Britain* (London: Longman, 1984), *Altering the Earth* (Edinburgh: Society of Antiquaries of Scotland Monograph Series 8, 1993) and *The Significance of Monuments* (London: Routledge, 1998); John Hedges, *The Tomb of the Eagles* (London: Murray, 1984); Timothy Darvill, *Prehistoric Britain* (New Haven: Yale University Press, 1987) and *Long Barrows of the Cotswolds and Surrounding Areas* (Stroud: Tempus, 2004); John Barrett, *Fragments from Antiquity* (Oxford: Blackwell, 1994); Christopher Tilley, *A Phenomenology of Landscape* (Oxford: Berg, 1994); Anna Ritchie, *Prehistoric Orkney* (London: Batsford, 1995); Alasdair Whittle, *Europe in the Neolithic* (Cambridge: Cambridge University Press, 1996), and *Sacred Mound, Holy Rings* (Oxford: Oxbow, 1997); I. J. Thorpe, *The Origins of Agriculture in Europe* (London: Routledge, 1996); Mark Edmonds and Colin Richards (eds), *Understanding the Neolithic of North-Western Europe* (Glasgow: Cruithne, 1998); Francis Pryor, *Farmers in Prehistoric Britain* (Stroud: Tempus, 1998) and *Seahenge: New Discoveries in Prehistoric Britain* (London: HarperCollins, 2001); Andrew Jones, 'Where Eagles Dare: Landscape, Animals and the Neolithic of Orkney', *Journal of Material Culture*, 3 (1998), pp. 301–24; Mike Pitts, *Hengeworld* (London: Century, 2000) (the reinterpretation of the Woodhenge child is on pp. 37–38); Ann Woodward, *British Barrows* (Stroud: Tempus, 2000); and Jan Harding, *Henge Monuments of the British Isles* (Stroud: Tempus, 2003). For a recent piece of research devoted to the issue of how earlier prehistoric communities may have reflected cosmology in their deposits and monuments, see Judith Currivan, 'Walking Between the Worlds: Cosmologies Embodied in the Landscape of Neolithic and Early Bronze Age Britain' (unpublished Reading University Ph.D. thesis, 2004).

Chapter Five: The Fraternal Druids

The general remarks on clubs and societies are taken from Peter Clark, *British Clubs and Societies, 1580–1800* (Oxford: Oxford University Press, 2000), especially pp. 1–25 and 470–91, with some data added from P. H. J. H. Gosden, *The Friendly Societies in England, 1815–1875* (Manchester: Manchester University Press, 1961), and Simon Cordery, *British Friendly Societies, 1750–1914* (Basingstoke: Palgrave Macmillan, 2003).

The Druidical Society of Anglesey is described in Mrs Pritchard, 'The Druidical Society', *Transactions of the Anglesey Antiquarian Society and Field Club* (1925), pp. 63–68, and M. F. Joliffe, 'The Druidical Society of Anglesey, 1772–1844', *Transactions of the Honourable Society of Cymmrodorion* (1940), pp. 189–99.

Accounts of the foundation and early history of the Ancient Order of Druids can be found in the order's journal, *The Druid*, for 1909, pp. 52, 71 and 83; Charles Beale, *A Short Account of Modern Druidism* (privately published, n.d.); Hugo Wiese, G. Wolfstoll and Karl Roeder, *Handbuch des Druidenordens* (Munich, 1931), pp. 146–52; Wilhelm North, *Who was Henry Hurle, the Founder of the A.O.D.?* (London, 1932); J. W. Shaw, *Historical Notes on the Order of Druids* (Manchester, 1936); and Ted Williams, 'A Brief Treatise on the History of Ancient Order Druidism', *The Druid's Voice*, 4 (Winter, 1994), pp. 6–9.

To these sources I have added material for the early nineteenth century from *The Ancient Order of Druids: Address, Constitutional Laws, Choruses and List of Lodges* (n.d., but 1820s); *The Druids' Magazine*, 3 (1832), pp. 2, 249; *The Druid* (1909), p. 100; the list of Druid orders compiled by John Goodchild and kept in his collection below Wakefield Public Library; Jacob Stanley, *An Address to the Lodges of Druids, Odd Fellows* … (Wednesbury, 1813) (quotation on p. 2); and *Rites and Ceremonies of the Loyal Order of Druids* (Bolton, 1848).

The crisis of 1831–34 is described as it unfolded in the *Druid's Magazine*, 3–4 (1833) and the *Druid's Monthly Magazine*, 1 (1834). I have added some context from Martin Gorsky, 'The Growth and Distribution of English Friendly Societies in the Early Nineteenth Century', *Economic History Review*, 2nd series 5 (1998), pp. 489–511. I am grateful to Martin for various helpful conversations when he was my colleague at Bristol, and since.

Material for the remainder of the nineteenth century is taken from *Ancient Order of Druids: Address, Constitutional Laws, Choruses and List of Lodges* (London, 1843); *Ancient Order of Druids: Introductory Book* (London, 1889); Shaw, *Historical Notes on the Order of Druids*; Beale, *A Short Account of Modern Druidism*; Gosden, *The Friendly Societies in England*, pp. 46–49; Worcestershire Record Office, 705:550/4600/6(i) (BA 4600) (constitutional laws of the United Ancient Order of Druids, 1846); Williams, 'A Brief Treatise', p. 8; John Goodchild's handlist of Druid orders; *Rules to be Observed by Members of the Druid Friendly Society* (Salisbury, 1853); Cordery, *British Friendly Societies*, p. 30 (the description of the Female Druids' initiation); *Rules of the Sheffield Equalised Independent Druids' Friendly Society* (Sheffield, 1898); *The Druid* (1911), p. 35; George Jones, *Druidism Historically Considered* (Bristol, 1856) (the Stanton Drew outing); R. A. Thomas Johnson, *History of the Ancient Druids* (Bradford, 1835); John Hoyle, *Lectures* (Manchester, 1861); and *Ceremonies to be Used in All Lodges of the United Ancient Order of Druids* (Hull, 1897).

Early twentieth-century material is taken from the *Druid* (1907–11); John Goodchild Collection, *Ceremonies to be used in all Lodges of the United Ancient Order of Druids* (1897, 1910 and 1923 versions), and *Lecture for the Inauguration of Past Arches* (3rd edition, Hull, 1906); *Devizes and Wiltshire Gazette* (31 August 1905); *Sphere*

(2 September 1905); *Salisbury and Winchester Journal* (19 June 1925) (which includes the anthem); *Times* (18 June 1931); National Archives, WORK 14/2135–6 (applications for rites at Stonehenge and letters of permission); Williams, 'A Brief Treatise', pp. 8–9; Wiese, Stoll and Roeder, *Handbuch des Druidenordens*; Edwin Harris, *A Short History of the Druids* (Rochester, 1909); Order of Bards, Ovates and Druids archive, manuscript of Ancient Order of Druids, Ritual of Primitive Degree, from 1920s; and *East London Observer* (24 September and 5 October 1932).

Chapter Six: The Rebel Druids

For Celtis and Trithemius, see Noel L. Brann, 'Conrad Celtis and the "Druid" Abbot Trithemius', *Renaissance and Reformation*, new series 3, no. 1 (1979), pp. 16–28. My opinion regarding Stukeley is argued, with full references, in 'The Religion of William Stukeley', *Antiquaries' Journal*, 85 (2005), pp. 381–94.

Material for Iolo Morganwg is taken from the *Gentleman's Magazine*, 62 (1792), pp. 956–57; Edward Williams, *Poems, Lyric and Pastoral, in Two Volumes* (London, 1794), pp. xix, 80–84, 104–8, 136–44, and 160–8; Prys Morgan, *A New History of Wales: The Eighteenth-Century Renaissance* (Llandybie: Christopher Davies, 1981), pp. 141–42; and *Iolo Morganwg* (Cardiff: University of Wales Press, 1975), p. 18; Elijah Waring, *Recollections and Anecdotes of Edward Williams* (London, 1850), passim; Dillwyn Miles, *The Secret of the Bards of the Isle of Britain* (Llandybie: Gwasg Dinefwr Press, 1992), pp. 66–67; Elwyn Davies, 'Iolo Morganwg (1747–1826): Bardism and Unitarianism', *The Druid's Voice*, 3 (1993), pp. 21–26; Mary-Ann Constantine, *'Combustible Matter': Iolo Morganwg and the Bristol Volcano* (Aberystwyth: University of Wales Centre for Advanced Welsh and Celtic Studies, 2003), p. 16; Damian Walford Davies, *Presences that Disturb: Models of Romantic Identity in the Literature and Culture of the 1790s* (Cardiff: University of Wales Press, 2002), pp. 136–64 (quotation from Southey on p. 136); Geraint Jenkins, *'Perish Kings and Emperors, but let the Bard of Liberty live* (Aberystwyth: Centre for Advanced Welsh and Celtic Studies, 2006); and National Library of Wales, MS 13145A, p. 205 (rules of the South Walian society of Unitarian Christians).

I have taken the cultural background for the Druids of Pontypridd and Llantrisant from Pontypridd Museum and Llantrisant Heritage Centre. The pioneering study of them is Roy Denning, 'Druidism at Pontypridd', in Stewart Williams (ed.), *Glamorgan Historian*, i (Cowbridge: D. Brown, 1963), pp. 36–45. The best yet written on Myfyr Morganwg is Huw Walters, 'Myfyr Morganwg and the Rocking-Stone Gorsedd', in Geraint Jenkins (ed.), *Rattleskull Genius* (Aberystwyth: University of Wales Centre for Advanced Welsh and Celtic Studies, 2005); I am very grateful to the author for the gift of this essay, as well as other kindnesses. I have added information from Dillwyn Miles, *The Royal National Eisteddfod of Wales* (Swansea: Christopher Davies, 1978), p. 56; Owen Morgan ('Morien'), *History of Pontypridd and Rhondda Valleys* (Pontypridd, 1903), pp. 82–92 (which contains the quotations about Isaiah and Morien's religion); Wirt Sikes, *British Goblins: Welsh Folk-Lore, Fairy Mythology, Legends and Traditions* (London, 1880), pp. 277–78; *Western Mail* (23 March and 21 December 1879, 20 March and 20 June 1881, 27 December 1882, and 24 February 1888); National Library of Wales, MS 21178E (Gwilym Morganwg to Taliesin ab Iolo); Central Glamorgan Gazette (28 March 1930); *Pontypridd District Herald* (29 June 1878); and (John Williams), 'Congress of Bards, Pontypridd', *Cambrian Journal*, 3 (1856), pp. 201–4.

The most interesting study of Morien yet published is John Michael Greer, *Phallic Religion in the Druid Revival* (Lewes, Sussex: Order of Bards, Ovates and Druids, 2004). The material used in my own interpretation has been drawn from Owen Morgan (Morien), *The Light of Britannia* (Cardiff, 1890); *Guide to the Gorsedd or Round Table and the Order of the Garter* (Cardiff, 1899); *History of Pontypridd*, pp. 26, 75–78, 254–61; *The Royal Winged Son of Stonehenge and Avebury*, also entitled *The Mabin of the Mabinogion* and *Kimmerian Revelations* (Pontypridd, n.d.) (quotation from p. 24); *The Battles of Wales* (Liverpool, 1920), pp. 11–23; and Meic Stephens, 'Sober Facts Too Much for Owen', *Pontypridd Observer* (3 January 2002).

The unpublished dissertation on William Price is John Cule, 'Dr William Price (1800–1893) of Llantrisant: A Study of an Eccentric' (Cambridge M.D., 1960), which not only uncovered most of the primary sources for his life but printed many of them. The published booklets on him, which add interesting details and (in the latter case) excellent illustrations, are T. Islwyn Nicholas, *A Welsh Heretic: Dr William Price, Llantrisant* (London, 1940), and Dean Powell, *Eccentric: The Life of Dr William Price* (Llantrisant: privately published, 2005); Cyril Bracegirdle's short and lively biography, from 1997, seems to be more of a work of historical fiction. Also important is Brian Davies, 'Empire and Identity: The "Case" of Dr William Price', in David Smith (ed.), *A People and a Proletariat: Essays in the History of Wales, 1780–1980* (London: Pluto Press, 1980), pp. 72–93. I have added material from National Archives, H.O. 40/57 (Marquess of Bute to Marquess of Normanby, 10 July 1840); Museum of Welsh Life, MS 50/5/, 28–30 (his genealogies); *Cardiff Times* (19 and 26 May and 9, 16 and 23 June 1888); *Western Mail* (23 March 1881, 15 and 25 January 1884, and 3 April 1884); and *Pontypridd Observer* (8 January 2004).

Any study of G. W. M. Reid must now build on the work of Adam Stout: 'Choosing a Past: The Politics of Prehistory in Pre-War Britain' (University of Wales, Lampeter, Ph.D. thesis, 2004), pp. 132–82; and *Universal Majesty, Verity and Love Infinite: A Life of George Watson MacGregor Reid* (Lewes, Sussex: Order of Bards, Ovates and Druids, 2005), available at http://druidry.org/pdfs/fifth mt haemus lecture. pdf. He has also supplied me with information and encouragement throughout my own work on the subject. His achievement drew at moments on two pioneering works by others: R. Bruce Aubry, 'George Watson MacGregor Reid' (unpublished manuscript of 1986 which now exists in various private collections; Philip Carr-Gomm sent me a copy of that in the Order of Bards, Ovates and Druids – hereafter OBOD – archive); and Alan Seaburg, 'The Last Two Universalist Parsons in the United Kingdom: George Watson MacGregor Reid and Arthur Peacock', *Transactions of the Unitarian Historical Society* 23, April 2004, pp. 530–62. I have added opinions or emphases of my own based on George W. Reid, *The Natural Basis of Civilisation* (London, 1895); Warburg Institute, Gerald Yorke Collection NS 29–31, 55 (five treatises by Reid); *The Nature Cure Journal*, volumes 1–4 (1906–9); 'Ayu Subadra', *The Path that is Light* (London, 1910); *The New Life* (1913) (I am very grateful to Philip Carr-Gomm for the gift of a copy of this from the OBOD archive); Rosita Forbes, *The Spirit of the Sahara* (London, 1921)(I am grateful to Philip Carr-Gomm for drawing my attention to this work); Andy Worthington, *Stonehenge: Celebration and Subversion* (Wymeswold, Leicestershire: Alternative Albion, 2004), pp. 14–18; *Salisbury and Winchester Journal* (all issues covering the summer solstice 1912–33); *Wiltshire Gazette* (ditto); *Sphere* (29 June 1912); *Salisbury Times and South Wiltshire Gazette* (26 June 1914, 26 June 1915, 28 June 1918, 25 June 1920, and 22 July 1932); *Wiltshire Times* (2 July 1932); *Daily Mirror* (23 June 1914); *Evening News* (22 June 1914 and 22 June 1915); *Sunday Express* (19 June 1932); *Times* (23 June 1924 and 22 June 1925); *Western Daily Press* (22 June 1925); *Illustrated London News* (29 June 1929); National Archives, WORK 14/2135 (the Office of Works's file on Stonehenge and Druids); Christopher Chippindale, *Stonehenge Complete* (London: Thames and Hudson, 1983), p. 204 (Atkinson's anecdote); *The New Life and Druid Journal* (Midsummer issues 1927, 1930 and 1931); Wiltshire Archaeological and Natural History Society Library, Devizes, Cunnington Cuttings 11, pp. 15–34 and 94 (collection of items relating to the cremations controversy); Earl of Crawford and Balcarres, 'Anniversary Address', *Antiquaries Journal*, 5 (1925), pp. 221–36; *Service Book of the South London Universalist Church* (photocopy in the OBOD Archive, kindly sent to me by Philip Carr-Gomm); and OBOD Archive, photocopies of correspondence between American Universalists and Reid's Church in the Andover-Harvard Theological Library. Sir Thomas Kendrick's book is *The Druids* (London, 1927) (quotations from pp. 29 and 121).

Godfrey Higgins's relevant books were *The Celtic Druids* (London, 1829) (quotation on p. 299) and *Anacalypsis* (2 volumes, London, 1833–36). For the impact of the latter, see Leslie Shepard, 'The *Anacalypsis* of Godfrey Higgins – Precursor of H.P.B.', *Theosophical History*, 1 (1985), pp. 46–63. For an example of the digestion of ancient Druidry by Theosophy, see Peter Freeman, *The Druids and Theosophy* (Glasgow, 1924), while the Ancient and Archaeological Order is described in Ithell Colquhoun, *Sword of Wisdom: MacGregor Mathers and the Golden Dawn* (London: Spearman, 1975), p. 120.

Dudley Wright's book was *Druidism: The Ancient Faith of Britain* (London, 1921–4) (the initiation ceremony is on pp. 59–65). Lewis Spence's was *The Mysteries of Britain* (London, 1928) (quotations from pp. 5 and 19, and initiations described on pp. 178–205). The Ancient Order of Druid Hermetists is recorded in Wiltshire Record Office, 2860/21, 'The Summer Solstice Celebration of the Druid Order'; *Salisbury Journal* (issues after summer solstice 1943 and 1946–53); National Archives, WORK 14/2135–6 (Office – later Ministry – of Works file on Stonehenge and Druids); *Pendragon* (Midsummer 1938); *Pendragon and Druid Guardian* (Summer Solstice 1948); *Wiltshire Gazette* (27 June 1946 and 26 June 1947); and Colquhoun, *Sword of Wisdom*, pp. 119–20.

A copy of the instrument appointing Robert MacGregor Reid chief has been acquired by the OBOD archive and was sent to me by Philip Carr-Gomm. Comments on his coup are found in Wiltshire Record Office, 2860/21 ('The Summer Solstice Celebration'). The feud with Smith is chronicled in the government file on Stonehenge at National Archives, WORK 14/2136. Copies of the rites of Robert's order, and of its promotional literature, are preserved in the archive of the Order of Bards, Ovates and Druids; the Museum of Witchcraft at Boscastle, Cornwall (in the Cecil Williamson papers; my heartfelt thanks to Graham King for inviting me to read these); the Wiltshire Local Studies Library, Trowbridge; the Wiltshire Record Office, 2860/21 (Austin Underwood Collection); Institute of Archaeology, Oxford University (Stuart Piggott archive); and Birmingham Reference Library. Publications not found in these are summarised in Colquhoun, *Sword of Wisdom*, pp. 124–27. Robert's relationship with Crowley is recorded in the Warburg Institute's Gerald Yorke Collection, NS 18 (22) and his attitude to the Golden Dawn in Colquhoun, *Sword of Wisdom*, pp. 117, 127–30.

Reports of the Universal Bond in the 1950s, mostly at Stonehenge, are found in press cuttings collected in the Wiltshire Archaeological and Natural History Society Library, Devizes, Scrapbook D; and in the *Daily Express* (21 March 1956); *Salisbury Journal* (22 June 1956, 28 June 1957); *Southampton Echo* (21 June 1956); *Daily Mail* (20 June 1956) and *Manchester Guardian* (23 June 1959). Its relations with the Office of Works over Stonehenge are recorded in National Archives, WORK 14/2136.

The controversy over Stonehenge in the 1960s is recorded in Daniel's editorials in *Antiquity* 35 (1961), pp. 171–74 and 260–62; 35 (1962), p. 167; 38 (1964), pp. 165–66; 40 (1966), p. 171; and 42 (1968), pp. 168–69; Wiltshire Record Office, 2860/20–2 (three files of cuttings, letters and papers on issue kept by Austin Underwood; the ministry statement quoted is in a letter from J. M. Melhuish, dated 10 July 1969); and National Archives, WORK 14/2136 and 14/2789 (the Ministry of Works files). Press reports not found in these are in *The Times* (29 May and 22 June 1961, and 3 June 1964). Comment on the affair is found in Adam Stout, 'The World Turned Upside Down: Stonehenge Summer Solstice before the Hippies', *3rd Stone* 46 (2003), pp. 38–46; and Worthington, *Stonehenge*, pp. 30–32. The quotations from Stuart Piggott, *The Druids* (London: Thames and Hudson, 1968), are on pp. 9, 23, 165, 175 and 180–81. Leslie

Grinsell's pamphlet was L. V. Grinsell, *The Druids and Stonehenge* (Guernsey: Toucan Press, 1978) (quotation on p. 23).

The fortunes of the Universal Bond between 1964 and 1984 are recorded in Austin Underwood's files of letters and cuttings in the Wiltshire Record Office, 2860/20 and 22 (the quotation from Maughan is in the cutting from the *Southampton Evening Echo*, 19 June 1968); in its magazine, *The Druid* (four issues, 1965–68) and its publication *The Most Ancient Order of Druids* (London: The Druid Order, n.d.); and in Chippindale, *Stonehenge Complete*, pp. 262–63, and Worthington, *Stonehenge*, pp. 32–45, 72–123.

Ross Nichols and the Druidry that has appeared since 1985 were both covered by my essay 'The New Druidry' in my book *Witches, Druids and King Arthur: Studies in Paganism, Myth and Magic* (London: Hambledon and London, 2003), pp. 239–58. Since it went to press the following additional studies and source material have become available: Philip Carr-Gomm (ed.), *In the Grove of the Druids: The Druid Teachings of Ross Nichols* (London: Watkins, 2002); Philip Carr-Gomm, *Druid Mysteries* (London: Rider, 2002), *Druidcraft* (London: Thorsons, 2002), and *What Do Druids Believe?* (London: Granta, 2006); C. J. Stone and Arthur Pendragon, *The Trials of Arthur: Being the True Tale of a Twenty-First Century King* (London: Thorson, 2003); and Emma Restall Orr, *Living Druidry* (London: Piatkus, 2004).

Index